The
NEW
Alchemists

The book is dedicated to health professionals and science and technology geeks everywhere.

The
NEW
Alchemists

The rise of
deceptive healthcare

Bernie Garrett

Hammersmith Health Books
London, UK

First published in 2021 by Hammersmith Health Books – an imprint of
Hammersmith Books Limited
4/4A Bloomsbury Square, London WC1A 2RP, UK
www.hammersmithbooks.co.uk

The information contained in this book is for educational purposes only. It is
the result of the study and the experience of the author. Whilst the information
and advice offered are believed to be true and accurate at the time of going to
press, neither the authors nor the publisher can accept any legal responsibility
or liability for any errors or omissions that may have been made or for any
adverse effects which may occur as a result of following the recommendations
given herein. Always consult a qualified medical practitioner if you have any
concerns regarding your health.

British Library Cataloguing in Publication Data: A CIP record of this book is
available from the British Library.

Print ISBN 978-1-78161-188-3
Ebook ISBN 978-1-78161-189-0

Commissioning editor: Georgina Bentliff
Designed and typeset by: Julie Bennett, Bespoke Publishing Ltd
Cover design by: Madeline Meckiffe
Index: Dr Laurence Errington
Production: Deborah Wehner, Moatvale Press, UK
Printed and bound by: TJ Books Ltd

Contents

Contents

About the author

Bernie Garrett is a professor at the University of British Columbia (UBC) School of Nursing with over 35 years of experience in both critical care nursing and nursing education in the UK and Canada. He is a registered nurse and holds a PhD in information science, and a number of specialist clinical and educational qualifications. He has authored several science and clinical textbooks, chapters in edited books as well as numerous research papers. His work is underpinned by a passion for health science and technology, and he holds provincial and national awards for his work in furthering nurse education. He is an Inaugural Fellow of the Canadian Nurse Educator Institute, and lives in Vancouver, British Columbia.

Acknowledgements

As with any venture of this nature, I am standing upon the shoulders of giants, and owe a huge debt of gratitude to numerous researchers, authors and practitioners whose work has helped inform this work, many of whom offered constructive critique. Firstly, a big shout-out goes to Tim Caulfield, who proved inspirational with his own work, and also a great source of encouragement. Secondly, thanks for inspiration and ideas to all those in the science and evidence-based health posse who are consistently challenging badly-evidenced therapies, poor practice, pseudoscience and health nonsense, including in no particular order: David Nunan, Edzard Ernst, Paul Offit, Ben Goldacre, Steven Novella, Simon Singh, Harriet Hall, Joe Schwarcz, Johnathan Jarry, Jennifer Gunter, Linda Girgis, Mark Crislip, Kimball Atwood, Scott Gavura, David Gorski, David Colquhoun, Stephen Barrett, Clay Jones, Jon Hislop, David Robert Grimes, Trisha Greenhalgh, Yoni Freedhoff, the Friends of Science in Medicine and Sense About Science organisations and of course, Bill Nye and Brian Cox. Additionally, thanks to several folks from alternative medicine who offered constructive suggestions and have challenged and critiqued their own professions (often with detrimental effects on their own livelihood): Matthew Bignall, Samuel Homola and Britt-Marie Hermes. Thanks are also due to my nursing colleagues who have provided support and encouragement over the years, including: Sally Thorne, Elizabeth Saewyck, John Oliffe, Paul Galdas, Paul

Ong and Martin Lipscomb. Also, thanks to the University of British Columbia for continuing to champion academic freedom, to the University of Portsmouth, who originally employed me as a lecturer, and Oxford Brookes University for supporting my PhD studies. Additionally, many thanks to Roger Cutting for his unerring science advocacy, and Georgina Bentliff at Hammersmith Books for editing advice. Also, cheers to Public Service Broadcasting who provided much of the soundtrack to my writing activities over the last few years. Finally, love and thanks to my long-suffering family for putting up with me over the course of writing this book.

Section I

Wellness is not something you can buy

Chapter 1

The art of the con

In 1404, King Henry IV of England signed a law making it an offence to create gold and silver out of thin air, known as the 'Act Against Multiplication'. Clearly, some rather strange ideas were afoot during the early Renaissance. Most people think of alchemists as crazed and fraudulent mediaeval experimenters trying to turn lead into gold, but in fact, a major part of their work focused on finding an 'Elixir of Immortality', essentially a potion to prevent ageing. Alchemists believed in the principle of transmutation, in that substances could be changed from one thing to another, and similarly in terms of health, illness changed to wellness. Much bad-press was received by alchemists, primarily arising from the fact the field was inundated with cheats and imposters who swindled unsuspecting people who had turned to them in desperation over their health and financial problems. These ideas were initially very popular, and persisted for several centuries, and even some of the great luminaries of the Enlightenment, such as Roger Bacon and Isaac Newton, were self-confessed Alchemists. Nowadays, modern science dismisses most of alchemy as pseudoscience and many of those early beliefs have been proved incorrect. Nevertheless, some important advancements arose from the early work of alchemists, such as enhanced processes of distillation and other important discoveries that led to the progression of chemistry.

The Act Against Multiplication was eventually repealed in 1689, after lobbying by the early chemist Robert Boyle. However, as an analogy to the current state of health science with regard to deception, there are some interesting parallels with these ancient alchemists. Unfortunately, even though healthcare knowledge and practice have improved immensely over the last century, healthcare remains riddled with deceptive practices and charlatans, probably more so than any other human enterprise. Separating the valuable from the worthless in terms of health practices has become more and more difficult, and this provides the focus for this book, where we explore some of the key areas of deception that influence modern healthcare practice.

Health is something that all of us have a vested interest in one way or another, but unfortunately deception in healthcare seems an ever-growing problem in modern life; something that the COVID-19 pandemic illustrates all too well. After a long career working in healthcare, I still never cease to be amazed by the number, ingenuity and sheer audacity of the latest health scams, and the variety of different forms of health deception is quite remarkable. In this book, we will explore a number of them, and the reasons why one might be inclined to engage with them. Over the years these have included: big pharma scandals, fake doctors, useless surgical procedures, counterfeit drugs, fake diagnoses, magic diets, millionaire health gurus, alternative health cons, Nobel laureates who went off the rails, celebrity health scams and even the marketing of radioactive toothpaste. The COVID-19 pandemic has also provided an opportunity for a new set of scams. Much of this growth of health deception has been fuelled by the development of the Internet and social media, and so we will also explore how this has helped support a growing range of successful deceptive health enterprises. However, the writing of this introduction has prompted a reflection on why I became so interested in all of this perverse activity in the first place.

All of us are shaped by our life experiences, and in reflecting on all of the factors that have influenced my own interest in this curious aspect of health, there are many; but I guess one in particular stands out. As an 18-year-old I was finishing up high school in 1970s' England. My parents had divorced a few years earlier and my mother had embarked on the world of dating as a mature woman. I can only imagine that this must've been quite a harrowing process in the pre-internet world. She had started corresponding with a man who was currently residing in an open prison in Somerset in the UK as a part of a 'Write to Prisoners' charitable activity. I have no idea how she got into this, but even as a somewhat naïve teenager, I considered this probably wasn't the best way for her to find a new suitor. Apparently, the gentleman she was writing to, 'Jeff', was a local businessman who had run afoul of the taxman and was now spending a couple of years at Her Majesty's pleasure to make amends. His incarceration was now coming to an end and his release imminent. My mother had started to visit him at the prison and also offered to be a named responsible person for him to visit as he started to make supervised trips out. Eventually, he was released and they continued their relationship. I finally met him when they had been seeing each other for about three months. He seemed quite charming, even to a somewhat angsty teen who naturally distrusted any adults and was keen to steer well clear of anything to do with his mother's love life.

My two older brothers and sister also felt he might be a somewhat sub-optimal new partner for our mother, and were keen to size-up this new man in her life. They visited one weekend to check him out. He seemed quite charming, and regaled us all with tales of his successful business ventures before his downfall, how his tax evasion had all been rather an unfortunate lapse of judgement, and how he had lost most of his investments in the process, including his beloved Jaguar. He was apparently now a reformed man rebuilding his business empire, and keen to reassure us that he was a genuine good egg, much akin to Toad of Toad Hall in Kenneth Grahame's *Wind in the Willows*, I couldn't help thinking. He also covered the bill for a quite expensive lunch for us all, and had also been generously bestowing various favours upon our mother, including jewellery, flowers and fine dining. Although we all remained somewhat suspicious, our mother seemed very happy, and Jeff appeared financially very secure. Their relationship flourished over the coming months.

At the time we lived in a small council flat, and one day Jeff came to visit to take my mother out for a dinner date. Whilst she was getting ready, he struck up a conversation about the month I had spent in Germany a few years ago on a school exchange as he had heard I collected German stamps. As a part of our school's German language programme. I had participated in this student exchange when I was 16, and stamp-collecting had been a hobby of mine as a kid. I had long since given this up as it was considered by my peers as being mortally uncool by this stage of adolescence, but the collection was in the bookcase and included some fairly rare items, some stamps over 80 years old procured from Hannover flea markets, and examples from the 1920s German hyper-inflation era where simple postage stamps cost thousands of Deutsche Marks; in 1923 a US dollar was worth 4,210,500,000,000 German Marks![2] It also contained some Nazi stamps and post-war examples, so was historically quite curious. I hadn't looked at it in ages, but recall my father had once advised me to hang on to it as he thought it could turn out to be quite a valuable collection in time. Jeff asked to see them, and looked suitably impressed when I fished it out.

A month later I had started at college and moved away to Portsmouth. One weekend, shortly after I had arrived, I got an urgent phone call from my older brother saying all was not well at home and I needed to make a visit to see our mother as soon as possible. You can probably guess what is coming. Jeff had absconded with all of my mother's jewellery, quite a bit of cash, and anything else of value that he could lay his hands on, including my brother's car. He had lent it to Jeff the previous weekend as Jeff had said he had a friend who was interested in buying it. My mother was devastated, not only because since her divorce she had few assets of any value in any case (she worked full-time in a retirement home as a cook to make ends meet), but also because she felt she had let us all down. She had not told anyone Jeff had disappeared for over a week since he vanished, and she had lent him a large part of her life-savings. He had told her he needed some money to tide him over as his assets were invested in some business deal. She couldn't believe she had been so easily duped. At first, I thought I could not possibly have had anything of value left at home Jeff might have taken, but then I had a thought; sure enough, when I checked my remaining belongings, my old stamp collection was gone.

Once the police got involved it turned out Jeff was not a businessman at all, but actually a serial con-artist. He had pulled this trick a few times, and currently there were at least three other women in exactly the same position, all of whom he had been visiting since his release. He had borrowed from one to give the impression of wealth to another, and so on in a cycle to keep his scams afloat. To this day it seems careless to me that the prison did not check that the women he was visiting on his supervised days out from prison were not fully aware what he was actually in prison for. Privacy issues notwithstanding, it would seem they had some responsibility for transparency in this to the public. Anyhow, as Jeff was not exactly a criminal genius, the long arm of the law caught up with him a few months later, but none of our things were ever recovered. Astonishingly, at his trial he claimed he had simply borrowed the money and items from his 'girlfriends', and couldn't see how he had really done anything wrong.

It is easy to say we all should have known better, but the fact remains despite all our misgivings, a whole family of people gave a guy they knew as a convicted felon who had just been released from prison the benefit of the doubt. Why? Because it is human nature. People can be easily manipulated as even though we may dwell on negative thoughts more in general, we naturally prefer to believe in something positive rather than negative and that there is more than the evidence might suggest; we mostly also tend to be forgiving. These are typical qualities of being social beings, and the traits that con-men like Jeff rely on as part of their 'art of the con'.

In exploring the growth of health scams, alternative health trends and fake health news over the last few years, I have witnessed these same characteristics in play repeatedly. It is not a matter of gullibility, but of people taking advantage of the human predisposition to like simple answers to complex questions and certainty rather than doubt, and to want to believe providers of health products and services are trustworthy and have your best interests at heart.[1] In the current climate of mistrust in authority, it is these same traits that lead people to buy into a whole raft of doubtful health trends and misinformation, from the health ideals of celebrities such as Oprah Winfrey, to the inexplicable health advice from some doctors such as Mehmet Oz, Andrew Wakefield or Joseph Mercola. Like Jeff, many of the people engaged in these activities will argue they are doing nothing wrong, but simply selling services and goods people want, or revealing the real *facts* in the face of conspiracies to cover up an underlying truth. This unerring sense of infallibility and self-righteousness is one characteristic of these people that should be a red flag to us all.

Curiously, the disgraced doctor Andrew Wakefield is also a prime example of the changing nature of public trust in our institutions. At one time, being struck off the medical register in any country would have been the kiss of death for a career as a public health advocate. However, he was struck off the UK Medical Register for deception in 2010, but remains a hero to many for his ongoing support of the links between the MMR vaccine and autism (now comprehensively proven false (see page 261). He has successfully reinvented himself using the narrative of the brave scientist fighting against the narrow-minded medical establishment, acquired a celebrity girlfriend, and cast himself as some sort of postmodern Galileo.[3] He was even invited to Donald Trump's inauguration ball, and made an appearance in two anti-vaccination propaganda films (*Vaxxed 1* and *Vaxxed 2*) – quite the reversal of fortune.

Although the majority of health professionals are good and honest people, after 35 years of working in professional healthcare I have also seen my share of dishonest practices: doctors and nurses who lied, drug companies that used deceptive marketing to sell products, and all sorts of alternative health practitioners selling fake remedies for profit. I decided that deceptive healthcare practices and the reasons why people engage in them offered a fascinating area to research further. Some colleagues actually advised me against doing this at the time: 'Don't go there, it's a rabbit hole!' they said, suggesting raising my head above this particular parapet would not bode well for my career. Yet, I found I was irresistibly drawn to trying to understand the nature of healthcare deception, and why intelligent and talented people end up engaging with it. So, I started work researching in this area, exploring health scams, medical fraudsters, celebrity wellness gurus and the weird world of alternative healthcare. It is a fascinating subject and there is no shortage of material in what seems to be a boom business.

Chapter 2

Are we obsessed with our health?

I really shouldn't have looked at Twitter this morning, I considered as I sipped my morning coffee one rainy January morning here in Vancouver, BC. The morning's stream was full of the usual bizarre health stories: dodgy doctors, Big-Pharma scandals, magical detoxes to restore wellbeing and vitality, vaccination conspiracy theories, mom's odd health tips, miracle diets and sound-baths that promise to increase your health and happiness – overall, more weirdness than you might expect to find in an episode of *Stranger Things*. Most of us have fallen prey to some aspect of this over the years, maybe buying a health product that guaranteed to provide miraculous results, or following some dubious health advice from friends or family. As I pondered this latest collection of bewildering health news over my coffee, I still wondered why society seemed increasingly obsessed about heath and 'wellness' these days when, in terms of public health (pandemics aside), we have probably never had it so good. In general, as both physical and mortal beings, we are naturally concerned with our welfare and those of our families, friends and wider society to a significant extent. With new diet fads, detoxes, health and fitness plans and wellbeing programmes now everywhere we turn, it is evident that being healthy has morphed into a lucrative commercial enterprise in modern society. But, maybe a good place to start is to consider how we actually define health.

What do we mean by 'health'?

In terms of human wellbeing, health was defined by the World Health Organization (WHO) in 1946 as not merely the absence of disease or infirmity, but a state of complete physical, mental and social wellbeing. This definition persists to this day, but has been argued as somewhat vague and also unattainable for many. For example, the physician and author Peter Skrabanek once joked this was a state only achievable at a moment of mutual orgasm![4] In 1984, a WHO discussion proposed moving away from viewing health as a state towards more of a framework that presented health as a process. This was exemplified in the 1986 Ottawa Charter for Health Promotion. Their definition stated that health is:

> The extent to which an individual or group is able to realize aspirations and satisfy needs, and to change or cope with the environment. Health is a resource for everyday life, not the objective of living; it is a positive concept, emphasizing social and personal resources, as well as physical capacities.[5]

This definition exemplifies the complexities in defining health, and how complex factors combine together to affect the health of individuals and communities. These are also known as the determinants of health. It is clear that whether people are healthy or not is determined by both their circumstances and the environment where they live and/or work. These determinants of health include: our physical environment, our social and economic environment, and a person's individual characteristics and behaviours. We certainly can't control many of the determinants of health, but should recognise that factors such as economics, gender, education and access to public healthcare services have a significant impact on public health.

Although there is a specialty of preventative medicine and all doctors engage in health promotion, modern medicine remains primarily focused upon illness and disease rather than health. Medical textbooks remain largely focused on ways the body and mind go wrong, and how to correct this, and medical research likewise remains chiefly disease focused. Contemporary medicine has put huge efforts into producing classifications of disease, and in mental health psychiatrists have identified thousands of ways in which our minds can go wrong. This has led to the label of *allopathic* medicine being frequently applied by alternative health advocates, suggesting medicine is simply focused upon symptom and pathology treatments, and flawed as it is not focusing on the *holistic* health of the person. However, this is a somewhat inaccurate and pejorative description of medicine used by its critics, as medicine is not by any means simply focused on symptomatic treatment or the suppression of pathophysiological processes. It is also only one profession working in modern multidisciplinary healthcare, where nurses, pharmacists, physiotherapists and multiple other professions work together to try to ensure a holistic approach to health is achieved. The biomedical approach focusing on illness has also resulted in massive health advances over the last century, but it can also lead us to unrealistic expectations in terms of personal health. In reality, the absence of disease remains something of an illusion. Using modern diagnostic techniques, including genetic profiling, biochemical analysis and imaging, every one of us can be found to have some dysfunctional element or be dis-eased in some way.

Nevertheless, this complexity in the nature of health, and the availability of new health technologies, has meant that healthcare has become one of the highest growth industries in the world today. Over $200 billion was generated last year in healthcare revenues in the United States alone.[6] In response to increasing public demands alongside the traditional healthcare production sectors of the life sciences, biotechnology, pharmaceuticals and healthcare equipment, a corresponding growth of healthcare services has also occurred. Aside from national public health programmes with nations attempting to improve the health of their citizens, in more economically developed countries, a corresponding growth in the consumer health sector has also occurred, including a social trend towards what has become known as the 'wellness' industry.

The wellness industry

When I was young, wellness wasn't particularly trendy or cool. Indeed, the nearest most of my friends and I ever came to preventative health and self-care was likely to be our irregular dental check-ups. Whilst eating a balanced diet and active recreation were certainly promoted, and there were plenty of sporting facilities, swimming pools and the odd gym, spas and natural health stores were a rarity. Today, these are commonplace in any city or major town in Europe or North America. According to the Global Wellness Institute (a self-styled institute that promotes the industry), the global wellness industry is worth around $4.2 trillion USD, and has surpassed both the pharmaceutical and diet industries (which are considered separately). Wellness sectors include healthy eating, nutrition, weight loss, fitness, preventative medicine, the spa industry and alternative healthcare (although most wellness definitions try to avoid the inclusion of medical therapeutics). Even though the wellness industry is booming, whether it's actually having any impact on public health is highly debatable. Its popularity has certainly proved beneficial for those working in this field (most of whom are independent practitioners), but compared with established health professions (doctors, nurses, dentists, physiotherapists, dietitians etc.) it remains relatively unregulated. The industry also targets the more affluent parts of society, as it requires customers with disposable income in order to thrive. It is also noteworthy that this social trend of wellness is actually making some people unwell. It has perpetuated unrealistic ideals of health and body-image for most of us, and has given rise to a new golden age of deceptive healthcare and scams as this book will show.

'Wellness syndrome' is one example, described by Andre Spicer and Carl Cederstrom in their 2015 book of the same name as: 'when you become conscious of your own health to the point that it provokes anxiety and guilt, in other words you develop an unhealthy relationship with your body'. They highlight the negative effects of being obsessed with wellbeing and health and describe how we can become so self-conscious about whether we take care of our bodies as well as we should, that we begin to live constantly feeling anxious and nervous about our health. The wellness industry provides a socially acceptable way to engage in thoughts of body dysmorphia and obsessive health behaviours, telling us which bodies and lifestyles are good and which are bad. Many advocates live their lives reading celebrity health websites, watching their shows, buying essential oils, drinking alkaline water, grounding their chakras, getting acupuncture, detoxing, taking homeopathic remedies and opening their 'third eye', believing they are engaging in personally meaningful health practices. Nevertheless, it is important to recognise the modern wellness businesses providing this are firmly focused on health as an arena for commercial gain, rather than being driven by any desire to promote spiritual or traditional healing. Often such purveyors of wellness products and services suggest an ancient, traditional or indigenous basis for their merchandise without any integration of the complex systems of beliefs and traditions of the cultures from which they arose. Most of the wellness practices employ unrealistic, idealised and trendy stereotypes of health, typically promoting the idea of able-bodied, thin, cisgender, stress-free, blissfully wealthy people. Anybody who possesses those attributes is seen as healthy, providing an unattainable goal for most people, and an ongoing source of revenue for those working in the field. In this respect, health is certainly a socially constructed concept.

Some might see this as a cynical interpretation, but public health services and the wellness industry are very different kettles of fish. People may find themselves discouraged by the failures of modern impersonal medical systems to resolve our contemporary health issues and seek alternatives. However, those alternatives more often than not present other issues and also often rely on predatory business models, as we shall see. Imagine a store that sells products with vague descriptions of what they do, how they work, based on a set of unconfirmed beliefs, with no warranty, and where if they do not work as suggested you are advised to try more of them or something else. If your local car dealer were to operate in this way, they would likely not last long. However, in wellness there are no absolutes, no meaningful guarantees, no professional requirements to use scientific evidence, and little regulation in the marketing of wellness products and services. This growth of the wellness industry and alternative healthcare is a huckster's dream and has led to the significant growth of health scams.

Science in the age of alternative facts

Another contribution to this new era of health scamming is the ongoing decline of trust in science and the return of belief-based narratives. Much of this has been fuelled by a perception that science has failed to address major societal issues, including many health problems. Whilst massive decreases in infectious diseases, infant mortality and smoking-related health issues have occurred together with improvements in cancer and cardiovascular disease statistics, chronic conditions such as asthma, allergies and autism have increased. While the age of popular science is now long-passed, scientific progress and research into these issues is ongoing. However, an interesting irony has arisen in how science is now negatively viewed by many, compared with how much it is depended upon in our increasingly technological world.

Science and the media

The media coverage of science has become polarised. Popular media often advocates for the benefits of science, and new forensic science and science-fiction shows arrive on our screens virtually every week. At the same time, a return to nature, the dangers of technology, conspiracy theories, the evils of the industrial-military-technological complex and Big-Pharma narratives pervade the Internet. Although we now live in a world that relies on science and technology to fulfil our daily needs, some academics question the fundamental principles of science and its value to society. People who put belief in expert opinion or other authorities frequently reject scientific findings in favour of testimonial, dogma or what are often referred to as 'other ways of knowing'. Naturopaths and media figures, such as Deepak Chopra (page 252) and Gwyneth Paltrow (page 256), tell people to ignore scientific evidence and trust in their vital energy and intuition in making their health choices. Many therapies, health machines, nutritional supplements and traditional folklore remedies proliferate without substantive evidence of benefits (other than monetary benefit to those who sell them). These therapies are usually supported by personal theories, beliefs and ideologies, rather than evidence, often promoted under the guise of recognising ancient wisdom or even 'new-science'. Nevertheless, many people swear by these remedies, and the public uptake of alternative medicine has increased significantly over the last few decades.[7, 8, 9] The reasons for this are complex, but an increasing suspicion of science by the general public has certainly been a contributing factor.

The growing misunderstanding of science has been compounded by incompetent and sensationalist reporting, and stereotyping in the media. This makes it difficult for researchers to get their work understood. Advertisers frequently make use of science to promote products (typically in iconic white lab coats), but science is frequently portrayed as nerdy, boring and difficult, whilst scientists are typically portrayed as either nerds, mad / evil villains, boffins, impersonal geniuses, eccentric loonies or morally negligent. A good example of this sort of imagery can be seen with the popular CBS comedy show *The Big Bang Theory*, and a quick flick through the latest Netflix offerings will reveal numerous others. Ultimately, such pop-culture typecasting of science and scientists does have an impact on public views and confidence in science, and in science-based healthcare.

During the current pandemic this has also been evident with the portrayal of immoral scientists rushing untested products to market for profit by the anti-vaccination movement. Additionally, the political manipulation of messaging, misusing science to suit particular agendas, has always occurred; an example is Donald Trump's 2018 doctor's letter claiming 'His physical strength and stamina are extraordinary'; another is his use of a personal physician's support to justify his experimental COVID-19 treatment.[10, 11]

The modern anti-science movement and alternative facts

An ongoing educational shortfall in science education in schools, together with growing anti-science narratives in social media, certainly hasn't helped in the ongoing rise in health scams and fraud. Shortly after I and my family moved to Canada, we attended a weather-themed primary school science fair at my daughter's school. Like many in her class, she had built a rain gauge and been recording precipitation in our garden over a month. As it was a science project, we, and a number of the other kids participating, were then somewhat surprised when one of her classmates received a prize for a poster explaining rainbows were caused by 'god's tears'. Certainly, it was a colourful and creative entry and we can understand a desire to reward all the kids for their contributions, but this was possibly not the best example of meteorological science to set for a school class. Without a good understanding of what science is and is not, it becomes difficult to discriminate effectively between a sound hypothesis and hyperbole. Currently, scientific illiteracy is not a major impediment to success in business, politics, the arts or, as we shall explore, even a career in healthcare.

The idea that science cannot explain everything and is flawed, and so we should turn to traditional or alternative narratives to explain phenomena which should be regarded as equally valid, has become increasingly accepted, even in many university departments as a part of postmodern thought. However, whilst certainly inclusive, it is also rather problematic as an approach to preventing errors in practical applications. One of the great advantages of a scientific approach is that, rather than telling us what to think, it provides a self-correcting process that tells us how to think and test our ideas against the real world. Reverting to ancient or alternative knowledge does not do the same, and instead can move us into a situation where we attempt to make the real world match our beliefs, rather than the reverse. Ancient health explanations were the cutting-edge of knowledge at their time, but were frequently wrong, as they were based upon understanding of how the body worked in a time before we even had a rudimentary understanding of electricity. Few people today would be impressed by their physician suggesting that one of their children's 'four humours' was out of whack, probably the black bile, giving rise to a melancholia. As a part of Greek or even Shakespearean cosmology, that might be an expectation for the level of knowledge at the time, but we have long-since dropped these ideas as a useful explanation of bodily functions.

We also now live in the age of mass communication and *alternative facts* that often run contrary to established scientific truths. Here, truth is seen as a relative commodity, dependent on your viewpoint. Former White House Press Secretary Sean Spicer's grossly inaccurate statement about the attendance numbers of Donald Trump's inauguration was seen as a perfectly acceptable alternative to photographic evidence to the contrary by many of his followers. Alternative facts are not really anything new, they've been used throughout history, usually by those in power to maintain control or further their own agenda. Classic examples include the notions that Jesus was a Caucasian man, slavery was good for black people, Jewish people were the cause of Germany's pre-war problems, HIV/AIDS was a gay problem and Iraq had weapons of mass destruction. This sort of thing was also the stock in trade of the ancient Greek sophists, who made a living out of rhetoric and popular public speaking. Whilst evidence to the contrary eventually overturns most false arguments in time, often they persist far longer than they should, and sometimes even return after a long period of absence.

Perhaps the most surprising alternative fact with a resurgence of late has been that of the flat-Earth movement, which has had a new spike of interest following the rapper B.o.B. making an argument on Twitter about a flat-Earth in 2016. This was followed by a GoFundMe campaign to research it. The US Flat Earth Society was also recently reported to have posted that it had 'members all around the globe' on Twitter. However, given the preponderance of ironic and parody accounts it has become impossible to tell if even this is genuine or not.

Alternative facts seem to run counter to the notion that a fact is a piece of information based on an objective reality, and rely on the idea that any piece of information has implicit values attached. Philosophers have been making such arguments for at least 2000 years, but these ideas have been taken up significantly to devalue science and often to promote health scams. Whilst science is definitely not value-free in the way it is implemented, the fundamental principles employed in public healthcare and the modern evidence-based practice movement rely on a belief in the value of evidence rather than theory to support practice. This basically opens up three choices to those who wish to sell a product or service which has no scientific basis for health benefits:

1. promote an anti-science argument that science cannot explain the metaphysical nature of the product,
2. suggest that science has yet to catch up with the well-known benefits of the product or
3. manufacture bad-science designed to support the product.

Sometimes all three techniques are used together in a kitchen-sink approach to provide an alternative narrative in a health scam, but all are fundamentally designed to make us buy something, and also designed to make us trust the person selling it.

Chapter 3

Trust me, I am not a doctor

In 2010 an Angus Reid Opinion Poll in Canada revealed an increasing number of Canadians did not trust their doctors.[12] In 1966, more than 75% of Americans reportedly trusted their physicians, whilst in 2014 only 58% of people agreed that doctors could be trusted, and more recent international studies have also suggested that trust in physicians is declining.[13] In the 2014 Ebola crisis, less than one-third of Americans said they trusted public health officials to share complete and accurate information.[14] Nevertheless, public healthcare professions still remain at the top of all professions in terms of perceptions of honesty and ethical standards overall, and nurses came out above medical doctors in both 2018 and 2019 Gallup polls.[15]

Deceptive divisions

As discussed earlier, a common justification given for the rise in trust in wellness and alternative health practitioners is that contemporary 'Western' healthcare is fixated on curing disease, whilst what has been termed 'non-allopathic' healthcare (based upon ancient and traditional remedies) focuses on holistic care, which is also argued to be what consumers really want. In actuality, this is rather an oversimplification of the complexities of modern healthcare and medicine. Firstly, there is really no

Eastern, Western, Southern or Northern Medicine; there is just bio-physiological medicine which is based on scientific evidence (drawn from multiple global sources) and other medical traditions which are based upon alternative socio-cultural traditions. The argument is usually used to imply an overly simplistic binary rhetoric of 'modern Western science', being bad, vs 'ancient Eastern philosophy', being good. Even a cursory deconstruction of this reveals a naïve anti-science agenda. Although still a widely popularised meme, any credible historical scholar will attest this is a poor reflection of the development of modern science, completely ignoring Asian and Middle-Eastern contributions to science.

Science is universal, and its methods contributed to by numerous cultures. In Section IV, I will explore how the term 'alternative medicine' is also something of a misnomer because it suggests a false dichotomy between two kinds of medicine, scientific medicine and alternative medicine. Science-based healthcare has become one of the greatest successes of human development, because of a focus on establishing evidence of efficacy of interventions. Anything that can be demonstrated to have a positive impact on people's health, be it herbs, diets, exercises or new drugs, becomes a part of it, irrespective of where it arises. For example, many drugs and practices have developed from traditional remedies such as Indigenous people's use of willow bark containing acetylsalicylic acid for pain (now available as aspirin), or by their treatment of scurvy through conifer-needle tonics, which actually contain high volumes of vitamin C. Sometimes, it takes time for beneficial new health practices to become adopted and less useful practices discarded, but medical science is rapidly advancing and changing the way we live. This raises the logical question of why we should want to seek alternatives to it. In this book I will explore some explanations that aim to answer this question.

Secondly, as discussed earlier, the term 'allopathic' medicine is usually used as a pejorative term to discredit any health science that employs the use of pharmacologically active agents or surgical interventions to treat pathophysiologic processes. Although there is some truth in the fact that the majority of medical treatments are aimed at specific physiological issues, and acute care services are designed at resolving disease and illness, the myth of allopathic medicine completely ignores the nature of modern medical care, primary healthcare services and the role of nursing in the system. Modern medical care is not simply focused on cure, or single organs or systems, and preventive medicine is practised by all physicians to keep patients healthy.

The role of nursing is typically ignored in arguments over allopathic modern medicine. As a nurse, I know that many people do not really understand what we do, but the whole ethos of nursing is about caring for the whole person, including their personal, psychosocial, family or community health needs. As nurses outnumber physicians by about five to one around the globe, the assumption we have no real influence in the healthcare system, or are simply hand servants of the medical profession, is misleading.

Promoting distrust

The idea that people are taking their health into their own hands and are interested in health promotion is certainly a positive thing, but such arguments used by the wellness and alternative medicine movement largely signify an argument for mistrust in scientific healthcare, whilst some providers imply they have specialist esoteric knowledge and can provide additional health benefits not available through public systems. In essence, people's trust in scientific healthcare and doctors appears to be declining, and even the title 'doctor' does not carry the same weight of expert authority as it used to. In the age of online diploma mills and private alternative-health-professional colleges, the reality is a professional wellness or alternative health qualification is easily obtained. Unfortunately, there is practically no meaningful regulation of these schools in much of Europe and North America, and it is a case of 'buyer beware' (see page 226).

Modern medicine is horrid

Like most human endeavours, modern medicine is indeed flawed and most of us do not enjoy a visit to the doctor or dentist. It usually involves a trip to noisy chaotic clinics or offices, with unpleasant diagnostic procedures, and mixing it up with lots of people who are ill. Let's face it, modern medicine is usually very disagreeable. To paraphrase Winston Churchill, modern medicine is probably the worst possible form of healthcare, apart from all the others we have tried. Although modern scientific healthcare and medicine have achieved numerous successes, most notably reduced infant mortality, prevention and treatment of infectious diseases and life-saving surgical procedures, all contributing to an increased lifespan, there are also numerous areas where problems remain. The treatment of chronic diseases and combating stress continue to be challenging. Cancer is still a major killer.[16] New strains of bacteria and viruses arise and antibiotics become less effective with resistant strains evolving, and issues of quality assurance with medical errors and adverse events make the headlines on a daily basis. Arguments citing the failures of medicine are frequently used as a justification for ignoring medical advice in favour of alternative sources of health knowledge.

Many of these criticisms of modern healthcare are spread by proponents of the wellness movement through modern social media, and the contemporary anti-vaccination movement is an interesting case in point, being one that was highlighted by the World Health Organization as 'a top threat to global health in 2019'.[17] The warning came after a 30% spike in measles cases had occurred internationally following drops in the uptake of childhood vaccination against the disease, including in several countries where the virus had been virtually eliminated.

Where's the harm?

Another argument that is frequently used in the wellness industry is the notion that, unlike medicine and modern healthcare, at the end of the day their products and services are all generally harmless and support consumer choice in their health. However, this argument is fundamentally flawed; as the old adage goes, aeroplane crashes do not really validate flying carpets. Whilst the majority of these practices may indeed be relatively harmless, the impact of them in terms of public health is actually not very well understood. Levels of risk in healthcare are difficult to quantify, but a significant clinical risk may be considered one where unnecessary harm is a likely outcome of a healthcare practice or choice (taking into consideration current knowledge, available resources and the context of care delivery), compared with the risk of non-treatment or other treatment. To date there is little quality research exploring the nature of the uptake of wellness health products and services in terms of risk, or into the factors that help explain people's desire to engage in potentially hazardous health practices.

Research has demonstrated that many patients use alternative remedies that are well known to cause serious adverse reactions or drug interactions, such as the use of the aristolochia root or Chinese knotweed.[18, 19, 20, 21] Other practices present significant risks in terms of people avoiding well-established effective public healthcare practices, in preference to alternative approaches. For example, the use of homeopathic vaccines in place of medical vaccines is well known to be ineffective. Herbal treatments have also been associated with adverse events through unwanted drug interactions, and psychological harm has also been documented where alternative medicine was employed as a substitute for medical treatment.[22, 23] Serious injuries with physical manipulative alternative therapies such as chiropractic have also been documented, and a 2002 systematic review of the research identified that elderly patients frequently suffered harm from the use of alternative medical therapies.[24, 25, 26]

Proponents of the wellness industry and alternative medicine will often contrast these events as rare compared with the huge number of medical errors that occur every year with conventional healthcare. Yet such comparisons are unsound, as we don't know the incidence of adverse events in these mainly private practices, and by their very nature the majority of customers of wellness and alternative health products and services are adults who are not acutely ill and do not require invasive life-saving interventions. In truth, these practices may be far from harmless, and we don't have a good handle on the actual risks associated with adopting them. Undoubtedly, many of these practices also involve deception with misinformation (either intentionally or not).

Misinformation and deceptive claims

In California in the USA, a woman died due to a reaction to an intravenous infusion of turmeric prescribed by a naturopath for a skin condition in 2017.[27] Though there is no medical condition whatsoever for which intravenous turmeric has been proven as an efficacious therapeutic intervention, it was promoted as an effective cure by the practitioner. In another sad case, a toddler died of meningitis in Alberta, Canada after his parents used coneflowers (echinacea), recommended by their naturopath to boost his immunity, and other natural remedies, instead of consulting a medical doctor. Again, echinacea is not an established effective treatment for meningitis or any infection compared to readily available antimicrobials. In the days leading up to his death, they treated their son, Ezekiel, with other home remedies, including maple syrup, water, juice with frozen berries and finally a mixture of apple cider vinegar, horseradish root, hot peppers, mashed onion, garlic and ginger root.[28] In British Columbia in 2018, a remedy derived from rabid-dog saliva was prescribed for the treatment of a toddler's belligerent behaviour; this resulted in professional sanctions against a naturopath from their regulatory body.[29] In all of these cases, licensed healthcare practitioners were involved who made seriously inaccurate claims of efficacy for the products they recommended based on claims of their alternative expertise.

In probably one of the most well-publicised cases, in 2014 the self-styled Australian wellness guru, Belle Gibson, claimed she had cured herself of brain cancer through dieting and promoted her healthy cookbook and application *The Whole Pantry* for cancer patients. The Instagram star had raised substantial funds through sales of the book with the help of her hundreds of thousands of followers and claimed it was going to charity. By early 2015, it was estimated that in excess of $1 million (AUD) had been made in sales of *The Whole Pantry*. However, it subsequently turned out she had never had cancer and had failed to donate the money, and instead lived a lavish lifestyle on the profits. In the subsequent investigation, Penguin Australia Pty Ltd, the publisher of the book, cooperated with the authorities and agreed to make a $30,000 (AUD) donation to the Victorian Consumer Law Fund, acknowledging that it had not taken adequate steps to verify Gibson's claims prior to publishing the book. Justice Debra Mortimer found that Gibson's claims had been misleading and deceptive, and that: 'Ms Gibson had no reasonable basis to believe she had cancer from the time she began making these claims in public to promote *The Whole Pantry* book and the apps in mid-2013.' However, there was insufficient evidence to prove that she was not acting out of delusion. At the time of writing, Gibson has yet to pay the $410,000 (AUD) fine levied by the Australian Consumer Court.[30] Sections II, III and IV of this book explore these and other cases of serious safety issues in depth.

I want to believe

Today, purveyors of deceptive healthcare have capitalised on a growing lack of public trust in science and medicine, and on our unerring ability to want to believe in things beyond the existing limits of scientific knowledge. Of course, science has certainly been misused a lot over the years and certainly has its limitations. Many conditions remain obstinately untreatable and public health services often struggle to meet public demands. On the other hand, wellness and alternative health services offer pleasant and relaxed therapeutic spaces and services generally designed to align with the customer's beliefs rather than challenge them. Commercial health gurus and celebrity doctors are transforming ancient healthcare practices into aspirational and desirable lifestyles. Movie stars and social media influencers sway our perceptions of health, social status and wealth. The wellness and alternative health movement has become a major industry.

The hyperbolic bandwagon

Many physicians, established health professionals and alternative medicine practitioners have capitalised on this trend. Undoubtedly, much wellness advice does have value in terms of general health promotion, and some alternative therapeutics do work, but most often not in any clinically useful way compared with conventional therapies. Other therapies and practices simply work due to the placebo effect, which we now know may account for up to 25% of the effect of any medicine. However, the hyperbole that now surrounds most of this industry is nothing short of astonishing. Inevitably, most wellness and alternative health offerings involve taking something with some small element of truth in it, transforming it with inflated claims of value in the treatment of an illness or benefits for personal health, and then marketing it with all of the modern tools of consumer culture. In this way, knowledge supporting the value of a simple whole-food, plant-based diet can be morphed into claims of preventing or treating cancer. Some practitioners are clearly well aware of the deceptive nature of the products and services they sell, whilst others have convinced themselves that they have unique cures, and their products and services are innovative, astonishing breakthroughs, despite all evidence to the contrary. Like our con-man Jeff, many who engage in these activities will argue that their behaviour is perfectly reasonable. Nevertheless, the majority of wellness and alternative health practitioners operate on a very different level of integrity from public health professionals, although, as we explore later in the book, they often mimic their educational and practice structures. The result is a self-sustaining business model providing intangible benefits to all but those providing them.

The modern healthcare paradox

We all care about our health at some level, and exploring why we are all susceptible to health misinformation and scams is a fascinating subject. This book is not about the case for or against medicine, wellness or alternative health, nor is it about celebrity influence and social media. It is simply about deception in the healthcare sector, how it works and how to avoid it. It remains a paradox that in our current, high-tech society, we have arrived at a new level of consumer-driven health nonsense fuelled by social media – one that targets the vulnerable and relies on our good nature and human fallibility to sustain deceptive business practices. On the one hand we embrace scientific and technological advances that have revolutionised human health and the miracles of modern medicine, whilst on the other we engage in unhealthy lifestyle choices, seek unrealistic wellness alternatives and support the licensing of dubious (and even dangerous) healthcare practitioners. Dissatisfaction with existing public health options can lead to people searching elsewhere for answers, and fundamentally, it is an issue of trust and where we place, or misplace, it.

Section II

Health scams

Chapter 4

What is a health scam?

Generally, the law defines fraud as the use of deceit, falsehoods or other fraudulent means to cheat a person of property, money, valuable security or any service, and health fraud is on the increase. In the UK, a 2012 report identified it as a significant and growing threat to patient care;[104] so much so that the government set up a special Health Authority in 2016 to counter fraud in the NHS and public health, the NHS Counter Fraud Authority (NHSCFA). A 2018 NHS report from the NHSCFA estimated that a staggering £1.29 billion could be lost to economic crime from the NHS alone on an annual basis due to health fraud.[105] The UK National Fraud and Cyber Crime Reporting Centre (Action Fraud) also identifies health fraud as a growing and problematic area of criminal activity. They particularly cite a growth in sales of health- and medicine-related products and services that appear to be a legitimate form of alternative medicine, after people receive an email or advertisement promising miracle cures that offer unbelievable results. Typically, fraudsters lead their victims to believe they'll receive quality products or services for a lower price than they are currently paying, or can provide guaranteed cures for acne, skin blemishes, AIDS, arthritis, baldness, cancer, impotence and weight loss.[106] In Canada, where I live, the Canadian Anti-Fraud Centre (CAFC) has documented a significant rise in health-related frauds (or scams as they are more commonly known) over the past decade, particularly in the area of cybercrime (criminal offences involving a computer to either commit or target crime). In 2012, only 10 victims of health scams were reported in Canada with a total financial loss of $741 (CAD), whilst by 2018 the figure was up to 332 complaints with $93,935 (CAD) of reported losses. CAFC also notes that these data are likely to represent less than 5% of actual fraud activity, as frauds are largely unreported.

Many dubious healthcare practices, whilst not obviously fraudulent, also exist in a grey area of legislation and remain unchallenged in case law, such as the promotion and/or sale of novel health products by celebrities or qualified health practitioners. However, all health scams involve an element of deception in some form or another, and can largely be characterised as opportunistic commercial gain involving sales of a product or service that is either fake or has a claimed effect with little to no substantive evidence of efficacy.[21] Before we look at some key examples, let us explore exactly what deception is and involves.

The nature of deception

Deception itself is an interesting phenomenon and not as straightforward a concept as it might at first appear. In simple terms, it can be considered as acting in such a way as to lead another person to believe something that you yourself do not believe to be true. If we consider deception as the spread of beliefs or statements that are not actually true, this also gives rise to problematic questions about how to verify truth and veracity. Nevertheless, deception can be considered as a simple communication process that always involves two (or more) individuals: the deceiver and the deceived. Deception can also be described as a relational transgression, in that it involves violating implicit or explicit rules of behaviour in relationships

– honesty and trust, for example. It includes a wide variety of behaviours, but usually results in feelings of betrayal and distrust when discovered, and is generally considered a human characteristic, although it also has roots in evolutionary biology. We might consider the example of animals that deceive through camouflage, or by attracting prey with deceptive lures, such as in the case of the anglerfish.[107]

Practically speaking, deception is some form of communication, involving distortion or omissions, that serves to misrepresent something that the deceiver themselves knows. It may take one of two forms: one where the deceiver is aware of the deception, and one where they are not. The first form is therefore, intentional (basically, this is the same as lying, as it simply involves propagating a deliberate untruth). The other form is more complex, as it involves some kind of self-deception where an intention to deceive is not necessary. This is different from lying, as here the deceiver has no knowledge that they are intentionally deceiving.

This notion of self-deception remains a complex and controversial idea. Whether it is possible for us to actually deceive ourselves has been a topic of hot debate for both psychologists and philosophers alike. Self-deception can be regarded as the process of convincing oneself of something, and at the same time, not revealing knowledge of this deception to oneself. This requires a person to reject or rationalise away the importance or significance of contrary evidence and logical argument that challenges the deceptive belief the person holds. Therefore, self-deceivers apparently must:

1. hold contradictory beliefs and
2. intentionally get themselves to hold a belief they know to be false.

This presents something of a paradox, because it seems to pose a logically impossible state of mind: expressly, consciously believing something and not believing it at the same time! Nevertheless, in the light of the substantial evidence that self-deception is not only possible but actually widespread, researchers have sought resolution of this paradox. Some approaches have attempted to use 'intentionality' as an explanation. Here, deceiving oneself is argued to require some kind of purposeful intent involving partitioning of the mind. This separation of the mind may be done over time, or by dividing concepts between different factions (such as the conscious and unconscious mind). In this way one might intentionally hide the deceit in the subconscious in some way. However, these ideas have generally fallen out of favour with psychologists who today prefer 'non-intentionalist' theories that suggest being deceived is nothing more than believing falsely, or being mistaken. Some non-intentionalist explanations even go so far as to suggest that self-deceivers actually recognise at some level that their belief is false, but they make an ongoing effort to resist the idea of this unwelcome truth, driven by the anxiety such recognition would cause. Self-deceivers, when challenged, will frequently claim that they are not misleading others, even though they may be withholding or misrepresenting important information. People may simply ignore, or filter out, contrary evidence or views. People sometimes like to think this way, because it makes it easier for them to continue an activity that they enjoy. Alternatively, self-deception may provide a social or economic advantage in some way. Whatever cognitive processes are involved, self-deception does seem to exist. For our purposes here, it can be considered as the ongoing belief, support and dissemination of an idea (or ideas) in the face of overwhelming contradictory evidence that it (or they) are untrue.

Deception and bullshit

The Princeton philosopher Professor Harry Frankfurt went as far as to suggest that there is a distinct form of self-deception observed in science, known fittingly as 'bullshit' (BS). He argued, BS is frequently seen in academic work where a person becomes indifferent to the difference between truth and falsehood as long as their position is supported. The motivation is not to find the truth or perpetuate a falsehood, but to serve some other purpose, such as to gain recognition, status or even notoriety. He argued that those who produce BS certainly aren't honest, but neither can they be considered liars, given that a liar and the honest man are linked in their common regard for truth.[108]

Often, perpetrators of BS demonstrate misleading arguments to support their position. I suspect all of us have some tendency towards this kind of self-deception. I guarantee, everyone reading this can think of sometime when they exaggerated somewhat in recounting something, either for humour or for some other effect. Politicians do it all the time, with former President Donald Trump's ongoing narrative on immigration fears being an excellent example. I would also guess everyone can also recall some child at school who exaggerated things to make him/herself more likeable, or would even admit to doing that themselves. It's a normal human trait, and generally a tendency that is fairly harmless and one that we grow out of. However, in some people it can become a problematic behavioural issue, as their being able to discriminate between fact and falsehood becomes blurred. An example would be a person advertising a new pain-relieving device by claiming that they have prestigious advanced degrees, when in fact these are worthless diploma-mill qualifications. The truthfulness of these claims is not important to the perpetrator, or even if the device works or not, as in terms of BS the argument is irrelevant to the main objective of increasing sales.

The motivation may not even be as simple as personal gain. Frankfurt suggested that sometimes proponents of BS have no financial interests but simply believe in something to the extent they are unconcerned with truth or falsehood as they are completely invested in their belief, accepting nothing that conflicts with it. For example, a hypnotherapist recently told me they had seen a hysterectomy performed using only hypnosis for anaesthesia. That sounds quite remarkable, yet I am sure they believed it. If the person telling you something like this is someone you would normally trust, then you might be inclined to believe them without further exploration. In this example, there is certainly some good evidence that hypnosis techniques can place people in a highly relaxed state where they are susceptible to ideas, and this can be useful for changing behaviours. Also, pain is known to be psychologically mediated. However, in exploring the claim further, it became apparent that what the hypnotherapist actually saw was a video, and it was not a first-hand experience. They also confirmed they actually had no idea if other drugs or local anaesthetics were used, and I could find no independent written accounts of it, or quality studies published that supported the use of hypnotherapy in such surgery. Additionally, no gynaecology units or anaesthetists are currently using the technique. It is possible, of course, that the claim is true, but it has shifted from a trustworthy truthful first-hand account to anecdotal evidence from someone with a vested interest in the technique.

The truth is more likely to be that they saw some questionable video evidence and accepted it as true because it fitted with their current views on the value of hypnotherapy and alternative health techniques. However, challenging the person making a BS claim with more detailed questions, though quite reasonable, does not usually go down well. Most of us tend to let these things slide without doing so when we hear them, as few people enjoy being characterised as narrow-minded sceptics. This is often how such ideas continue to propagate, and how faith-healers continue to succeed in their businesses (see Section IV). However, this sort of bias is something we are all susceptible to, and we will come back to this later in the book.

Delusion

Deception is also quite different from delusion, although it may be practically indistinguishable from it. However, the latter is considered the result of some kind of neurological dysfunction or mental illness, rather than a normal cognitive process.[107] For example, children often hang on to belief in the invulnerability of their parents, and parents often enact deceptions on their children to make them feel safe. These are normal rather than delusional processes, whilst the QAnon-promoted idea that Satan and the government are trying to deliberately infect you with the SARS-CoV-2 virus using the CIA or MI5, does involve delusional thinking; notwithstanding, similar ideas have actually been promoted by several influential preachers.[109] Delusions may also be accompanied by hallucinations and other signs of mental illness in more extreme cases.

The nature of deception in modern healthcare is, then, a complex issue. It is readily apparent that some of those who perpetuate health scams are being deliberately deceptive for personal gain, and are essentially crooks. On the other hand, those who actively promote misinformation and falsehoods may simply be demonstrating a form of self-deception with practices that require their willing suspension of disbelief in the face of conflicting evidence, and acceptance of alternative (often mystical or supernatural) explanations. Nonetheless, for those of us who experience the effects of health deception, the results are essentially the same in both cases, and typically negative.

Chapter 5

A profusion of health scams and devious practices

Health scams take a wide variety of forms, through simple misrepresentations of the efficacy of health products to unlicensed practitioners selling health services. They involve fraudulent or deceptive acts or operations and have been perpetuated by all types of practitioner and business, from massage-parlour owners to licensed physicians. Here, we will explore the most common scams that involve direct marketing to the public rather than other types of health-related fraud which also exist (such as tax-evasion by doctors and pharmaceutical companies). The growth of information technology and the Internet has also supported a massive growth of these, alongside other fraudulent activities, as it has opened up the opportunity for practically unregulated global mass-marketing.

Theft and reselling

A simple health scam is the theft and resale of stolen health products, most often drugs or single-use medical equipment. You might think it would be hard to sell-on stolen medical goods, but apparently it is not that difficult. Here in British Columbia, the College of Pharmacists recently fined a pharmacist $25,000 for reselling pharmacy supplies and prescription medications stolen by a hospital employee – typical of this sort of activity.

According to the outcome of a complaint, an investigation found that pharmacist Laurent Pierre Roy was very likely to have been aware of the doubtful nature of the supplies he was receiving, which he had been purchasing for at least five years.[110]

In 2006, specialist medical diagnostic equipment worth around £1 million was stolen in a spate of thefts from several NHS hospitals. Police and health officials reported concerns that criminal gangs were stealing diagnostic equipment to order, to be exported and sold abroad.[111] Theft remains a massive ongoing problem, and in the UK the NHS Counter Fraud Authority reports that theft is likely to cost the NHS around £1.25 billion a year.[128] In a recent example, £160k-worth of coronavirus personal protective equipment was stolen from a Salford warehouse in May 2020.[112]

Fake products and services

More commonly, health scams involve selling some sort of fake products or services. In the past this was most likely to happen through door-to-door sales, magazine or newspaper advertisements, or pop-up outlets hawking 'snake-oil' remedies or cure-alls. Examples of this are abundant from the past, such as *Dr Miles Restorative Nervine*, a remedy marketed in the 1880s in America for a wide variety of illnesses, including exhaustion, headaches, insomnia, backaches, epilepsy, miscellaneous pains and spasms, heart trouble, side-effects of smoking, ageing and the frustrations caused by annoying children. It was actually a bromide-sedative syrup, and simply a forerunner of modern tranquilisers. Today, the majority of health scam activity occurs through the Internet.

In a research project undertaken between 2016 and 2017, several colleagues and I set out to explore the nature of health scams and the techniques used to market them on the Internet. We found a surprising amount of deceptive healthcare practices in a number of different areas.[21] Most of those we identified involved products of some kind, and a major area, where we found huge amounts of deceptive products being sold, was in marketing that targeted people with concerns about their body image.

Body-building supplements

Nutritional body-building supplements, for example, were predominantly targeted at adolescents and young men. Research into adolescent and adult male perceptions of body image has established clear links between feelings of confidence and power in social situations and body image, making this population very susceptible to misleading marketing.[113, 114, 115] Products range from protein cocktails to ginseng, and of particular concern here were the unsupported claims of efficacy, extensive use of testimonials and unrealistic before-and-after imagery used to market them. For example, although there is no good evidence that it has any effect on libido, one nutritional supplement vendor quite unrealistically claims that its D-aspartic acid product: '… can have a profound effect on strength, muscle size, density, thickness and fat loss, …can also lead to increases in libido, a general feeling of well-being and sexual performance enhancements'.[21]

Weight loss products

Similarly, weight loss products were predominantly marketed to younger women, in the form of metabolic stimulants or body training gimmicks such as weight loss wraps. Examples here also have virtually zero evidence of effectiveness for weight loss, and included apple-cider vinegar, green coffee and waist training bands. Exposure to media depicting a thin-ideal body has long been related to body image concerns for women, and adolescent women are known to be particularly vulnerable to such concerns.[113, 116] These scams targeting individuals with body dissatisfaction made extensive use of the Internet as a powerful and relatively unregulated communication channel for deceptive media and persuasion techniques to sell products with minimal, or no, effectiveness. As many studies have confirmed, body dissatisfaction can be a precursor to other negative mental health issues, and activities preying on these concerns have the potential to do serious harm.[116, 117]

Miracle medicinal products

Scams selling medicinal products were also highly prevalent in our research. Most of these deceptions are characterised by unrealistic claims of efficacy for natural and herbal remedies, specifically for conditions where there exists no or poor supporting scientific evidence. Products were often sold using deceptive and/or celebrity promotion (sometimes even by physicians). Additionally, aggressive subscription strategies for exclusively branded products were frequently used. Some examples included:

- Arthri-D3 (N-acetyl-glucosamine with turmeric and other herbs) – this purported to reduce joint inflammation in arthritis
- bee propolis – this claimed to have antiviral effects for HIV
- chaga mushrooms – these were claimed to have an anti-carcinogenic effect
- aloe vera juice – this was claimed to be beneficial for psoriasis
- Radionics machines – these were claimed to increase personal energy levels (see page 198).

A large group of remedies in this category targeted skin conditions, with acne remedies being particularly prevalent (24% of those identified in this category).[21] For example, acne-control programmes, such as Proactiv, are marketed on the web and in shopping malls as subscription-based services. They sell a range of branded products claimed to be highly effective, and some even offer 60-day money-back guarantees. However, the ingredients are simply over-the-counter acne products available in your local pharmacy with minor additions, repackaged more expensively in a proprietary package. To get them you have to sign up to a subscription service with payment up front and with instalments for a programme. This is very clever marketing, as acne control takes months and is notoriously difficult to manage (especially in teenagers – the target market). By the time customers have figured out it's just the same products they had been using previously and the miraculous effects advertised do not happen, it is usually well beyond two months of use.

The marketing also cleverly used celebrity endorsements, with phenomenal before and after videos and photos to lure customers in. Whilst some of these products marketed might have some limited medical value, others were completely fake, such as the companies selling 'DNA repair' and Radionics machines (explained on page 198).

Bogus claims by alternative health service providers

Another major area of highly exaggerated claims of efficacy was found in the marketing of health services by alternative medicine practitioners. Most of these scams required consultation with a practitioner who would claim to have an effective treatment or cure for a specific medical condition, when in reality no such treatment was known to be effective – for example, chiropractors claiming they could resolve asthma through spinal manipulation, or naturopaths claiming they could treat cancer with intravenous (IV) vitamin supplements. The majority of these scams were offered by naturopathic practitioners, including such things as food allergy testing for asthma, or cryotherapy for inflammation. Faith-healing was also evident, with one practitioner, known as the 'Dreamhealer', based here in Vancouver, claiming to be able to teach people to reverse their illness symptoms through distance energy healing. Overall, the use of inflated claims of expertise on websites and testimonials was highly prevalent, and also strategies designed to remain technically within the law, such as sales of self-help faith-based seminars or the promotion of donation-based services. In terms of health scams, alternative medicine has a whole set of issues of its own, and we will explore these in the next chapter.

Healthy lifestyle and wellness products

A further significant class of scams (by number of instances identified) consisted of those broadly defined as healthy lifestyle products. In particular, these scams involved selling anti-ageing, sexual enhancement, and nutritional booster products. Like most health fads, scams in this category seem to come and go. One developing trend in 2018-19 was that of promoting alkaline water for its anti-ageing and detoxifying properties (see page 286). These scams were characterised by vague claims of enhancing and improving your life in some way, such as boosting your energy. I actually had a young product representative follow me around my local supermarket last year trying to sell me this stuff, arguing with me about its radical health-giving properties. Finally, a small but developing number of diagnostic testing services were also identified, including mail-order genetic diagnostic services and even a mail-order postural assessment service.[21]

Health insurance scams

Apart from individuals, or groups of individuals, making fraudulent claims against insurance companies, of which there are numerous well-documented examples, scams selling bogus health insurance are another area of fraudulent activity.

These are rare in the UK and Canada where there is universal health coverage. However, in the United States there have been numerous insurance frauds. Schemers have proven very willing to take advantage of uninsured people's vulnerabilities and exploit them by offering bogus insurance policies. As with other frauds, they manipulate people's expectations and concerns, often using popular terms and buzzwords and jargon like 'healthcare reform' – to gain trust and credibility with their victims. Whilst genuine programmes must explain the key points before they ask you to sign up, scammers gloss over the major points or leave them out altogether. They are well prepared for questions, and often direct potential clients to sophisticated websites, demonstrating promises of great coverage with enticingly low premiums. The problems arise when clients attempt to claim and their coverage proves to be non-existent or practically useless.

James Lee Graff, Kari Hansen and William Kokott operated one of America's most brazen health insurance schemes and sold phony health coverage, through the company Employers Mutual LLC, to more than 30,000 Americans citizens between 2000 and 2001. The total damage was estimated at more than $42 million USD including over $14 million in stolen premiums and the medical bills that ill policyholders had to pay from their own pockets when their coverage turned out to be bogus. Graff and Hansen received lengthy jail terms in 2007, whilst Kokott died during the trial.[118]

More recently, in October 2018, Federal authorities shut down a network of Florida companies under the Hollywood-based Simple Health Plans LLC, citing the use of aggressive and deceptive sales tactics to sell inadequate health insurance products that fell short of the requirements of the Affordable Care Act and left tens of thousands of people around the country with unpaid medical bills. 'There is good cause to believe' that the Florida companies have sold shoddy coverage by falsely claiming that such policies were comprehensive health insurance or qualified health plans under the Affordable Care Act, Judge Gayles of the Federal District Court in Miami noted in a restraining order issued at the request of the Federal Trade Commission. Telemarketers had lured consumers through websites offering 'Trumpcare' and 'Obamacare', using the logos of well-known insurers to make the coverage appear credible.[119] Others simply used completely fake companies to scam money out of unsuspecting victims, and a growing trend of overseas telesales health insurance scams seems to be arising. The Insurance Bureau of Canada has noted concerns here and confirms that legitimate insurance companies, brokers, agents and direct writers will never request a signing fee, or that a payment be sent through an electronic or wire transfer, or to an unidentified post-office box.

Illicit billing

As we have seen, healthcare providers from a wide range of health professions have been caught engaging in fraudulent activity over the years. Apart from the ones involving corruption through kickbacks for prescribing certain drugs, or the unnecessary issuance of prescriptions, the most common such frauds usually involve illicit billing. These again are much more common in North America where private health insurance is a major industry. The following are the main classes of such practices:

- **Billing for services not rendered:** Here the service provider submits claim forms to government healthcare plans and/or insurance companies for services and care that was never provided, and the corresponding patient files have no supporting documentation. Such was the case of Dr Kaim Lalini, a dentist in British Columbia who owned several clinics across Vancouver and was ordered to pay $30,000 and stop practising for six months in 2018 after admitting to charging for unnecessary procedures.[120]

- **Billing for a non-covered service as a covered service:** Here, the provider delivers a treatment which is considered experimental and therefore not approved by government healthcare or other insurance plans. However, by coding it as something else that is covered by insurance, they can submit claim forms and still get paid for utilising the experimental treatment.

- **Misrepresenting dates of service:** Providers can make more money by reporting they visited with and/or treated the same patient on two separate days rather than one day. Each visit is considered as a separate billable service. By using false dates, it is more profitable for the provider.

- **Misrepresenting locations of service:** Here several clinic visits are billed even though patients may be self-medicating for some of them. For example, allergy patients may be given four pre-loaded syringes of drugs to administer at home during the month, and attend the clinic once a month. However, the clinic charges the insurer for four separate clinic sessions to administer the injections. Most insurers do not accept self-injection as a reimbursable expense.

- **Misrepresenting providers of service:** As seen with the cases of Rajdeep Kaur Khakh and Malachi A Love-Robinson, impersonation of a physician and billing for treatment does happen. More frequently than those extreme examples, practitioners sign insurance claim forms showing that they have provided care when, in reality, lesser-qualified healthcare professionals or assistants actually provided it. This was the case with Kermit Gosnell's notorious Women's Medical Society Clinic, where unlicensed doctors and nurses were employed to perform treatments.

- **Waiving of deductibles and/or co-insurer payments:**
  Some providers have been identified waiving patients'
  deductibles (the amount they agree to pay out of your own
  pocket) or co-insurer payments in order to treat them. This
  can be more profitable than not treating, or, by submitting
  other false claims to insurance companies to make up the
  difference, they can make up this difference. The providers
  know that patients are unlikely to complain because their
  co-payments and deductibles were waived.[121]

- **Incorrect diagnoses or procedures:** Unscrupulous
  providers can bill for extra services if they report false
  diagnoses or procedures performed. For example, if a
  parent goes to a chiropractor with a perfectly healthy
  infant for a check-up, they can intentionally misdiagnose
  non-existent issues and charge for unnecessary tests and
  treatments. If an elderly patient falls inside a nursing home,
  a crooked doctor could intentionally misdiagnose a head
  trauma requiring the (unnecessary) use of a computed
  tomography (CT) scan and/or blood tests. The potential
  for fraudulent provider claims with the elderly, children
  and/or those with mental health issues is considerable.
  Arguably, some of this could be simple professional
  incompetence. Nevertheless, misdiagnoses do allow for
  potentially significant income generation.

In 2014, an undercover investigation for BBC 1 South's '*Inside
Out*' accused the Twyford physician Dr Julian Kenyon of using
false diagnostic tests at his clinic. Dr Kenyon had been using a
technique called electrodermal testing (see page 199), claiming
that ailments and allergies could be detected by measuring
the skin's resistance to a small electric charge with a device.
The programme showed Dr Kenyon testing a six-year-old boy
with the device and then claiming that he was sensitive to dust
mites.[122] In December that year, Dr Kenyon ended up in front of

a General Medical Council (GMC) conduct tribunal. The panel heard that, after a 20-minute consultation, which cost £300, Dr Kenyon told one terminally ill man with late-stage cancer: 'I am not claiming we can cure you, but there is a strong possibility that we would be able to increase your median survival time with the relatively low-risk approaches described here.' He was referring to an expensive experimental therapy called sono photodynamic therapy (SPDT). This involves using a combination of low-intensity ultrasound and drugs known as sonosensitisers, and light sensitive drugs and light exposure, to target and kill cancer cells. He also made exaggerated claims about the treatment's supposed benefits to an undercover reporter who posed as the husband of a woman with breast cancer. As an experimental and expensive therapy, with no referral from a GP or cancer specialist, it was inappropriate for Dr Kenyon to make these claims. After considering the full details of the case, the GMC allowed him to keep his job but imposed restrictions on his licence for 12 months.[123, 124]

Overutilisation of services

This classically involves billing for unnecessary services. Unscrupulous providers typically use this technique on patients with chronic conditions or a tendency towards hypochondria. They order numerous tests and examinations as long as a patient still has coverage or is able to make payments. Substance rehabilitation facilities and scam cancer clinics are prime exponents of this. According to a US National Survey on Drug Use and Health in 2017, 20.7 million people aged 12 or older needed treatment for an illicit substance use problem (7.6% of people aged 12 or older). There remains significant potential for fraud in this area.[125, 126]

Unlicensed practitioners

Unlicensed practitioners are another form of health scam many people worry about, but thankfully this type of deception is fairly uncommon. However, cases regularly arise and they are often well publicised in the media. In 2008, an Australian man, Vito Zepinic, was criminally convicted by a Sydney magistrate on six counts of falsely holding himself out to be a doctor. He avoided jail in Australia, and was placed on a good behaviour bond. However, he moved to the UK and in September 2009 obtained a Senior Lecturer position at the Unit for Social and Community Psychiatry, Queen Mary University of London. He had claimed a qualification as a medical doctor to gain the position at this prestigious school. Five months after he had started the job, Zepinic's conviction in Australia was brought to the institution's attention and he was immediately suspended. Zepinic had trained as a psychologist at the University of Sarajevo, but no evidence of him having qualified as a medical doctor was ever produced.[127] Also, his registration as a clinical psychologist had been removed in New South Wales, Australia in 2010, although he had applied for reinstatement in 2018. However, the tribunal found that '...far from demonstrating any reflection on or attempts to address the shortcomings identified in the 2010 decision', Zepinic had continued 'to exhibit behaviour that is completely inconsistent with the standards of honesty and integrity expected of a health practitioner'.[128]

Another more infamous case is that of Kermit Gosnell in the USA in 2011, where a number of unlicensed doctors were found to be employed in his Women's Medical Society Clinic in Philadelphia, Pennsylvania, where he performed late-term abortions. Gosnell and various employees were charged with eight counts of murder, 24 felony counts of performing illegal abortions beyond the state of Pennsylvania's 24-week time limit and 227 misdemeanour counts of violating the 24-hour informed consent law. The murder charges related to a woman who died following an abortion procedure, and of seven newborn infants killed by having their spinal cords severed after birth. His clinic was found to employ numerous unqualified, unlicensed and unsupervised staff who misrepresented themselves to patients as qualified doctors and nurses. In 2013, a jury convicted Gosnell on three counts of murder and one count of involuntary manslaughter, and he was sentenced to three life terms in prison without the possibility of parole. Some of Gosnell's employees had little or no medical training, and one was reportedly a teenager still in high school.[129]

In 2012, a health worker who had invented an impressive medical career to secure work as an NHS practice nurse, physician's assistant and doctor was jailed for 15 months. Abdul Pirzada, originally from Afghanistan, came to Britain in 2001, forged a degree and falsely claimed to have worked in global hot spots for the French Red Cross and United Nations. He also landed three jobs at health centres in Birmingham between February 2004 and April 2011, working first as a healthcare assistant and eventually ending up working as a locum general practitioner. Prosecutor Robert Davies told the court: 'In simple terms, the CV is almost entirely a work of fiction or misleading claims.'[130] His claims of medical qualifications gained in Pakistan were false, along with his assertions he had worked as a doctor in Bosnia and Glasgow, although he was thought to have a genuine medical qualification from a Russian university. He was eventually arrested in 2011 when a pharmacist noted that his name on a prescription did not appear on the NHS-approved list; police were alerted to this suspicious behaviour and found a large quantity of drugs at his home.

In Canada in 2013 the College of Dental Surgeons of British Columbia shut down an illegal dental practice run by Tung Sheng Wu, a man with no known training in dentistry. College investigators and police officers entered Wu's residence and found a dental office in a bedroom along with 1500 client files. He escaped to Ontario, but eventually turned himself in and was sentenced to three months in jail and ordered to pay the College's costs. Wu had previously agreed to stop practising dentistry in 2003 after being ordered to do so by a court.[131]

In another Canadian case in 2015, the College of Physicians and Surgeons of British Columbia (CPSBC) challenged a woman named Rajdeep Kaur Khakh who was posing as a doctor and unlawfully injecting people with Botox and other cosmetic filler substances, and ordered her to stop. She signed an undertaking to stop the procedures and to stop using the title of doctor. Once more, in 2019 the CPSBC sought an injunction against Ms Khakh, as it had been reported that she was continuing to provide cosmetic injections under the Instagram name of 'Dr Lipjob'. She was eventually given a suspended 30-day sentence and two years' probation in January, and ordered to pay fines and costs for illegally pretending to be a doctor and injecting dermal fillers despite a previous court order.[132] In a similar case in 2017, police arrested another teenage fake-doctor in Toronto, a 19-year-old woman who had allegedly offered plastic surgery as 'Dr Kitty' in an unlicensed basement medical clinic through advertisements placed in local restaurants.[133]

In one American instance, the fake doctor was actually an errant teenager. Malachi A Love-Robinson was only 18 when he was convicted of practising medicine without a licence in Boynton Beach, Florida. He had been taken into custody in January 2015 after walking the halls of a hospital wearing a lab coat and a stethoscope, but also operated his own office in 2016, called New Birth New Life Medical Center & Urgent Care, in West Palm Beach. He was arrested in October 2016 for practising medicine without a licence after an undercover officer attended his clinic and was given a physical exam and medical advice. He pleaded guilty to several charges in 2018 at the age of 20, and was sentenced to three and a half years in prison.[134]

You would think it would be hard to keep up such deception for any length of time, but in other fascinating examples, Zholia Alemi, 56, worked as a psychiatrist within the NHS and in private practice for more than 22 years despite never qualifying, and in Quebec, Nathalie Bélanger, who had no professional nursing qualifications, worked as a nurse for 20 years.[135] A newspaper investigation in 2018 revealed how Alemi had passed herself off as a senior doctor in the UK despite dropping out of medical school at the University of Auckland in the early 1990s. Her only medical qualification was a degree in human biology. However, she managed to fool medical authorities for 23 years, even passing assessments that allowed her to qualify as an NHS consultant. She was jailed for five years in 2018.[136] In Quebec, Nathalie Bélanger had managed to get hired and keep her job at Jonquière Hospital for 20 years by providing the nursing licence number of someone with the same name. She was eventually discovered when she enrolled in a continuing education course, and someone noticed that the age listed on her licence number did not match up with her actual age. She was immediately suspended pending an investigation, which led to her dismissal. She has since been charged.

In fact, fake clinicians, clinics and dubious qualifications are to be found all around the world. In India in 2014 a number of doctors were accused of fraudulently obtaining licences for medical practice in collusion with middlemen and officials of the Medical Council of India.[137] In most cases in North America, the employment of physicians, nurses and other professionals in positions of trust in public health is rigorously policed, and exceptions of fake practitioners like these rare. That said, a case recently came to light here in British Columbia of two South African doctors, Rosemarie and Sean Cambridge, who had migrated to Canada in 2010 and had been practising medicine here for seven years without a full licence. They operated under a provisional licence, but astonishingly had both repeatedly failed their qualifying exams in British Columbia on at least four occasions over the period. It also came to light that the couple had also unsuccessfully attempted to gain licensure in Saskatchewan in 2010, prior to moving to British Columbia. At least they both had medical qualifications, but were finally removed from the register in 2018 by which time they had a reported 1200 patients on their books.[138]

Pandemic scams

The most recent examples of health scams are likely those that suddenly emerged in the face of the 2020-2021 COVID-19 pandemic. Unfortunately, global disasters and misfortune seem to bring out both the best and worst in human nature. The 2020 outbreak formed a perfect opportunity for scam artists, according to the Royal Canadian Mounted Police (RCMP) and Federal Bureau of Investigation (FBI), with a surge in cases of hucksters targeting people using the Internet searching for help.

In Croydon, in south London, the National Crime Agency reported that a 46-year-old pharmacist was arrested in April 2020 on suspicion of making false and misleading claims about the capability of coronavirus testing kits he had allegedly been trying to sell. In a separate incident, a 39-year-old surveyor from Uxbridge was also charged for the same offence.[139] The test-kits were not officially approved test products and their safety, performance and accuracy were highly suspect.

In the USA, Dr Jennings Ryan Staley, a 44-year-old licensed physician in San Diego, was arrested for allegedly marketing packages of drugs that he said could provide six weeks of immunity from COVID-19. He charged $3995.00 a throw for them.[140] Some fraudsters set up fake pop-up testing sites. At one in Louisville, Kentucky, the providers charged $240 a test, swabbing mouths and gathering personal information whilst using the same gloves between clients.[141]

The rapid increase in such activity led to Operation Quack Hack being initiated by the US Food and Drug Administration and the Federal Trade Commission to clamp down on fake coronavirus medications and cures. It exposed a health underground in America abounding with distrust of medical and governmental authorities.[142] Dr David Brownstein, a physician marketing a bizarre and almost certainly useless range of therapies for COVID-19, argued the two agencies had gone too far. Brownstein said he used his intense regimen of megadose vitamins and iodine for four days, followed by nebulised hydrogen peroxide, iodine, then intravenous treatments of hydrogen peroxide, vitamin C and ozone, on more than 100 COVID-19 patients during the outbreak in the Detroit suburbs in March and April 2020.[142] He was quoted as saying: 'My partners, nurses and I were going out to see patients in their cars in the parking lot in 30-degree weather in March. We were giving them IVs in their cars, and as soon as we started treating them, they got better. We saw 107 patients. Only one was hospitalized. No one died and no one had to be ventilated.'

The FTC did not agree, and ordered him to take down his reports of his novel therapy from his website, to which he complained that, 'It sends a chill out that you can't report anything about COVID that's positive'. The reality is that Brownstein chose to market an expensive and outlandish therapy through a website as 'research' without any obvious prior ethical review or no comparative control group (i.e., patents who did not receive his made-up treatments) rather than attempt to undertake good science and publish a study in a peer-reviewed journal. This is actually quite easy to do for potentially useful Coronavirus research, as ethical review boards and journals have instigated accelerated review processes for COVID-19 research. Instead, he took shortcuts to self-publish his findings from a small confirmatory experimental design, with a huge risk of confirmation bias (see page 134) and the FTC, quite rightly in my view, regarded this as misleading to the public.

The most common forms of deception involved the sales of fake remedies, including some promoted by TV celebrity physician, Doctor Oz (see page 249), who advised the use of supplements and vitamins to boost immunity. Other people recommended more controversial alternative remedies, like using colloidal silver, chaga mushroom blends, 'miracle mineral solution' (bleach) or oil of oregano.[143] None of these had any evidence of value in the treatment or prevention of COVID-19.

Some fraudsters were more inventive, and both the Canadian Anti-Fraud Centre (CAFC) and the FBI posted warnings about the upsurge in COVID-19 scams. Reported scams included sales of fake tests, cures or preventative immune-boosting agents, telephone frauds offering loans and financial services, financial advisors pressuring people to buy COVID-19 stocks in medical or pharmaceutical companies, door-to-door decontamination services, fake charities asking for donations, and even telephone calls from fake Centers for Disease Control and Prevention (CDC) agents offering sales of lists of the names of locally infected people.[144]

Chapter 6

Conspiracy theories –
Just because you're paranoid...

Conspiratorial thinking

One way in which health scams continue to prevail is in the spread of conspiratorial thinking. Intriguingly, a University of Chicago study in 2013 suggested that almost half of Americans believed at least one medical conspiracy theory, with 37% believing that the FDA deliberately suppressed natural cures due to influence from the pharmaceutical industry.[145] These ideas are, of course, completely unsound but overall, they represent a way for people to exert some personal control in complex systems that are difficult to understand without the use of overly-simplistic arguments. People do not become conspiracy theorists overnight, but gradually move from one tenable position (e.g. pharmaceutical companies have a history of behaving badly) through leaps of illogical reasoning to irrational ones (e.g. Big-Phama and the global biomedical healthcare system is suppressing the cure for cancer).

COVID-19 conspiracy theories

The COVID-19 pandemic has proved a fertile ground for the development of such conspiracy theories, particularly by alternative health activists. The upsurge of COVID-19 deniers and conspiracy theorists has been fuelled by social media. A 2020 study in Canada reported almost half of Canadians believed at least one unfounded theory about COVID-19, and a look at UK media reveals similar themes.[146] Many of these theories are promoted by existing anti-vaccination activists such as Del Bigtree and Sherri Tenpenny in the US. Some have focused their attention on the efforts to create and test a vaccine. For example, the Children's Health Defense anti-vaccination organisation, founded by Robert F Kennedy Jr, suggested the rush to find a vaccine, instead of focusing on treatments, is being driven by profit.

Amongst the most outlandish claims are those that viruses cannot be transmitted between people, 5G cell phones are responsible for decreasing immunity and activating the virus, and even that the Bill and Melinda Gates Foundation is running a scheme to depopulate the planet using COVID-19. The theory suggests that wealthy globalists, including Bill Gates and Anthony Fauci, actually unleashed the coronavirus from Wuhan, China, alongside their immune-system-weakening 5G wireless technology, and they now intend to install digital ID tracking chips in our bodies during vaccination against the virus.[142]

The anti-vaccination website Vaxxter.com owned by Sherri Tenpenny published multiple articles promoting such false and unsubstantiated claims about the COVID-19 virus. For example, an April 2020 article was headlined 'China Cures Coronavirus with Vitamin C' and another, headlined 'Is 5G a Deadly Trigger for the Coronavirus?', suggested that 5G radio waves were linked to outbreaks of the new strain of coronavirus in Wuhan, China; Milan, Italy; and Iran, comparing the effects of 5G to starving the brain of oxygen.

Del Bigtree, a media sensationalist and producer of the controversial anti-vaccination film *Vaxxed: From Coverup to Catastrophe*, followed Luc Montagnier's lead and asserted that SARS was a lab-made virus from China. He also claimed that the pandemic wasn't serious as, 'Italy goes through this every year. We just don't report on it', in a web-based question and answer session. Even US President Donald Trump got caught up in spreading unsubstantiated information. An Arizona couple poisoned themselves by ingesting chloroquine phosphate, a chemical used to clean home aquariums, after getting the idea from Trump, who publicised the potential benefits of the drug chloroquine during a televised news conference. The man died and his wife was left in a critical condition. Health Canada became so concerned about this spread of misinformation and the threat to public health that they issued a warning to Canadians not to consider false or misleading claims about COVID-19 spread on social media.[146]

The Big-Pharma conspiracy theory

Not surprisingly, the significant issues in the pharmaceutical industry have resulted in the growth of distrust in modern healthcare provision, and for some, this has developed into belief in the Big-Pharma conspiracy theory. Every day memes flash across social media feeds with texts like 'Big-Pharma is suppressing the cure for cancer. Here's why…' or 'Vaccines are designed to depopulate the world…' or, more recently, 'COVID-19 was created by Bill Gates and Big-Pharma to sell vaccines' or the latest one that new COVID-19 vaccine contains microchips so Bill Gates can track us. The images accompanying them are usually highly emotive and often depict such things as doctors forcing pills down a child's throat, or ludicrously large needles with screaming children. Versions of the Big-Pharma conspiracy theory generally suggest some (or all) of the following are true. The pharmaceutical industry (and associated businesses, professionals, pharmacists, doctors, nurses etc) are:

- trying to extract every last penny out of the pockets of the sick, injured and dying to maximise their profits,
- inventing new maladies so people will buy more drugs,

and inventing more addictive drugs so more people will become addicts,

- concealing cures for all the major diseases (such as cancer), as selling drugs is more profitable than healing people,
- suppressing natural and alternative cures on the principle that they are not patentable and thus not profitable to sell, and only market patented, expensive and less effective drugs,
- renaming old illnesses so people will think their conditions are more serious, making them more willing to pay higher prices for prescriptions,
- in league with governments, or Satan to depopulate the planet, using techniques, such as dumping chemtrails of poisons from commercial aircraft.

A simple internet search for the term 'Big-Pharma' will reveal all of these themes. Narratives from alternative medicine providers also often promote this theory, particularly by suggesting that doctors only treat diseases rather than people and their main motivation is to profit and earn kickbacks from pharmaceutical companies by prescribing as many expensive drugs as possible, and to keep patients on those drugs as long as possible.

Even with all of the well-documented misdeeds of the pharmaceutical industry, these theories are, of course, irrational. Firstly, the conspiracy does not seem to be as successful as its proponents claim as fraudulent practices are discovered and eradicated in the business all the time, as indicated by the number of whistle-blowers and settlements. Likewise, the alleged global depopulation strategy does not seem to be working too well, as the global population is still increasing. Additionally, most drugs sold by Big Pharma are based upon natural products, and some entirely so. Choose any natural substance you can think of, and chances are you'll find that it is being sold by some pharmaceutical company.

The idea that suppressing cures is more profitable than selling them is also illogical. If the idea were to maximise sales of products that treat diseases, marketing vaccines would not make sense. For example, it would be far more profitable to sell more tuberculosis drugs and therapies rather than to cheaply vaccinate people against it. Prevention is cheaper than cure, and more profitable for the company in the long term. If a pharmaceutical company did manage to develop and patent a cancer-curing drug, the profits would be astronomical. Additionally, no single company has a monopoly on developing cures (as is illustrated by the multiple companies engaged in COVID-19 development), and much basic drug research is done in public universities. So, the conspiracy argument relies on accepting there is a global collusion to supress information. Likewise, the idea that hundreds of thousands of healthcare practitioners are conspiring to hide the truth from the public is also absurd. The sheer number of practitioners that would need to be in cahoots to make the conspiracy work is unlikely in the extreme.

In Europe and North America, people tend to spend the same amount of money on pharmaceutical products as they do on unregulated nutritional supplements, vitamins and other herbal or natural remedies, so once again that argument fails a simple test. Nevertheless, those promoting conspiracy theories are usually trying to sell something else, be it a book, membership of a society/club, or a product. The herbal remedy and supplement industry is a multi-billion-dollar business in itself, and (as we shall see) a particularly deceptive one, that makes good use of the Big-Pharma conspiracy theory.[97, 98]

Overall, scams and deceptive practices can be readily found across all spheres of professional healthcare. They have a long history, and the nature of these swindles varies over time, often in unison with changing technology and changes in popular health fads (such as the popularity of alkaline water last year, or at the time of writing, apple cider vinegar and paleo diets).

Unlike simple financial frauds, however, they can have serious implications for your physical and psychological welfare and can cause significant personal harm as well as financial loss. Let's start with a look at one area that frequently makes the headlines, the case of 'bad medicine' and medical malpractice. Unfortunately, there is a lot of it about.

Section III

Bad medicine

Chapter 7

The chequered history of modern medicine

The rise of biomedicine

Most people would be likely to agree that biomedicine, pharmacology, nursing and associated specialist professions dominate professional healthcare delivery in most of the world today. Overall, they have proved very effective, but it hasn't always been that way. Modern healthcare has evolved into a highly specialised, science-based, multidisciplinary industry, and the dominance of medicine and pharmacology within it has mainly been achieved as a result of the adoption of a scientific basis for its practice over the last century. In doing so, medicine has established a significant track-record of success. This, together with legislation controlling the prescription of medicine, has led to it attaining a primacy in modern healthcare provision. Nevertheless, prior to the last century, the success of physicians or surgeons was not that much better than that of any other practitioners. Even the father of medicine, Hippocrates of Kos (460 – 370 BCE), identified that more than half his patients perished due to the diseases he was treating them for.

Back in the 17th century there were significant divisions between medicine, surgery and pharmacy and no clear leader in terms of effective practice. Apothecaries made and sold a variety of dubious medications, including herbal folk remedies, whilst physicians held university degrees and prescribed a range of treatments, including effervescent salts, medicinal snuffs and painkilling necklaces. Physicians were also rather contemptuous of surgery, as surgeons did not have degrees and frequently served in the dual role of barber-surgeon, practising tooth extraction and bloodletting (hence, the red stripe on barbers' poles, symbolising blood).[33] Some surgeons also experimented with tooth whitening by applying nitric acid, with a dramatic whitening effect. Unfortunately, this also destroyed the unfortunate recipients' teeth in the long run.

Eventually, with the increasing success of surgery (particularly following Joseph Lister's antiseptic surgery innovations in 1865), this distinction between medicine and surgery ceased to survive. Today the professions are combined, although interestingly, in the UK when surgeons qualify (they already hold a medical degree), they generally revert to using the title Mr or Ms rather than Dr to emphasise the distinction and their historical medical snub.

As English physician and writer Ben Goldacre wrote in his 2008 book, *Bad Science*, prior to 1900 we had very few effective medical treatments for any of the major illnesses and maladies affecting people of the time.[31] For example, tuberculosis, a major killer, was only identified as being caused by a bacterium in 1882, and a successful means of immunisation against it by Bacillus of Calmette and Guérin (BCG) developed in 1921 in France. Even then, it was not until after World War II that BCG received wider acceptance in the rest of the world. The use of sound scientific practice by physicians was yet to occur more widely at the start of the 20th century, and many doctors were prescribing dangerous treatments well into the 1920s, such as chlorine gas for the common cold. There were narcotic analgesics and insulin, but precious little else in terms of substantial effective therapies prior to 1935. This was rapidly to change with the massive increase in effective therapeutic interventions, ushering in what Goldacre has described as the 'golden age of medicine'.[32]

This era was heralded by the advent of a huge range of more effective medical and surgical interventions and health knowledge including antibiotics, anaesthesia, thoracic surgery, vascular surgery, neurosurgery, solid organ transplantation, dialysis, radiotherapy, intensive care and establishing causative links between diet, exercise and smoking on cardiovascular and respiratory diseases. These rapid developments in effective therapeutic interventions were the product of progress in scientific knowledge and technology during this time, including pharmacology, the discovery of DNA, medical imaging and information technology. However, the effectiveness of modern medicine is a relatively new phenomenon, and even in relatively recent history modern biomedicine has made some serious missteps causing significant harm. This has inevitably impacted on public trust in both medicine and the pharmaceutical industry over the years.

Ineffective remedies and diagnoses

Ancient practices

Bloodletting is probably the best-known medical practice that has been thoroughly discredited. However, it was once considered one of medicine's most ancient and successful practices and persisted as a treatment until well into the 20th century. It was even recommended in the 1923 edition of the bestselling medical textbook, *The Principles and Practice of Medicine*. Bloodletting is believed to have originated in ancient Egypt and spread to Greece, where physicians in their wisdom supposed that all illnesses stemmed from an overabundance of blood. In mediaeval Europe, bloodletting became the typical treatment for various conditions, from plague and smallpox to epilepsy and gout. Veins or arteries in the forearm or neck were cut, sometimes using a special tool known as a fleam, or leeches applied to drain blood.

In 1163 a church edict prohibited clergy, who often stood in as doctors, from performing bloodletting, but doctors and barbers continued to offer bloodletting services. The practice remained popular with the wealthy, and new multi-blade devices were developed, such as the scarifcator that made multiple nicks to vessels all at once.[29, 33] Marie-Antoinette was reported as having bloodletting performed while giving birth to her first child in 1778, whilst George Washington is probably the most famous victim of it. Physicians drained an estimated 2½ litres (the average adult has about 5 litres of total blood volume) in a day from him for a troublesome sore throat in 1799; he died four days later. Not surprisingly, there has been intense speculation as to whether the blood loss or infection acquired during the procedure contributed to his demise.

By the late 1800s bloodletting had largely been discredited through scientific studies of its effectiveness, although, interestingly, it was abandoned in practice long before it was challenged in theory as new and more successful treatments of diseases took its place. One might ask why the practice did persist for so long when discoveries in the 16th and 17th centuries by anatomist Andreas Vesalius and physician William Harvey identified serious flaws in Greek anatomy and physiology? It is likely bloodletting survived for as long as it did more as a result of social, cultural and economic factors, and these most likely continue to influence modern healthcare practices as much as evidence does today.[34]

Another interesting example of an ancient medical practice that persisted long after it should have been discarded was the use of weapon salve to heal injuries. Weapon salve was a treatment for injuries based upon the occult belief that there was a causal metaphysical link between a wound and the weapon that had caused it, and that this link persisted after the injury. This idea was popularised by Swiss physician Paracelsus in the 16th century, and was promoted by the English diplomat Sir Kenelm Digby's as the 'Powder of Sympathy', and by the English physician Robert Fludd. It became a widespread practice throughout the 17th century. The salve was usually made of fat and the patient's blood along with other ingredients. This was applied to the weapon or article that had caused the injury. Francis Bacon even described how a salve was believed to cure a wound made by it in his *Sylva Sylvarum*, or *A Natural History* in 1627. The practice of applying weapon salve began to disappear after 1650, as it was found ineffective and challenged by physicians adopting more rational methods. However, like bloodletting, the social belief persisted up until the beginning of the last century with a reported case in the *British Medical Journal* of a woman, Matilda Henry, in 1902 using it for an injury from a nail (from which she died shortly afterwards from tetanus).[35, 36] The acceptance of the more complicated explanatory theories of the germ theory of disease, micro-organisms and infection have taken the place of such beliefs in medicine today. However, as I shall explore later in the book, magical beliefs are still frequently used to support healthcare practices.

Hysteria

Not all of these examples of bad medicine are in the distant past, however. The diagnosis of female hysteria is a more recent example. Female hysteria was once a common medical diagnosis for women, but is now no longer recognised as a medical disorder. The diagnosis was in reality a term that was used as a way to explain female sexuality and the female sexual response in medical terms. The diagnosis and treatment of female hysteria were practised by physicians until quite late in the 20th century. Once again, this was more a result of socio-cultural factors rather than good science.

The origins of female hysteria are thought to be in ancient

Egyptian and Greek beliefs, in that the womb was thought capable of affecting the rest of the body in a negative way. The classical Greek physician Galen, who practised around 180 CE, believed that the retention of 'female seed' within the womb was to blame for irritability, fainting, anxiety, insomnia, depression (and practically any other symptoms) in women. The suggested treatment was to promote expulsion of this 'fluid'. Marriage with regular sexual intercourse was the prime recommendation, but for single women or married women unable to achieve orgasm through intercourse, midwives were employed to stimulate the genitals, and release these troublesome 'fluids'. These ideas were further developed by the French neurologist Jean-Martin Charcot in 1880, who suggested hysteria was caused by an unknown internal malady affecting the nervous system. One of his students was none other than Sigmund Freud, the founder of psychoanalysis. Freud took up this idea with considerable enthusiasm, carrying out several studies on female hysteria between 1880 and 1915.[37] He concluded that it was the result of a 'psychological scar produced through trauma or repression' rather than any physical cause. As with much of Freud's work, his ideas revolved around human sexual behaviour and he believed that women experienced hysteria because they were unable to come to terms with the loss of their 'metaphorical penis'.[27] Strangely enough, as previously recommended, treatment involved marriage and regular sexual intercourse, or alternatively genital stimulation for single women. However, a more scientific approach to the latter was recommended by Freud called uterine or gynaecological massage.

A Swedish physiotherapist named Thure Brandte had developed a massage and exercise regimen for issues of uterine prolapse with some success in the 1860s. A form of this uterine massage quickly became the norm for treating female hysteria. One of the recommended techniques used a bimanual massage, meaning one hand was placed on the front, and the other inserted into the vagina to perform a massage, until a 'paroxysmal convulsion' was achieved. Today this would simply be called an orgasm, but Brandte opened several extremely successful clinics, with numerous doctors apprenticing at them. The therapy was remarkably popular for some reason, and he reported that he was treating as many as 117 patients a day! As these treatments were considered physically exhausting for doctors, a technological solution was developed in the form of mechanical stimulation devices, or as we know them today, vibrators.[38, 39] The 2011 romantic comedy film *Hysteria* explored how the Victorian medical management of hysteria led to the invention of the vibrator quite humorously. However, this subject continues to raise much controversy and ire in some conservative cultures today. For example, in the US state of Texas a person can go into a gun store and purchase any manner of lethal armaments quite legally, but should they wish to purchase a vibrator, the vendor would be breaking the law. In 2008 a US District Judge released a report declaring it to be 'facially unconstitutional and unenforceable', but it remains technically against the law to sell sex-toys in Texas.

After about 1915, gynaecological massage fell out of favour with conventional medicine as a treatment though it continued as a form of alternative medicine. Modern advancements in medical knowledge and the rise of feminism, and more socially open attitudes to sexuality, have led to the understanding that the womb is not actually the cause of most female medical issues. However, it was only in 1952 that the American Psychiatric Association finally dropped the term 'female hysteria' from its diagnostic manual, and somewhat astonishingly the actual concept of hysterical neurosis was only finally removed in the 1980 edition of the manual.[35, 36] This only serves to demonstrate how difficult it is for health professionals to let go of popular ideas, even when they are completely wrong.

Radioactive therapies

In the late 19th century, the discovery of radioactivity also led to some dubious medical uses. Before people understood that radiation exposure could be deadly but had value for destroying cancer cells, a number of physicians thought it was a useful new medical ingredient. Radithor was a solution of radium salts which was claimed by its developer, William J A Bailey (who also falsely claimed to be a doctor of medicine), to have significant curative properties for multiple conditions. Its value was based on the now generally discredited idea of 'radiation hormesis'. Radiation hormesis is a hypothesis that suggests low doses of ionising radiation (just above natural background levels) are beneficial, stimulating the activation of repair mechanisms that protect against disease. This belief was promoted by a number of physicians at the time, and even today has some support. In a 2008 report, the US National Research Council suggested that there was no evidence for hormesis in humans, whilst the risks associated with radiation exposure were well known.[40] However, back in the 1920s it was unknown what dose of radiation was harmful to humans. The Pittsburgh physician C C Moyar was one proponent, who prescribed Radithor as an aid to the healing process to the wealthy industrialist Eben Byers, who ingested large quantities of it between 1927 and 1930. He stopped drinking Radithor in 1930 when his teeth started falling out, but died quite gruesomely, as his jaw and skull degenerated in 1932 from excessive radiation exposure. After this and similar cases, its popularity and uptake in the medical profession rapidly declined.[41]

Outside of medicine, radioactive cosmetic and other products enjoyed a brief popularity also. Thor-radia beauty crème was marketed in France in the 1930s, and Doramad Radioactive Toothpaste in Germany in the 1940s. Both claimed to produce glowing effects! The most curious example was probably the

NICO Clean Tobacco Card, which was exported from Japan to the United States in the late 1960s. It consisted of a small metal plate impregnated with uranium. The idea was to put it inside a pack of cigarettes where it was claimed the radiation it emitted would reduce the tar and nicotine content.[42]

Although radiation hormesis is now a generally debunked medical therapy, and the once-claimed health benefits now described by most doctors as 'radioactive quackery', there are still many alternative practitioners and people who believe in it. Each year in Montana, thousands of people seek relief from a variety of ailments, from cataracts to arthritis, at the radon health mines of Boulder and Basin in the USA. Owners of the Merry Widow Health Mine in Basin, where these radiation aficionados congregate, dismiss the EPA warnings about radon as government propaganda.[43]

Psychosurgery

Another fascinating example of an ineffective and seriously harmful medical practice was the neurological surgical treatment of people with mental illness, known as psychosurgery, common between 1940 and the late 1960s. Working at psychiatric institutions in the 1920s, the US physician Dr Walter Freeman observed at first-hand the suffering of mentally ill patients, which encouraged him to further his studies in the field. He gained a PhD in neuropathology and a position at George Washington University as head of the neurology department. In 1935, Freeman learned of a surgical technique performed by Yale physiologists, John Fulton and Carlyle F Jacobsen, on the frontal lobes of the brains of chimpanzees. It had the claimed effect of calming their aggressive tendencies. That same year, a similar procedure intended to treat mental illness was performed by Portuguese neurologist Dr Egas Moniz's team, which he termed a 'leucotomy'. Moniz hypothesised that mental illness was caused by abnormal neural connections in the frontal lobe of the brain. His surgical procedure removed small cores of tissue from the brain, and he argued that removing white matter fibres from the frontal lobes would improve a patient's mental health. The procedure enjoyed a surge of popularity which resulted in him being awarded a Nobel Prize for his discovery of the therapeutic value of leucotomy for certain psychoses in 1949. Critics, however, accused him of understating the complications, providing inadequate documentation and not following up on patients' recoveries.

Freeman modified the Moniz procedure, renaming it a 'lobotomy', and together with the neurosurgeon James Watts developed a more efficient way to perform it without drilling into the skull. Instead, it involved rendering a patient unconscious by electrical shock before inserting a small ice-pick-like instrument above the patient's eyeball. The instrument was hammered into the skull and wiggled back and forth in order to sever the connections to the prefrontal cortex in the frontal lobes of the brain. Four hours later, patients were said to awaken without any anxiety or apprehension. Freeman and Watts performed a number of lobotomies at a private practice in Washington, DC, and by 1949, 5000 lobotomies were being performed annually in the USA.

In reality, the procedure simply resulted in patients becoming brain damaged and entering a vegetative state, or being reduced to only being able to perform simple behaviours. Many hospitals adopted the procedure and it spread internationally. A likely reason for its popularity in mental health institutions was that lobotomised patients were far easier to manage than ones with severe psychotic symptoms. The first such operations in the UK were performed in late 1940, and by the end of 1944 about 1000 had been carried out (known as the standard Freeman-Watts prefrontal leucotomy in the UK). By 1954 that UK figure had risen to about 12,000, with the number of procedures peaking in 1949 at around 5000 a year.

During the 1950s, increasing concerns about the procedure developed, with numerous deaths and extensive functional damage caused by the operation. This led to the number of operations performed declining rapidly. The treatment of mental illness was also changing, with the introduction of new drugs and new ideas about the nature of mental illness itself. The procedure was also very negatively publicised by Ken Kesey's 1962 novel *One Flew Over the Cuckoo's Nest* and later in Stanley Kubrick's celebrated film of it in 1975. Freeman performed his last lobotomy in 1967 during which he famously severed one of the patient's arteries, resulting in their death three days later. By the mid-1970s the use of psychosurgery had declined still further, and virtually disappeared by 1980. In total, about 50,000 people received lobotomies in the USA and around 20,000 in the UK, with patients suffering significant irreversible brain damage as a result. As a nursing student in the UK in the 1980s, I can recall attending a lecture in an old disused psychosurgical operating room in a large mental hospital during our psychiatric rotation. We were all surprised by the large skylight in the ceiling, which we were informed was designed to let as much natural light in as possible for the surgeons performing lobotomies.

Today, most countries have abandoned surgery for mental illness altogether. However, despite poor evidence of benefits versus risks for patients, and dubious evidence of clinical efficacy, psychosurgery is still carried out on occasion today in both the USA and the UK. Today, most procedures are aimed at brain stimulation, rather than destruction (ablation) of tissue, for conditions like severe depression or obsessive-compulsive disorder (OCD). Nevertheless, in the US, the Massachusetts General Hospital has a neurosurgery department that offers cingulotomy (a procedure to cut a connection in a part of the brain known as the cingulate gyrus) for severe depression and OCD, and a woman with OCD underwent cingulotomy at the Frenchay Hospital in Bristol in the UK in 2010.[44, 45]

Spock's infant sleep advice

Another well-documented episode of extremely bad medical advice was that provided by the paediatrician Dr Benjamin Spock in 1946 in his book *Baby and Child Care*, published that year. He advised that babies were best placed upon their front (or prone) to sleep. This was the first book to give this advice from a paediatrician, and it was rapidly taken up by many other parenting guides, rapidly becoming the prevailing wisdom. Unfortunately, this advice was not based on evidence and it has since been proven dangerous, as it is now known that placing a baby in a prone position for sleep is a significant risk factor for sudden infant death syndrome (SIDS). 'Cot-deaths', or SIDS, became a subject of intense scrutiny between 1970 and 1991, as healthy babies in economically developed countries were inexplicably dying at the rate of one in every 250 live births each year.

In 1978, the UK physician, Dr Peter Fleming, Professor of Infant Health and Developmental Physiology, returned to Bristol in the UK from a job at the Toronto Children's Hospital in Canada. He had acquired funding from the US National Institutes of Health that enabled him to set up his own lab. Fleming was particularly interested in the relationship between breathing and temperature control in infants and read a Dutch report that suggested putting babies to sleep on their fronts led to a high risk of cot death. He then went back and analysed his own data and found that 93% of the babies who had died had been put to sleep on their front! Initially Fleming struggled to get his findings accepted over the now orthodox understanding that putting babies in a prone position to sleep was best. Researchers refused to accept that something as simple as this could have such a profound effect. It wasn't until a follow-up study in 1991 that Fleming was confident enough to approach the government with his findings. A high-profile NHS 'Back to Sleep' campaign on the issue was launched in the UK and was rapidly followed elsewhere. Rates of SIDS fell dramatically, clearly indicating Fleming was indeed right. Nevertheless, in a 2005 review of SIDS research, it was estimated that, between the 1950s and the early 1990s, over 60,000 infant deaths worldwide were likely attributable to the harmful health advice favouring prone sleeping for infants.[46, 47]

Major medical blunders

Contaminated medicines

Jim the horse

At the turn of the last century, diphtheria was a major killer in North America, being an infectious respiratory disease that causes inflammation and thickening of the back of the throat that can lead to difficulty breathing, heart failure, paralysis and even death. An antitoxin against the bacterium causing the disease was developed in the late 1800s, produced by exposing horses to the toxins produced by diphtheria bacteria. These stimulated horses to produce their own antibodies against the toxin which were then harvested and purified before being administered to humans. In 1900 in St Louis, USA, a former milk wagon horse called Jim was used to produce serum containing diphtheria antitoxin. However, on 2 October 1901, Jim displayed signs that he had contracted tetanus and was euthanised. It was then discovered that some of Jim's serum from September 1901 contained tetanus following the death of a girl in St Louis that was traced back to Jim's contaminated serum. This oversight in distributing a contaminated diphtheria antitoxin led to the death of 12 more children. This contamination could have been easily discovered if the serum had been tested for tetanus prior to its use. This incident (known as the 'Jim the horse episode'), and a similar one involving a contaminated smallpox vaccine, eventually led to the passage of the Biologics Control Act of 1902 in the USA. The ensuing tragedy and reaction established a precedent for the regulation of biological materials, eventually leading to the formation of the US Food and Drug Administration, or FDA, in 1906 and similar legislation in other countries.

Factor Concentrate

Unfortunately, this was not the last episode of errors of contaminated biological products leading to fatalities or serious adverse effects. Probably the most recent and well known is the case of contaminated blood products distributed in the UK in the 1970 and '80s to patients with bleeding disorders. People with bleeding disorders lack specific proteins, known as clotting factors, that enable their blood to clot effectively. In the 1970s treatment for these people improved considerably when a new agent replaced the previous fresh-frozen plasma and cryoprecipitate containing the missing proteins that had been used for treating them when bleeds occurred. The new product was called 'Factor Concentrate' and for the treatment of haemophilia it was a major step forward, allowing patients for the first time to be treated preventatively to reduce the likelihood of bleeds and resultant joint pain. However, the concentrates were produced using a process involving the pooling of human blood plasma from thousands of donors to extract the required clotting factors.

At this time, it was known that blood products were also able to transfer viruses such as hepatitis, and this risk was vastly increased when pooled blood products were used. In 1974, the scientist Judith Graham Pool (who had previously helped develop the frozen blood product cryoprecipitate) described factor concentrates as 'dangerous' and 'unethical' and warned against their use.[48] These risks were further exacerbated when supplies of UK-produced factor concentrates proved insufficient to meet demand, and products were sourced from commercial suppliers in the United States. In the US, high-risk paid donors, such as sex workers, were used as sources; blood was also collected in prisons. As the material was combined, one infected donor could potentially contaminate an entire batch and this could then infect all of the patients that received the material. However, these risks were ignored by leading clinicians and government, who then failed to take appropriate action to end the use of high-risk sources in combined products. There was also some evidence that pharmaceutical companies and leading clinicians did not appropriately share information about the risks of contamination, or even concealed it from patients. Unfortunately, many people were infected with viruses from contaminated blood products during this time. In 1983, Dr Galbraith, Director of the Communicable Disease Surveillance Centre in England and Wales, sent a communication entitled *Action on AIDS* to the Minister for Health and Social Security in London, informing him of the death from AIDS of a haemophiliac patient who had received factor concentrate imported from the USA. He stated: 'I have reviewed the literature and conclude that all blood products made from blood donated in the USA after 1978 should be withdrawn from use until the risk of AIDS transmission by these products has been clarified ... I am most surprised that the USA manufacturers of the implicated blood products have not informed their customers of this new hazard. I assume no critical warning has been received in the United Kingdom?'

Despite Galbraith's warning the products were not withdrawn, and a Department of Health letter considered that his suggestion was 'premature'.[49] The NHS continued not to clearly communicate the known risks to patients at this time, or change practices to avoid using high-risk blood products for patients who could have been treated with safer alternatives. By 1983, heat-treated factor concentrates that inactivated the HIV virus became available and were used. Additionally, improvements in donor testing and alternative blood products meant safer treatment options were available. Eventually, all factor-concentrate products were heat-treated to destroy viruses, and in the 1990s the use of synthetic clotting factors became available in the UK, effectively eliminating the contamination risk.

Nevertheless, successive UK governments refused to hold a public inquiry into these events. Eventually, an independent public inquiry was held under Lord Archer, supported by the UK Haemophilia Society. It gathered evidence and reported in 2009, making strong recommendations to the government on the supply and use of blood products, some of which have now been implemented. In 2008 the Scottish Government set up a public inquiry under Lord Penrose, which was also damning on the lack of government and NHS responsiveness to the issue.[49] Over 4500 people with haemophilia and other bleeding disorders were infected with HIV, hepatitis B and C and a range of other blood-borne viruses as a result of the use of contaminated blood products. The UK Haemophilia Society reports that, to date, over 2000 of them have since died and of the 1243 people known to be infected with HIV, less than 250 are still alive.[50]

Inadequate testing and manufacture of medical products

Thalidomide

Yet another famous medical and pharmaceutical catastrophe was the thalidomide disaster of the 1960s. Thalidomide was a drug developed in the 1950s by the West German pharmaceutical company Chemie Grünenthal GmbH, originally as a new anticonvulsant drug; instead, it made users sleepy and relaxed. It seemed a perfect example of new form of tranquiliser, and animal testing had demonstrated it was practically impossible to achieve a toxic or deadly overdose of the drug. However, even though animal tests had not tested for the effects of the drug during pregnancy, in July 1956 thalidomide was licensed as an over-the-counter medicine, initially in Germany and shortly after in most other European countries. As the drug was known to reduce morning sickness, it became very popular with pregnant women. However, by 1960 suspicions with the drug's safety were being expressed by some doctors. Some patients using thalidomide had reportedly developed nerve damage in their limbs as a side-effect of long-term use. Grünenthal could not provide substantial clinical evidence to refute these concerns. However, due to such concerns over its safety, the Canadian-American pharmacologist and physician Frances Oldham Kelsey, who was a reviewer for the Federal Drug Administration (FDA) in the USA, refused to authorise thalidomide for the US market. Nonetheless, in 1961, the Government of Canada did authorise the marketing of the drug under the names Kevadon and Talimol (in Quebec), but as a prescription-only medication.

In Europe, a sudden increase in births of babies with neurological and severe limb deformities, and miscarriages or stillbirths, was noted. A typical characteristic was missing or deformed limbs. Nevertheless, the conclusive link with the drug was not made until 1961, where it was confirmed that nearly all these cases were in women who had used thalidomide. The drug was only taken off the market after the German paediatrician Widukind Lenz and the Australian obstetrician William McBride independently suggested a link. Damage from the drug was significant, and the severity and location of the deformities was dependent upon how well developed the foetus had been before the drug was taken. If taken on the 20th day of pregnancy it caused brain damage, and if taken between days 24 and 28, arm and leg damage would most commonly occur. After 42 days' gestation, it did not damage the foetus. It is not known exactly how many children were born with thalidomide-related disabilities worldwide, but estimates range widely from 10,000 to 100,000. Thousands of miscarriages and stillbirths are also suspected to be a result of the use of the drug.[51]

The aftermath of the catastrophe included a British newspaper campaign against the drug's use by the *Sunday Times*, and a long criminal trial in Germany. These forced Grünenthal and its British licensee, the Distillers Company, to support victims of the drug financially, although, astonishingly, some cases for compensation are *still* ongoing.

The thalidomide catastrophe has also led to tougher testing and drug approval procedures in many countries, including the UK, USA and Canada, ensuring that studies include testing for effects on pregnancy. There has recently also been some renewed interest in the drug's potential use for leprosy, AIDS and cancer treatment. However, due to its history its use remains controversial.

Breast implants

As with thalidomide, other health problems arising from medical products have provided the impetus for positive change. This was the case with the Poly Implant Prothèse (PIP) breast implant issue, where economising decisions during manufacture resulted in injuries that eventually led to major regulatory change. In 1965, the French plastic surgeon Henri Arion introduced breast implants. These were originally used for reconstructive surgery in breast cancer patients, but were also rapidly adopted by the cosmetic surgery industry. Arion teamed up with Jean-Claude Mas, a former butcher turned medical sales representative, and they worked together on developing these products until Arion's death in 1989. Mas went on to launch Poly Implant Prothèse (PIP) in 1991. That company would produce approximately two million sets of silicone breast implants over the course of a 20-year period, and set off a global health scare.

The problem arose when PIP started to manufacture silicone-based implants using a cheaper, industrial-grade silicone, not approved for medical use, in 2001. Concerns surfaced in France when surgeons started reporting high rupture rates as early as 2003. By 2009, these implants were rupturing at a rate that was well over double the industry average across the globe. When released, the silicone gel caused inflammation and sometimes scarring in the chest. Surgical removal was required, and questions over any potential harmful long-term effects were also raised. A flood of legal complaints followed and the company's bankruptcy resulted in 2010. In 2013, Mas was sent to prison for four years, fined 75,000 Euros, and banned for life from working in medical services or running a company. The French government recommended that 30,000 French women seek removal of breast implants made by PIP in 2011, and in the UK an estimated 40,000 women had been affected (although the government did not recommend precautionary removal).[52] Saline-filled implants from PIP were also sold in the USA (but not Canada) and in many other countries until the company's demise, and also suffered similar quality control issues, resulting in many rupturing prematurely (though without the same side-effects as from silicone gel release).

As a result of the PIP scandal, the European Commission ordered a full overhaul of medical device regulations to improve safety levels and to restore public confidence in the manufacture and testing of medical devices. The new regulatory framework around the medical device industry, called the European Medical Devices Regulation (MDR), came into effect in 2017, and has influenced other countries to review their own regulations and seek improvements in medical product safety. In the next chapter we will explore how the pharmaceutical industry continues to operate without significant consequences in some of its more harmful business practices, and how this has fuelled an increased mistrust of scientific medicine more broadly.

Chapter 8

Big Pharma

Another issue that has led to the growth of mistrust of modern biomedicine is the development of questionable business practices in the global pharmaceutical industry. Today this industry has grown into one of the most powerful players in modern economies. It discovers, develops, produces and markets pharmaceutical drugs for use as medications. Pharmaceutical companies manufacture and sell generic or brand-named medications and also develop and market medical devices. They are subject to laws and regulations that govern the patenting, testing, safety, efficacy and marketing of these products, which vary greatly, depending upon the country in which they are marketed. For example, melatonin is an interesting example. In most of North America this drug is sold over-the-counter as a supplement whereas, in the UK, it is only available on prescription.

There has been increasing controversy surrounding pharmaceutical marketing and influence. The term 'Big Pharma' was coined as a pejorative nickname given to it to highlight these problems. Criticism involves accusations and findings of undue influence on doctors and other health professionals through drug representatives, including the provision of marketing 'gifts' and biased information. As a nurse in the 1980s and '90s I recall the drug representatives regularly providing high-end buffet lunches on the medical unit whenever they were introducing a new product. To their persistent annoyance, most were consumed by hungry nurses between shifts rather than doctors. This practice has generally ended now, but, as we shall see, drug companies still use a variety of incentives to encourage doctors to use and recommend their products.

The drug approval process

The process of bringing a medicine to the market generally takes around 10–12 years, from initial discovery and lab work, through the phases of clinical testing, to being licensed and available on the market. Once a potential new drug has been discovered, it undergoes extensive laboratory testing, initially in vitro (in the lab), followed by animal testing in order to show its safety and its potential value as a therapeutic agent. The results from this pre-clinical phase are then submitted to the governing regulatory bodies (e.g. the Medicines and Healthcare products Regulatory Agency in the UK, Health Canada or the Food & Drug Administration [FDA] in the USA) for approval to be tested on humans in clinical trials. The clinical trial stage consists of three phases, and new medicines have to successfully pass these before they can be prescribed to patients:

- Phase 1 trials involve a small number of volunteers. These usually focus on healthy individuals, who are paid for their participation. This phase is about establishing whether the drug is safe to use in humans, rather than how effective it may be at treating a specific disease. This is when the optimal dosage is established and any side-effects identified. Many drugs that have been shown to work in vitro or in animals do not work in humans, or have undesirable side-effects so go no further.
- Phase 2 trials involve a larger number of participants to assess how well the drug works at treating a particular

disease and what might be the best method for delivery, e.g. tablets, injections, inhalers etc. Many drugs that look promising prove unsuccessful in phase 2 trials.

- Phase 3 trials require much larger groups of participants, usually hundreds to thousands, and the aim is to compare the effects of the new drug with either a placebo or an existing treatment. A range of different types of patient is required that should be representative of real-world patients who are likely to use the drugs. Again, many drugs do not pass phase 3 trials, as they are found not to be effective enough, to have undesirable side-effects, or not to interact well with other medications.

Independent ethical review is also required for each phase of drug trials, and once these stages of clinical research have demonstrated a drug is effective and safe, the treatment can be approved and registered with the country's regulatory authorities as an approved new agent for public use. Ongoing research also occurs following the marketing of the drug and involves monitoring long-term use, side-effects and uptake. As one might imagine, this route to developing and marketing any new drug is extremely expensive, and many more potential medications fail than are successfully brought to market. Furthermore, the success rate has declined according to a 2016 study. The overall likelihood of approval (LOA) from Phase 1 alone for all candidates was reported as 9.6%, and 11.9% for cancer drugs. Chronic diseases with high prevalence had lower LOA from Phase 1 trials compared with the overall dataset. Phase 2 clinical trials experienced the lowest success rate of the development phases, with only 30.7% of developmental candidates advancing to Phase 3. Overall, the chance for a new drug to actually make it to market is around 1 in 5000.[53]

The evolution of this approval process continues, and even this current version remains contentious, with many ethical challenges around the use of paid subjects, and animal testing. Nevertheless, there are also many opportunities for problems and errors to occur along the way, including the undue influence of commercial pressures. It has become evident that the development of new drugs is not simply an altruistic process. Issues of using approved drugs for purposes which they have not been approved (off-label prescribing), and offering incentives or 'kickbacks' to doctors and pharmacists to recommend drugs are commonplace. There is some good evidence that in the past, industry-sponsored clinical trials have been more likely to provide positive results for the drugs they test, that drug company sales representatives are motivated by financial incentives, and that sometimes academic authors, and even whole journals have been paid by drug companies to promote their products (and failed to openly disclose this).[54]

Big-Pharma settlements

Worryingly, multi-billion-dollar settlements against big drug companies have become almost routine over the last two decades, particularly here in North America. Here are some of the most prominent examples.

2007: The Abilify scandal

In 2007, the US drug giant Bristol Myers Squibb (BMS) had been heavily marketing its antipsychotic Abilify (aripiprazole) to treat symptoms of dementia in the elderly and to treat behavioural problems in children, conditions the drug was not approved for (i.e. off-label use), despite an FDA warning against potentially fatal side-effects of Abilify in the elderly. BMS had sent teams of sales representatives to nursing homes to promote the drug. They were also accused of paying medical professionals to promote and use their products, offering them cash incentives and expensive vacations to luxury resorts. In a legal action over this and other drug marketing infractions BMS paid a $515 million settlement to the government.[55]

2008: Opioid medication over-zealous sales campaigns

Another well-known case was that of the US private drug company Purdue Pharma L.P. over its OxyContin painkiller. A large settlement of over $600 million USD was made by the company that year after it had undertaken a massive sales campaign that made exaggerated claims that the drug was less addictive and less likely to cause withdrawal symptoms than other opioid medications. This was widely advocated to be a significant factor in the massive increase in deaths from overdoses that increased six-fold, from about 6000 deaths in 1980 to more than 36,500 deaths in 2008 in the USA alone. The CDC (Centers for Disease Control and Prevention) and the Obama administration suggested that improving the way these narcotic drugs were prescribed could help prevent continued misuse of the medications and curb the overdose death rate.[56, 57] At the time I am writing this, Purdue Pharma L.P. just agreed to a $270 million settlement with the state of Oklahoma to avoid going to a state court trial over the company's role in the opioid addiction epidemic. Purdue had also reportedly explored the possibility of declaring bankruptcy to address potentially significant liabilities from around 2000 ongoing lawsuits alleging the drug contributed to the deadly opioid crisis that has swept across the United States and Canada.[58] Another $1 billion lawsuit was filed in May 2019 against the makers and distributors of the Oxycodone drug Percocet (Apotex Inc, BMS, Johnson & Johnson and others) in Ontario. This class action lawsuit asserts that the Canadian drug makers enriched themselves at the expense of vulnerable patients by deceptively promoting highly addictive opioids. Nevertheless, the situation and causes of what has become known as the opioid crisis are complex. The legitimate prescribing of opioid medication is unlikely to be the only cause of the opioid crisis of the last decade, as the availability of illicit narcotics (from both stolen prescription and illegally manufactured drugs) has also increased dramatically. This has been the major cause of deaths here in BC, and has likely had an impact elsewhere.

2009: Risperdal prescription incentives

In 2009, the US-based medical devices, pharmaceutical, and consumer company Johnson & Johnson paid a reported $2.2 billion to settle a civil and criminal lawsuit against it for promotion of its drug Risperdal and others for uses unapproved by the FDA, and for paying kickbacks to doctors to recommend the use of the drug. Risperdal was promoted to treat anxiety, agitation, confusion and hostility in elderly dementia patients. At the time the company's transgressions occurred, Risperdal was only approved for treating schizophrenia.[59]

2010: Seroquel off-label prescribing

In 2010, the British-Swedish multinational drug company AstroZeneca paid a $520 million settlement over promoting off-label use of its antipsychotic drug Seroquel (quetiapine). It had been illegally marketing Seroquel to the elderly and children to treat insomnia, anxiety and other conditions for which it had not been found to be effective or safe. It was known at this time that using Seroquel in this way could increase the risk of death in these populations. AstraZeneca also promoted a study linking Seroquel with weight loss, while they were accused of burying other clinical data, particularly from a study that found that taking the drug was associated with significant weight gain, at an average of nearly 5 kg a year.[60]

2011: Vioxx drug safety

In 2011, another North-American drug company, Merck & Co., Inc., settled a lawsuit made against it by shareholders for false claims about drug safety and the illegal marketing of its painkiller Vioxx. This was the second time the company had settled a lawsuit over this drug. The drug had been removed from the market in 2004 when studies had demonstrated that it doubled the risk of heart attack and stroke in those using it long-term. It had been marketed for use for a number of conditions such as rheumatoid arthritis. The drug was estimated to have contributed to at least 47,000 heart attacks, many of them fatal. About 50,000 people sued Merck, claiming they or members of their family had suffered medical problems after taking Vioxx. In November 2007, Merck agreed to pay $4.85 billion to settle most of the pending Vioxx lawsuits, costing an estimated $8.5 billion in total. In 2011 Merck agreed to pay a further $830 million to resolve a class-action lawsuit brought by shareholders, who alleged the drug maker and its executives made false and misleading statements about the safety of Vioxx between its introduction in 1999 and its eventual withdrawal in 2004.[61]

2012: Antidepressant deceptive marketing

In 2012 a $3 billion judgment was made against the British pharmaceutical company GlaxoSmithKline (GSK) in part for illegally marketing the antidepressants Paxil and Wellbutrin and withholding data on the health risks of the diabetes medication Avandia. Another large case that settled that year, was from the American multinational biopharmaceutical company Amgen. Federal charges were made public as Amgen pleaded guilty to il-legally marketing the drug Arenesp for off-label use, and agreed to pay $762 million in criminal penalties and the settlements in a whistle-blower lawsuit. Amgen was accused of promoting the use of Aranesp to treat anaemia in cancer patients who were not undergoing chemotherapy, even though the drug's approval was only for patients receiving chemotherapy. Also, that Amgen had been overfilling vials of Aranesp so that doctors could give the extra 'free' drugs to patients, and then bill insurance companies for it.[62, 63]

Price-fixing

In another example where a pharmaceutical company exhibited questionable business practices, a number of drug companies in 2013 in the UK were accused of overcharging the NHS by using a legal loophole to inflate the price of medicines, at a cost to the taxpayer of tens of millions of pounds a year. At least 15 drugs were found to have substantially inflated prices after being sold-on from one company to another, and sold-on according to information highlighted by the British Medical Association. The controversial practice involved the firms selling on commonly used NHS medicines to businesses acting outside the government's price-regulation scheme. The purchasing firms then increased the prices they charged the NHS, who were forced to buy the limited supplies from these providers. In one of the worst examples, the cost of an epilepsy drug manufactured by the American pharmaceutical giant, Pfizer Inc., prescribed to thousands of patients, was claimed to have increased by 24 times the original price. In another, testosterone patches prescribed for hormone imbalances, jumped from £26 per 300 g to £395 after being sold on. Dr Peter Holden of the BMA, noted: 'This is the drug companies flipping the drugs over to another firm for personal gain and milking the NHS for more money. But the patient is also being inconvenienced because we may have to find another treatment.'[64] As a result, Pfizer was fined a record £84.2 million by the UK's Competition and Markets Authority (CMA), for overcharging the NHS for its anti-epilepsy drug in 2016, and the company it sold the drugs on to, Flynn Pharma, was fined £52m.[65] However, technically what they had done in terms of fixing the prices of these drugs was found not to be illegal, and the companies won an appeal in 2018, and a subsequent appeal by the CMA in 2020 quashing the fines.[66, 67] In a similar example, in 2017 the CMA found the drug company, Concordia International Corp., to have increased the price of liothyronine, a drug used to treat hypothyroidism, by nearly 6000% over 10 years![68] The legal challenges illustrate the CMA's continued interest in the pharmaceutical sector and a concern to weed out anticompetitive practices in this industry, although at the time of writing, due to a lack of success in the courts, it does not look like another legal challenge is likely unless the law changes.

Ongoing litigation

It does seem these cases did have some effect on these companies' business practices, as the number and size of settlements against the pharmaceutical industry have decreased significantly since 2013. In 2012-2013, pharmaceutical companies in the USA reached 22 settlements totalling $8.7 billion (an average of $394 million per settlement), whilst in 2016-2017, they reached 29 settlements totalling $2.8 billion (now averaging payment of a mere $97 million each).[69] However, a number of large settlements continue to arise. The painkiller Vioxx (rofecoxib) continues to cost Merck & Co money, more than 11 years after the company pulled the drug from the market and they settled another class action lawsuit in 2016 over ongoing issues related to its use for $830 million.[70] The US pharmaceutical company Celgene agreed to pay $280 million to settle claims that it marketed the anti-cancer drugs Thalomid and Revlimid (lenalidomide) for off-label uses in 2017. The lawsuit filed, by a former sales representative turned whistle-blower, identified that Thalomid (a derivative of Thalidomide) was being marketed to oncologists for a variety of cancers before it had been approved for this, and that Revlimid was being marketed for a broader range of cancers than approved for by the FDA.[71] Another big settlement in 2017 was that of the Dutch pharmaceutical company Mylan NV, who paid a $465 million settlement with the US Justice Department, resolving claims that it overcharged the government for its EpiPen emergency allergy injection treatment.[72] In 2018, AstraZeneca agreed to pay $110 million to settle a Texas claim alleging that the company cheated the state's Medicaid programmes by fraudulently marketing two medications to it. AstraZeneca was accused of promoting Seroquel for off-label use in children, and falsely promoting its anti-cholesterol drug Crestor as being superior to other statins.[73]

A number of pharmaceutical manufacturers (Purdue Pharma LP, Cephalon Inc, Janssen Pharmaceuticals Inc, Endo Health Solutions Inc. and Actavis plc), have been sued for allegedly marketing their highly potent opioid painkillers (e.g. Oxycontin – generic name, oxycodone) for more minor aches and pains, while masking the risks of addiction. This rising tide of lawsuits against opioid companies was recently joined by the Government of British Columbia, Canada, who launched a class-action lawsuit in 2018 on behalf of all federal, provincial and territorial governments and agencies, who paid healthcare, pharmaceutical and treatment costs relating to opioids. The suit alleges that by falsely marketing opioids as being less addictive than other painkillers, drug companies helped trigger the opioid overdose crisis that has resulted in the deaths of thousands.[74]

A number of lawsuits were filed against the German drug company Boehringer Ingelheim Pharmaceuticals Inc recently over their anticoagulant Pradaxa (generic name, dabigatran). This drug was marketed as a new drug to prevent blood clots and reduce the risks of stroke. The drug was approved by FDA in 2010, but it is alleged that Pradaxa had the severe side-effects of gastrointestinal bleeding, heart attack, stroke, brain haemorrhage, kidney bleeding and death in some patients. It is alleged the drug company withheld important analyses in the original clinical trial by excluding data from older patients that would have been much more representative of the patients who would actually take the drug. This resulted in biased results, and the FDA approving a drug that ultimately impacted on patient safety. The original and highly criticised 2009 paper that reported the original trial eventually had a post-publication correction to acknowledge these issues in 2010.[71, 72, 73, 74, 75, 76, 77, 78] In 2014, the drug maker agreed to settle more than 4100 lawsuits for $650 million. More than 2400 lawsuits have been filed since then, and many are pending at the time of writing.

Unfortunately, even these huge settlements probably make little impact on the profits of these companies. For example, the GSK $3 billion USD settlement in 2012 accounted for just 11% of the companies declared revenue that year.[79] Cases rarely result in criminal charges, and drug companies continue to fund clinical trials. Additionally, the pharmaceutical lobbying industry in North America is huge. Pharmaceutical companies spend far more than any other industry on influencing politicians and poured around $2.5 billion into lobbying and funding members of Congress over the past decade. In healthcare, the laws and regulations should ideally be in place to benefit consumers and protect us all from unlawful practices. Pharmaceutical companies and the taxes on their products make a large contribution to government funding. Given this sorry state of affairs, and the strong ties of the pharmaceutical industry to medicine, it is unsurprising that many people have lost trust in the biomedical establishment.[80]

Chapter 9

Dubious private clinics

One significant area of growing concern in modern healthcare has been the growth of controversial specialist experimental medical clinics. A number of these private medical clinics are now well established, and by all accounts are making significant profits. They may offer some conventional medical treatments, but generally offer unproven and experimental procedures and treatments not available in public healthcare, and provided in luxurious settings. They are also frequently the target of legal action by dissatisfied patients or relatives. The conditions targeted by such clinics are usually chronic and serious health issues that medicine has had limited success in treating, or conditions where the medical treatments are particularly invasive or aggressive. Naturally, these are areas where people have often lost trust in public healthcare (see page 23). Typical examples include clinics that offer specialist treatments for cancer, amyotrophic lateral sclerosis (also known as ALS, Lou Gehrig's disease or motor neuron disease), post-traumatic stress disorder (PTSD), depression, anxiety disorders including obsessive-compulsive disorder (OCD), substance and behavioural addictions, attention-deficit hyperactivity disorder (ADHD) and other mental health issues. They may be found globally, and because of regulatory issues are often located in economically developing countries. However, they are also to be found in Europe, and

North America. The clinics usually exploit a lack of regulatory protection or legislation for the specific conditions they treat. Many are run by alternative health practitioners, but many also by licensed physicians, surgeons and psychiatrists.

The Burzynski Research Institute and Clinic

One such infamous clinic that has experienced several legal actions is that of Polish physician Dr Stanislaw Burzynski, based in Houston, Texas. His cancer clinic has been the subject of multiple claims of deception and it has been the subject of serious ethical concerns raised by the surgical oncologist Dr David Gorski in his blogs and by others on a number of occasions.[81] In the 1970s, Dr Burzynski claimed to have made a breakthrough in cancer research through the discovery of substances that limited the growth of cancer cells. He called these substance 'antineoplastons', which are actually made from peptides and amino acids (the building blocks of proteins) isolated from human blood or urine. More recently, Burzynski has produced these compounds synthetically. He then founded his clinic in 1977 and has since been using antineoplastons to treat cancer patients. Antineoplaston therapy is not approved for general use, and the compounds are not licensed as drugs but are instead sold and administered as part of his research programme at the Burzynski Research Institute, and used in clinical trials at his Burzynski Clinic (humility does not seem a large part of his persona).

Supporters of the therapy claim that antineoplastons affect the growth of cancer cells, and that people with cancer do not have enough naturally occurring antineoplastons. Antineoplaston therapy is said to replenish the body's supply of the compounds to help the person fight the cancer naturally. It also reportedly costs around $9000 USD a month. However, it is notable the only clinic that has ever reported positive results with these compounds has been Dr Burzynski's own clinic. These were in case reports, and phase 1 or 2 clinical trials. Other researchers have not been able to get the same results, so there is no good quality evidence that this type of treatment helps to treat cancer. Since 1983, the American Cancer Society has stated that there is no evidence that antineoplastons have any beneficial effects in cancer and recommended that people do not buy these products in case of serious health consequences. Neither Cancer Research UK nor the Canadian Cancer Society recommend the therapy, and have expressed concerned about those seeking treatment with antineoplastons because not enough is known about its benefits or side-effects.[82] In fact, to date, antineoplaston therapy is not an approved cancer treatment anywhere in the world.

On the legal side, Dr Burzynski has had numerous run-ins with the law. In 2009, the FDA issued a warning letter to him stating that an investigation had determined that the Burzynski Institutional Review Board (IRB – designated to review and monitor biomedical research) '…did not adhere to the applicable statutory requirements and FDA regulations governing the protection of human subjects'. In January 2012, Lola Quinlan, an elderly cancer patient, sued Burzynski for using false and misleading tactics to 'swindle her out of $100,000'. She sued for negligence, negligent misrepresentation, fraud, deceptive trade and conspiracy, but was ultimately unsuccessful. Another warning was issued to Burzynski by the FDA in October 2012, requiring cessation of dubious promotional activities, including use of testimonials and promotional interviews with himself. In June 2013, the FDA inspected Burzynski's clinic in Houston and his ethical procedures for consent following the deaths of two child patients in January and February 2013. It then issued further notes and warning letters highly critical of his research procedures. Despite this, the Burzynski Clinic has continued to be able to offer antineoplaston therapy by numerous compassionate use exemptions. This is the ability to use unproven treatments in terminal illness on compassionate grounds. According to an investigative report by STAT News, published in August 2016, the clinic also benefited from the political lobbying of supporters, and particularly from the families of patients with terminal diagnoses.

In November 2015, the Texas Medical Board took Burzynski to court in Houston, Texas, where he was accused of bait-and-switch methods (advertising expensive therapeutics and then substituting inferior ones), improperly charging patients, not informing patients that he owned the pharmacy where they had to redeem their prescriptions, and the off-label prescribing of drugs (medications used in a manner not specified in their approved packaging label). In 2017 the Texas Medical Board found against Burzynski and issued an order that placed him on probation and ordered him to pay $360,000 in penalties and more than $20,000 in restitution for violating standards of care in his treatment of patients between 2009 and 2013.[83] At the time of writing, both the Burzynski Clinic and the Burzynski Research Institute are in full operation. Since 2011, the clinic has also offered 'personalised gene-targeted cancer therapy', which has stirred further controversy. In August 2015, Burzynski was identified by the Houston Press as number eight on the list of the 'Ten Most Embarrassing Houstonians', suggesting he was 'Truly an embarrassment to such a medical city where some of the best cancer medicine in the world is performed'.[84] Overall, it is quite astonishing that despite all of this Burzynski has been able to retain a medical licence and continues to run a successful medical business. The reasons why clinics such as Burzynski's are so successful are more to do with marketing and persuasive techniques, rather than clinical effectiveness. This is discussed further in Section VI (see page 313).

The Hippocrates Health Institute (HHI)

Another US private cancer clinic with a very dubious history is the Hippocrates Health Institute (HHI) in West Palm Beach, Florida, run by Brian Clements and his wife, Anna-Maria Clements. Both have been named in several separate lawsuits filed in Palm Beach County. Neither of the Clements is a medical doctor, though they did employ physician Dr Paul Kotturan in the clinic. Legal action was taken against them by the Florida Department of Health in 2015 requiring them to cease and desist representing themselves as doctors, and from the unlicensed practice of medicine.[85] Brian Clements has reportedly claimed to be a doctor of naturopathic medicine and has a PhD in nutrition from the University of Science Arts and Technology (USAT).[86] However, this is an offshore private university with an administrative office in Colorado and a campus located on the Caribbean island of Montserrat. Its accreditation by any reputable external academic body is highly questionable. The American Association of Collegiate Registrars and Admissions Officers (AACRAO) stated that 'USAT is not a legally recognized degree-granting institution of higher education approved by the Ministry of Education of Montserrat'. It has been referred to as a 'diploma mill' by University of Illinois professor George Gollin.[85] Interestingly, the HHI is actually registered as a massage and health spa in Florida, not as a medical establishment. A former nurse, Stephen Pugh, who worked at the HHI, recounted that even though they were not medical doctors, the Clements routinely interpreted laboratory blood tests, ordered intravenous treatments, prescribed supplements and told patients, 'We're going to cure your illness'. He also detailed how they placed restrictions on when staff could call an ambulance to take patients for emergency medical care at local hospitals.[87]

At the time of writing, the clinic names its cancer specialist as a Dr Janet Hranicky, who is also not a qualified physician.

Nevertheless, this is not clear on the clinic's website, where she is simply described as Dr Janet Hranicky who has '...extensive multi-disciplinary training with a number of world experts'. Her PhD thesis, entitled *The Pleasure Freeze: A Psychological Theory of Cancer*, is from a US college, the Fielding Institute, from 1986. This is a college that specialises in graduate programmes for 'mid-career professionals not being served by traditional universities'. Her thesis on file there simply presents a theory suggesting cancer has a psychological origin. It includes no actual research other than a literature review and presentation of her theory. Her area of expertise is apparently bio-energy fields and 'psychoneuroimmunology'. This is a theory most scientists regard as pseudoscience as it has virtually no supporting evidence. It has been well understood the immune system is neurologically mediated for at least 70 years (neuroendocrinology), but there is no good evidence that any immunological disease can be controlled by psychological methods. On her web resume, she also claims to be completing a medical degree at the International University of Health Sciences. This is an online university that claims accreditation by the Government of the Federation of St Christopher & Nevis in the West Indian island of St Kitts. Dr Hranicky is also pleased to claim she '... trained with doctors Brian and Anna Maria Clement in their renowned work in Nutritional Medicine and Integrative Wellness at the Hippocrates Health Institute'.

Another listed HHI team member actually is a licensed physician. He is Dr Robert D Willix Jr, who is identified as: 'A former board-certified cardiac surgeon with a passion for integrative healing', and one who '...travelled the world to study acupuncture, ayervedic [sic] and shamanic medicine'. The HHI website also indicates he is an '...accomplished author of five books and hundreds of articles'. However, a simple search in Pubmed, the online medical research bibliographic database, reveals only six papers to his name, and only one where he is first author... from 1976. Several books appear available under his name, all of which seem to be self-published on the CreateSpace, Real Health Books and eBrandedBooks.com platforms. One of them, *Age Proofing*, suggests it will reveal how you can be water-skiing rather than playing shuffleboard in your nineties! Nevertheless, later on, the same HHI bio page states: 'He has authored five books and hundreds of newsletters'. Overall, it is difficult to make sense of what this proclaimed 'ahead of his time' doctor's contributions to medical science actually are. Overall, this seems to represent a pattern of dubiously qualified practitioners, with inflated biographies operating at HHI.

The clinic has a well-publicised history of scandals and law suits and gained some notoriety in Canada and the media when the families of two young Canadian Indigenous girls with aggressive forms of leukaemia from the Six Nations withdrew their children from medical treatment and enrolled them at the HHI in 2014. Clements had claimed in presentations that, 'We have had more people reverse cancer than any institute in the history of health care.'[88] This is an absurd statement for any clinician to make, and totally uncorroborated by any evidence. The mother of one of them, an 11-year-old girl (simply known as JJ, because of a publication ban) said the clinic's director, Brian Clement, told her leukaemia was '...not difficult to treat'. Both families travelled to West Palm Beach and paid more than $18,000 each for the clinic's 'Life Transformation Program' at the HHI. This programme uses no medical cancer interventions, but includes laser light therapy, vitamins administered intravenously, a strict organic raw food diet and positive thinking exercises, all claimed to treat the cancer (none of which have any good evidence of effectiveness).

A legal case was instigated in the case of one of the children, 11-year-old Makayla Sault, and an application was made to the Ontario court by McMaster Children's Hospital to have the girl apprehended by Brant Family and Children's Services and returned back into medical treatment. Their case was based on the fact that other children with the same type and stage of cancer as Makayla had experienced a 70% or better cure rate with the conventional medical treatment. Children's Services refused to intervene, and the case became a political issue over First Nation rights in Canada. Ontario Court Justice Gethin Edward ruled on November 14th 2014 that constitutional protection of Aboriginal culture gave parents the right to choose traditional healing over chemotherapy for their children. Six Nations' Chief, Ava Hill, was quoted as stating that: 'This is monumental for our people all across the country.' Tragically, as predicted by the doctors, Makayla died in January 2015, less than a year after she had left chemotherapy for the HHI alternative treatments. The other girl, JJ's, leukaemia had also returned by March 2015.[89] The parents in these examples saw their children suffering horribly with chemotherapy and put their trust in a questionable clinic and practitioners rather than medical advice. Desperate parents are particularly vulnerable people and particularly susceptible to predatory marketing (see Section VI, page 313).

Following the controversy caused by the Makayla case, a number of medical ethicists demanded the Ontario Attorney General have a higher weigh-in on such rulings, suggesting the decision wrongly put Aboriginal rights ahead of the rights of a child. However, this type of ruling, or a reluctance of authorities to follow up with parents to enforce parental compliance with medical treatment of children, is not uncommon in North America. There have been a number of other cases that represent a view that children are essentially the property of their parents, who are free to take decisions, even if they will likely result in harm to their child, or even to other children. This view has most recently been seen in arguments over mandatory measles vaccinations for children attending public schools in the USA in 2019. However, Margaret Somerville, director of the Centre for

Medicine, Ethics and Law at McGill University, noted that: 'When the life of a child is at stake that is one of the clearest situations in which other rights should not prevail.'[90] Parents sometimes do make bad decisions, and especially when influenced by misinformation. Ironically, the Makayla Salut ruling actually resulted in Indigenous children having less legal protection than other Canadian children, and ultimately this decision provided the HHI with an ongoing source of clients from vulnerable Canadian families.

These were obviously factors that weighed heavily on Justice Gethin Edwards' mind, as in April 2015 he revised his 2014 ruling. In order to avoid putting the other girl, JJ, and her family through a legal appeal, the Ontario Attorney General, physicians, judge and family, all co-operated to come to a resolution. The Justice clarified his original controversial ruling to make it clear that the interests of the child were the key consideration in all cases like this. In the clarification of the decision, he stated that: 'Implicit in this decision is that recognition and implementation of the right to use traditional medicines must remain consistent with the principle that the best interests of the children remain paramount.' The parents agreed to a treatment plan with a new paediatric oncologist that included medical cancer treatment and traditional remedies.[89]

Today, the HHI Clinic continues to do business, and offers one- and three-week private cancer wellness programmes. It also claims to welcome '...medical doctors, physicians and other healthcare professionals to our Institute on our Doctor Days Immersion Experience as VIP Guests'. It was reported to have earned $22 million US in revenue and the Clements took home over a million dollars alone in 2013, so would certainly seem to have captured a lucrative business opportunity.[85]

Faith-based conversion clinics

In the area of mental health and even human sexuality other questionable private mental-health clinics have emerged. Dr Joseph Nicolosi was a clinical psychologist who advocated for so-called 'conversion therapy' for homosexuality to diminish same-sex attraction (also known as 'reparative therapy'). This widely discredited practice was designed to change an individual's sexual orientation through a range of methods, including religious rituals, behavioural modification and even electro-shock therapy. Nicolosi, a devout Catholic, operated a conversion therapy clinic in California for a number of years and was a major figure in the what has become known as the field of 'ex-gay treatment'. He founded the National Association for Research and Therapy of Homosexuality (NARTH), an organisation focused on attempting to turn gay people into straight people. This marginalised him within the mental health profession, before his death in 2017. Today, most physicians and psychiatrists regard conversion therapy as a religiously motivated harmful and inappropriate treatment, as homosexuality is not a medical condition. In 1973, the American Psychological Association (APA) voted to remove homosexuality from the *Diagnostic and Statistical Manual of Mental Disorders (DSM-II)* after finally recognising that being gay was not an illness.

California passed a law to ban provision of conversion therapy to minors, including some of Nicolosi's existing patients, in 2012. Nicolosi challenged the law on constitutional grounds in a law suit, but the law, effectively barring his clinic from taking on patients under the age of 18, was subsequently upheld. The psychiatrist Peter Gajdics suggested: 'It's just torture, abuse, and people still need to be educated.'[91] A number of other US states (15 at the time of writing) have also banned the practice for minors. In Ontario, a legal statute to protect minors from being subject to conversion therapy was passed in 2015. That same year, Manitoba adopted a regulation by its Ministry of Health, stating, 'It is the position of the Manitoba Government that conversion therapy can have no place in the province's public health-care system'. In Vancouver, Canada, the City Council passed a motion in 2018 to ban conversion therapy. The unanimous City Council vote made Vancouver the first city in Canada to approve such a ban. My colleague, Professor Elizabeth Saewyc, who studies youth health matters, noted: 'It's hard to know how prevalent conversion therapy is in BC, because it's mostly advertised through word of mouth. Medical professionals rarely offer it these days, and it's mostly provided by faith-informed practitioners.'[92] This is actually not uncommon with addiction programmes today also. For example, one of the most well-known and commonly used types of substance rehabilitation and recovery support is the '12-Step Program'. Just about everyone has heard of Alcoholics Anonymous, the organisation that originated the idea. The 12-Step Program remains a commonly used treatment choice for various types of addiction, although it arose from a spiritual, Christian inspiration that identified seeking help from a greater power as well as from peers with addiction struggles as key. This has led to criticisms of its universal applicability and evidence of efficacy of this and other religiously affiliated programmes.

In attempts to circumvent these criticisms and bans, some mental health practitioners have rebranded conversion therapy as 'Christian counselling'. Dr Nicolosi's son, Joseph Jr (a licensed clinical psychologist), has followed in his father's footsteps by offering a new form of conversion therapy to people in California, the latest version of which is called 'reintegrative therapy'. He took place in a well-publicised interview with the anti-lesbian, gay, bi-sexual, transgender and queer (LGBTQ) website Christian Militant in 2018 to promote his practice and denounce those states banning conversion therapy.[93] Dr Nicolosi Jr has also set up his own Reintegrative Therapy Association to license his now trade-marked form of treatment. He is named as the clinical director of his for-profit Breakthrough Clinic in California, where three-month outpatient programmes are offered for $4000, or for $200 per 45-minute session by telephone.

A growth industry

There are, unfortunately, numerous other clinics with such problematic histories – enough to fill a book in themselves. These include Dr Joseph E Rich at his Center for Environmental and Integrative Medicine in Knoxville, Tennessee (offering detoxification and weight-loss therapies), who had his licence suspended in 2008 after he was found to be 'unprofessional, dishonourable, negligent or incompetent' in the course of medical practice. Dr Jonathan Wright of the Tahoma Clinic, in King County, Washington, offering holistic anti-ageing therapies, was fined $7500 and received a 30-month professional probation for employing an unlicensed physician in 2013. Dr Rick Sponaugle of the Florida Detox and Wellness Institute currently offers anaesthesia-assisted addiction, rapid detox and chronic Lyme disease therapies (a disease that is thought not to exist by most physicians). He settled a number of cases against him out of court, and successfully defended others, including one where an ex-patient's wife filed a lawsuit against him in 2007 alleging that as direct result of the negligence and deviations from the acceptable standard of professional care, her husband suffered permanent brain injury. Dr Sponaugle's clinic treats around 400-500 patients a year and he has said that: 'A lot of us have brain trauma we don't realise we have.' Despite his claims of being an expert in novel addiction treatments and offering advanced treatments for mould toxicity, he has yet to publish any research on these treatments.

There are other examples of bogus cancer clinics around the world, in Germany, China, Hungary, Mexico, the USA and elsewhere, and the latest trend in specialist experimental clinics appears to be offering stem-cell treatments, either as disease or anti-ageing therapies.[94, 95] Many are run by, or employ, licensed physicians, whilst others are staffed by alternative health practitioners. The one thing they all have in common is claims of astute expertise in having discovered unique therapies that conventional science and medicine have yet to catch up with – that, and the use of testimonials from satisfied patients to support their practice, rather than reputable clinical research. These cases serve to illustrate the desperation of patients and their relatives with severe and chronic medical conditions to grasp at any potential remedy, no matter how doubtful. They also exemplify the lack of effectiveness of contemporary regulatory systems to protect people from opportunistic predatory practitioners, misinformation or health scams.

In the private and alternative health care sector the reality is there is often very little regulatory oversight. For example, in Hawaii, the Kokolulu Farm and Cancer Retreat is run by nurses Karin Cooke and Lew Whitney, and markets itself as an idyllic cancer retreat and claims their qigong retreats have resolved cancer tumours, back problems, lupus and migraines, controlled epileptic and Parkinson tremors/seizures without medication, and healed without surgery. They also claim '...those affected by cancer and other chronic illnesses are able to fully access a deeper healing, while nurturing body, mind and spirit through scientifically proven integrative techniques.' However, they offer no evidence of any of this outside of a few testimonials. They are registered as a public charity, but charge $6300 for a 14-day retreat and did not respond to written requests for information, and declined to be evaluated in relation to Better Business Bureau Standards for Charity Accountability in 2018. They also referred to an ex-intern who complained about their clinic online as a woman who '...spent her free time sitting in her room stuffing her obese body with chips and candy'. Not quite what one might expect from masters of tension management and tranquillity. In reality, a stay in a pleasant island retreat with other people with similar health issues may prove empowering, but the claims used to market their retreats prey on vulnerable people by providing unrealistic expectations and inflated benefit claims.

Another worrying case is that of Jason Klop, a Canadian naturopath who charges $15,000 US for children with autism to have faecal transplants at his clinic near Tijuana, Mexico. He claims to have successfully treated children as young as 2 years old from around the world using pills and liquids made from the stools of two American adolescents.[96] The process isn't approved in the UK, Canada or the United States for the treatment of autism, and the therapy has no quality evidence of any efficacy currently, and is completely experimental. However, setting up a clinic in Mexico offers him a way of legally doing business, and charging absurdly high fees for a comparatively cheap therapy. Many alternative clinics advertise in this way using unsubstantiated hyperbole to attract clients, and in this sector even qualifications may not mean what we may think they do.

Chapter 10

Is modern medicine safe?

The changing landscape and risks of modern medicine and public health create new challenges for all of us. Nothing is risk free, and every health intervention has multiple factors to be considered when comparing the risks and benefits. With our better understanding of human physiology, disease processes and new health technologies, the complexity and diversity of these decisions has increased considerably. There are the broad considerations, such as the existing evidence base of effectiveness, benefits and risks and possible harmful outcomes. Then there are more specific ones, such as selecting the appropriate therapy for the specific patient, the ability to deliver the therapy, the endurance of the beneficial impact, and the associated risk in not using it. A good example of this complexity is in the treatment of rheumatoid arthritis (RA). Traditionally, RA has been treated with anti-inflammatory drugs, which can reduce the pain associated with the condition but do not help the underlying causes. These drugs also have significant side-effects (e.g. Vioxx). However, a new class of drugs has been developed, known as 'tumour necrosis factor (TNF) inhibitors', that have provided hope for the millions of patients with RA. These new drugs target the underlying disease process for RA by acting on the specific immunological factors that cause the inflammation. Because they act on the causes of joint destruction, they begin working rapidly and can keep a patient's arthritis from worsening, and, if given early enough, can even prevent joint damage occurring. Nevertheless, they also have some undesirable side-effects. They can reduce the immune system's ability to fight off infections, and possibly may increase the risk of certain forms of cancer (although this remains unclear). Therefore, patients and physicians must balance the potential benefits of using TNF inhibitors with known side-effects and theoretical risks.[99, 100]

Evidence-based practice

Despite these complex questions and issues with modern medicine, professional healthcare continues to evolve, and one of the most important innovations in the last 30 years has been the development of the evidence-based practice (EBP) movement. This is certainly one of the best examples of the benefits of the application of science in modern society. EBP is generally recognised to have arisen out of the evidence-based medicine (EBM) movement. In 1972, the innovative Scottish doctor, Professor Archie Cochrane, published a book *Effectiveness and Efficiency: Random Reflections on Health Services*. In it he suggested that thorough reviews of research findings from a variety of disciplines were the best way to inform healthcare practice and policy.

The EBP movement probably represents one of the most important innovations in healthcare progress in the last century. Arguably, the nature of evidence-based practice also represents one of the least understood concepts in healthcare. This has led to various derivations of the term (such as evidence-informed practice) which have caused further confusion. A useful working definition of EBP is: 'The conscientious, explicit and judicious use of current best evidence in making decisions about the care of individual patients.'

Cochrane insisted that all clinical disciplines should be

required to summarise the scientific evidence concerning their practices to justify them, and that patients should only accept healthcare that was based on good scientific evidence. These ideas were driven by his observations that a lot of medicine was based on eminence or tradition rather than evidence, and we now had the tools to develop a sound scientific basis for all medical treatments and should endeavour to do so. Particularly, this referenced new developments in understanding biases in research, and new statistical and meta-analysis techniques that now enabled us to explore large data sets. These ideas have developed into a broad scientific healthcare movement today that suggests the key elements that should be considered for any clinical healthcare practice as:

1. Scientific evidence of a demonstrated positive (or negative) effect of a specific healthcare intervention
2. Social and personal acceptability of the intervention (patient choice)
3. Clinical expert judgement as to the efficacy of the intervention in the specific case considered, or any adaptations required in its implementation
4. Economic viability of the intervention.[101, 102]

EBP assumes the adoption of a scientific approach to healthcare inquiry and means supporting clinical decisions for therapeutic interventions on the best scientific evidence available. This evidence represents the collection, interpretation and integration of valid, applied empirical experience from research-derived, clinician-observed and patient-reported evidence. The aim is that the best available evidence, cost-effectiveness, practical patient circumstances and preferences are all considered in decisions to increase the quality of care delivered. This is a tall order, but the EBP process has delivered a systematic way to achieve this.[98] EBP is fundamentally based upon empirical science and one of its most innovative features is the clear identification of what represents the best evidence to support clinical decisions. EBP is particularly effective where research has provided evidence of the quantifiable (i.e. statistically significant) effectiveness of specific interventions for specific problems. However, this is not always possible. Sufficient research studies may not have been undertaken, and so other forms of available evidence may need to be considered. Therefore, EBP inevitably involves some sort of hierarchy of evidence. A number of different versions of these hierarchies have been proposed over time, and which one represents the best classification remains a matter of considerable debate. However, most present a similar pattern, and generally sort published evidence into two broad categories: evidence from multiple sources that has been systematically and rigorously evaluated (such as systematic reviews of multiple studies), and evidence that has not (such as individual clinical trials). We can think of this as information that has been filtered to produce the best possible results and information that remains unfiltered, but may still prove a valuable source of evidence. In the top category of evidence that has been systematically evaluated is the gold-standard of evidence, that which has been evaluated through systematic reviews. A systematic review explores a specific clinical question, with a comprehensive literature search, eliminating the poorly done studies, and makes practice recommendations based on the most academically rigorous studies. The Cochrane Database of systematic reviews is one of the best examples of this approach, and such reviews are powerful tools in identifying effective interventions. A meta-analysis is another form of systematic review that combines all the results of several good quantitative statistical research studies on a specific condition into a single statistical analysis of results producing very high quality evidence. As this requires data from multiple similar quantitative studies this approach has limitations.

It is important that we strive for a sound empirical basis for all healthcare practices to justify their use, but recognise that although modern healthcare science strives for objectivity, its application is always somewhat subjective. Given this complexity, as might be expected, the scientific justification of any practice requires considerable technical and scientific expertise, especially with the considerable specialisation of modern biomedicine. It is often difficult for the general public to differentiate fact from hyperbole, and this opens a vulnerability that health scammers and deceptive practitioners can exploit. Although regulatory approval may permit products and services with an acceptable risk-benefit profile to be sold, it cannot provide absolute assurance that any therapy is safe or effective for everyone. However, as physician Ben Goldacre notes in his 2013 book *Bad Pharma*, without medication there would be no medicine, and the sheer number of benefits that modern medicine has provided massively outweighs its problems, even though these remain significant.

A matter of trust

Unfortunately, the history of professional healthcare is littered with examples of ineffective and harmful practices, and questionable practitioners. This even reached the stage where it has been parodied in popular culture. In the Simpsons cartoon series, the character Dr Nick Riviera has a medical degree from 'Hollywood Upstairs Medical College', and regularly swindles or gives out useless or dangerous medical advice on the show (though he has avoided being successfully sued to date)! As with any human endeavour, people make bad decisions, errors occur and there are, of course, unscrupulous practitioners in all professions. This is something that those promoting deceptive health practices are well aware of, and capitalise upon to undermine a potential client's trust in public healthcare. The historical and current problems with modern health services present an opportunity for those who wish to sell ineffective therapies to the public, or promote an alternative ideological standpoint. This is well illustrated by the current successes of the anti-vaccination movement who have used social media to cultivate distrust in public health policy. The successful marketing of health misinformation and scams relies fundamentally on who you trust, not what you think.[103]

Trust (or the absence of it) is an essential element of any human relationship. Some of the most successful health scams have capitalised upon this and used anti-intellectualism to promote a growing mistrust of authority, science and medicine. For example, in the USA in 2020, Republican voters appeared far more likely than Democrats to believe the coronavirus pandemic had been exaggerated and mistrust expert scientific sources. Their scepticism was aggravated by right-wing media outlets such as Fox News, and even Republican officeholders (including Donald Trump in the early phases of the pandemic).[99] This distrust eventually demonstrated itself by the President himself, apparently distrusting the 2020 election result, which eventually resulted in the storming of the US Capitol by his supporters (and in his second impeachment trial). In the next section, we explore the nature of health scams before exploring further how health scammers have exploited peoples trust with underhand schemes to part people from their money.

Section IV

Alternative medicine

Chapter 11

What's in a name?

The use of alternative medicine has risen significantly over the past 50 years. Far from being a cottage industry, it is now a major and booming economic sector. A 2018 survey, funded by the National Institute for Health Research, undertaken by Ipsos MORI, found the use of complementary and alternative medicine (CAM), such as acupuncture, massage, osteopathy and chiropractic treatment, had risen from 12% of the population in 2005 to 16% by 2015.[148] Another 2016 report indicated that Americans spent more than $30 billion on alternative therapies. This includes treatments, a wide range of therapies and remedies such as homeopathy, chiropractic, reiki and acupuncture as well as nutritional supplements. The US report, released jointly by the government National Center for Complementary and Integrative Health (NCCIH) and the Centers for Disease Control and Prevention (CDC), found that 59 million Americans had sought out some type of alternative therapy.[149] More than 70% of Canadians also regularly use some form of complementary and/or alternative healthcare therapy today such as vitamins and minerals, herbal products, homeopathic medicines and other alternative medicine products to stay healthy and improve their quality of life.[150] In a 2016 survey of Canadian complementary and alternative medicine by the Fraser Institute, found increasing use over the past decade; approximately 80% of Canadians had used at least one form of complementary therapy, spending more than $8 billion on them. This included $6.5 billion spent on complementary services, such as homeopathy, chiropractic, reiki and acupuncture, and another $2.3 billion on herbs, vitamins, special diet programmes, equipment and literature.[151] A 2019 industry report suggested that the global market would be worth $210 billion by 2026.[152]

The rapid growth and commercialisation of alternative healthcare has led to much research into the possible factors associated with the use of alternative medicine. Psychological theory has suggested several personality traits that correlate with its uptake. One systematic review of beliefs associated with its use found that those with strong personal beliefs about self-control and holistic health and with a desire for natural, non-invasive treatments, had an increased likelihood of using alternative medicine.[153] Other significant driving factors are those that push people away from conventional medicine. These include negative beliefs about science, and a dissatisfaction with medical services.[8]

Overall, rather than people living alternative lifestyles, the research suggests that alternative healthcare users are mainly female, well educated, employed and often have chronic health issues.[9, 147, 154, 155] People with chronic illnesses that conventional medicine cannot cure are often challenged with the ongoing process of self-care management, and so they seek alternative options, often out of despair. The supplementary use of alternative medicine is well known here. For example, people with inflammatory bowel disease (IBD), multiple sclerosis (MS), arthritis and cancer, are all significant users of alternative medicine, with reported usage rates of 52% for IBD, 57% for MS and diabetes, 66% for arthritis, and as high as 80% for cancer.[22, 156, 157, 158, 159, 160, 161] Generally, alternative medicine advocates will argue this growth in popularity is because it focuses on prevention of illness rather than cure, and forms of holistic medicine that are wholesome, natural and harmless. Unfortunately, upon closer examination, it becomes apparent that none of these things is necessarily true and the alternative medicine universe is poorly regulated and rife with deceptive practices.

Problematic terminology

Alternative medicine has multiple names and definitions, so before we explore its merits and problems, defining what it actually is might be a useful exercise. However, defining it is one of the main challenges as there appears no overall consensus for use of the term. Common terms used in the field include 'alternative medicine', 'complementary and alternative medicine' (probably the most widely used – CAM), 'alternative health', 'traditional complementary and alternative medicine' (TCAM), 'integrative/integrated medicine', 'holistic medicine', 'traditional folk medicine', 'salutogenic medicine' and 'non-allopathic medicine'. This gives rise to many confusing and confounding issues, such as, what is alternative medicine an alternative to? What exactly is being integrated with what? What are salutogenic and allopathic medicine? Why should we classify a specific group of therapies differently based upon their use in combination with other therapies, and if we do, why then combine this class with other stand-alone therapies? Logically, such divisions make little sense.

Alternative to what?

Although, along with CAM, alternative medicine has become the most commonly used term, the nature of the term 'alternative' remains anything but clear. The Finnish physician Pekka Louhiala once suggested that in reality there is no alternative medicine, as it is really unproven medicine, arguing there is only scientifically proven, evidence-based medicine supported by good data, or unproven medicine for which scientific evidence is lacking. He also argued that bundling all these alternative therapies under one umbrella was misleading, as it implied that there are two kinds of medicine, each alternative to each other. Due to the rather arbitrary nature of the term 'alternative' there seems to be no clear consensus of meaning of alternative medicine in any significant sense. The British comedian Tim Minchin also highlighted this problem in his well-known comic monologue *Storm*, where he suggests that alternative medicine that works is called... *'medicine'*.[162, 163] Professor Richard Dawkins, voiced the same idea in that 'Either it is true that a medicine works or it isn't. It cannot be false in the ordinary sense but true in some "alternative" sense'.[164]

Complementary or complimentary?

Another significant part of the language of this wellness and alternative healthcare movement is the notion of 'complementary therapies'. The term CAM has become well established, but people still seem to disagree about what it really means, even its proponents. If someone calls themselves a CAM practitioner, one may assume this to mean they possess healthcare tools and techniques outside of the scope of physicians and allied health professionals (nurses, physiotherapists, dietitians etc) that they use in combination with established treatments. Whilst in essence this argument suggests 'complementary' refers to additional health-promoting activities used in conjunction with conventional medicine, rationally it makes little sense to differentiate therapies based upon whether they are used in combination with, or in addition to, other treatments. The term infers some kind of exclusivity, and that the intervention is somehow additional to a medical focus of treating disease. However, its use probably has more value to those marketing such therapies than as a meaningful way of classifying them. The term 'complementary therapies' presents us with the problem of devising meaningful ways to classify such treatments, which isn't as simple as one might think. For example, if an acupuncturist applies needles to treat shoulder pain, is this a complementary therapy or a primary treatment? If a physician prescribes analgesics to a patient after surgery to help manage their pain, is that a complementary therapy? If a nurse sits and has a conversation with a patient about their family support and home situation over a cup of tea, is that a complementary therapy?

I have also encountered complementary misspelled as 'complimentary' on many signs, which is possibly something even more cryptic! What really seems to differentiate those working in CAM healthcare from those in public healthcare is not if the therapies are used alone or in combination with others, but more if the therapies have an established scientific basis, or are more belief-based practices.

Allopathic dinosaurs and salutogenic positivity

The terms *'allopathic'* and *'salutogenic'* medicine have also become more frequently used in the alternative medicine movement and tend to be used as antonyms. The term *allopathic medicine* was coined by the homeopath Samuel Hahnemann in 1810 to distinguish his new practices from those of conventional medicine. Allopathic medicine was seen as the conventional practice of science-based curative biomedicine in which medical doctors and other healthcare professionals treated symptoms and diseases using drugs and other biomedical therapeutics. Hahnemann argued such practices were archaic, whilst his practices were more holistic, treating the whole person using the principles of spirituality and vitalism (see page 151). The problem is that technically this definition presents something of a straw-man argument. As discussed earlier, modern medicine is not simply focused on curative practices, but also employs preventative and holistic care, and so in practice the term tends to be used as a pejorative term used to infer biomedical practices are really some form of prehistoric nonsense.

Salutogenic medicine is described as a new paradigm in healthcare incorporating positive psychology and employing positive organisational behaviours. In the 1970s, the sociologist Dr Aaron Antonovsky coined the term *'salutogenesis'* when exploring the sociology of health. Rather than focusing on biomedicine and pathogenesis, the focus of salutogenesis was described as the 'birth of health', helping the individual pursue wellness, both mentally and physically, with the hope of preventing illness and achieving overall wellbeing. It is frequently espoused by chiropractors and naturopaths, and if it sounds a bit like impenetrably vague postmodern language, it's probably because it is.

Geographical divisions

To confuse matters even further, many alternative health proponents frequently try to explain complementary and alternative medicine in terms of non-western scientific and medical traditions. This is illustrated by the following examples:

> *'Alternative Medical Systems are complete systems of medicine that use different theories than western medicine.'*

> **US National Center for Complementary and Alternative Medicine, 2019**

> *'Integrative medicine offers a balanced, holistic approach to health. It combines the latest breakthroughs in western medicine with the centuries-old wisdom of natural therapies.'*

> **Virginia Mason Medical Center, Seattle, 2019**

As discussed in Section I, the notion of western science or medicine versus other (eastern or otherwise) is rather misleading and logically represents a false dichotomy, or at the very least an oversimplification. Apart from the fact much of contemporary science and medicine is based upon the historical work of multiple cultures (including significant Persian and Chinese influences), the idea promotes simplistic stereotypes. There are plenty of Indian, Iranian and Chinese nuclear physicists, biologists, chemists, medical researchers and rocket scientists who would likely balk at being labelled as representing western science or medicine. They simply regard themselves as scientists.

In short, a practical description of alternative medicine is that it represents a range of therapeutics that largely originate from traditions and theories distinct from contemporary biomedical science, and which claim mechanisms of action outside of those currently accepted by scientific and biomedical consensus.[6, 160, 161, 165, 166]

Some therapies are certainly used to supplement other forms of biomedical healthcare, such as meditation or acupuncture for anxiety and pain management. Nevertheless, the key feature of alternative medicine is that a scientific consensus on its efficacy has not been established. Even so, many alternative medicine practitioners will argue that their practices are science-based, when in fact they are clearly not. Some also argue that their practices are beyond scientific analysis, and in any case many of these practices (such as faith-healing) are impossible to validate in scientific terms.

Integrative medicine and research

The problems inherent in our current public healthcare systems, along with arguments for more compassionate care, have given rise to attempts to incorporate alternative medicine into medicine and public healthcare, usually referred to as 'integrative medicine'. Examples of this trend include several clinical and academic centres, including the UK College of Medicine and Integrated Health at Guy's Hospital, the University of Toronto, McGill University, University of Alberta, Mount Royal University, Harvard University, the Mayo Clinic and the University of Texas. Many leading US cancer centres increasingly present integrative medicine content on their websites, and many provide these services to patients.[167] There is also an *Integrative Medicine Research* journal published by Elsevier. At the time of writing, the University of Arizona had just received a US $15 million grant to support a new integrative medicine centre. The aims of these approaches sound highly laudable in terms of health promotion, in that they argue that integrative health emphasises therapeutic relationships and makes use of all appropriate therapies – conventional, complementary and alternative – to provide a holistic approach. They also promote the goals of researching alternative therapies through scientific research.

Nevertheless, a significant criticism of this approach is that it is grounded on flawed assumptions. A significant issue is that it neglects the existing interdisciplinary nature of contemporary public healthcare, and particularly the role of nursing within it. Nursing is focused upon holistic integrated person- and community-centred care. It will be the nurse who, in addition to providing medical care, also asks the patient how they are feeling overall, what else helps them relieve their symptoms, what supplements are they taking, how this illness is affecting their lifestyle/employment, how the family is coping, are their religious/spiritual needs being catered for, and who is looking after their pets. In the community, nurse-led clinics support a wide range of health promotion initiatives, from quitting smoking to breastfeeding programmes. In addition to doctors and nurses providing treatment, other science-based professionals in the system support people's specialist healthcare needs, such as dentists, physiotherapists, psychologists and social workers.

So, it is rather a misrepresentation to suggest that the current system is solely disease focused and non-holistic in its approach to health, unless one adopts 'holism' as an exclusively spiritual term.

What is being integrated?

Another problem is that this concept of integration involves bringing together different things to improve practice as a whole. In the public view, integrative medicine appears to equate the value of conventional and alternative treatments. However, combining faith-based and science-based therapies together with the notion of inclusivity may well result in a mélange of practices that is difficult to defend. In bringing together things we know work with things that are dubious, we could then well make things worse. As infectious disease specialist Mark Crislip wryly suggested: 'When you integrate cow pie with apple pie, the cow pie is not made better; the apple pie is made worse.' In effect, science-based medicine that works is seen as having the same value as faith-based treatments, whilst faith-based treatments become elevated to academic respectability (an example of how this has occurred with acupuncture is given below).

Science or magic?

Many proponents of integrative medicine will suggest that this is the whole point, and there is nothing wrong with that. Often, it is argued that, 'Maybe we simply don't understand it yet?' As science-fiction writer Arthur C Clarke famously suggested, 'Any sufficiently advanced technology is indistinguishable from magic'. So maybe alternative health practices are simply something we don't yet understand. However, there are a number of problems with using this argument.

Firstly, there has been significant progress in healthcare and medicine in the last 200 years through scientific medical research.

The exclusion of therapies identified as harmful or useless in favour of those that work has led to significant progress. We know that if therapies do work well, we can demonstrate this with scientific evidence. We can measure their effectiveness relative to other treatments, develop a solid evidence base and engage in deeper research into how they work. Alternatively, where we don't understand mechanisms, we can propose new theories regarding human health, and test them and produce new therapies. Therefore, if therapies that are not currently supported by science do work, then we should be able to gather evidence they are effective. This has been the basis of scientific progress for hundreds of years. Therefore, there is good reason to continue to apply a scientific approach to medical and healthcare research.

Secondly, the 'indistinguishable from magic' argument concedes that magical explanations are really explanations of technologies beyond our current level of knowledge, not ineffable divine explanations that are beyond knowing. If they are not considered advanced technologies then magical thinking is required to explain them, which presents even more problems. Magical thinking involves the acceptance of mysterious or supernatural forces to explain things and usually includes prescribed rites of precisely defined actions (often verbal) which are believed to produce mysterious effect. This often involves the use of mystical forces to cause a specific effect, or ritualistic acts that are believed to produce results elsewhere.[168, 169] Most modern theories tend to explain this as a belief that forces beyond scientific understanding can effect causality in some way. Belief in the paranormal represents a modern manifestation of this. An example would be: 'I broke a mirror; therefore, I will get seven years' bad luck.'[169, 170] In health terms, another example would be the belief that a blocked root chakra can cause arthritis, or that most ailments come from an acidic body.

If we take alternative medicine human-biofield energy

theories (e.g. reiki, acupuncture and therapeutic touch) as examples, they all propose unmeasurable life-force energies. They are often suggested as being beyond current scientific understanding (or even that they don't work unless you actually believe in them).[171] Although as Clarke suggested, phenomena that we don't understand might look like magic, as scientists we would expect to be able to explore them using scientific methods, and conclusively demonstrate they exist (even if we don't know what they are). If we cannot do so, they remain ideas that require acceptance of magical-thinking, i.e. faith rather than evidence.

The downside of integrative medicine

Despite their popularity, there is also a serious downside to integrating these approaches into public healthcare. Firstly, these practices are so poorly regulated it becomes practically impossible to discriminate those who are using them to scam people from the genuine believer, and opens up public susceptibility to deceptive practices by fraudsters. Secondly, the use of faith-based therapeutics has associated costs. In a resource-restricted system, the question arises, does it make sense to employ unproven therapies in public health simply because some people want them, or should we only allocate public funds to those therapies for which we have good evidence they work? This very issue came up last month in the news here in Canada, when it was revealed that Quebec-based Terre Sans Frontières (TSF) had spent $200,000 in aid money (with a further $150,000 budgeted) from Global Affairs Canada to send a dozen volunteer homeopaths to Honduras over five years to help treat the tropical infection Chagas disease (trypanosomiasis). As there is no evidence that homeopathy can treat this disease (or come to that, any other), and plenty of research that demonstrates antiparasitic drugs are effective, a media furore ensued. This was followed by a rapid cancellation of public funding for this aid.[172]

Integrative medicine also presents the potential for quality and ethical issues to arise. Even some proponents of integrative healthcare have acknowledged this. Doctors Melinda Ring and Sandy Newmark, of integrative medical centres in Chicago and San Francisco respectively, noted in a 2018 paper that a lack of evidence of safety and efficacy poses a problem for integrative medicine.[173] Also, little basic research is being undertaken to demonstrate the theoretical basis for the alternative therapies that are being applied in these new centres. For example, there are literally thousands of acupuncture studies reporting its clinical use. However, the hypothetical principles of *Qi* energy (also known as *Chi*), meridians, and acupuncture points that are a part of it remain speculative.

Integrative research and confirmation bias

Those who advocate for integrative medicine often argue that it is beneficial to do scientific research into these therapies to better understand them. This would be a good argument if these centres restricted themselves to researching these therapies before advocating them, and if such research were carried out in a rigorous and independent way. So, if integrative medicine research represented the positive evolution of health science and medicine, then we should expect it to demonstrate the same stringent high-quality scientific evidence that is now required in the development of conventional drugs or medical device. Yet large-scale, well-designed, randomised clinical trials (RCTs – typical medical studies where a therapy is tested in one group of people, and a similar control group does not receive the therapy, and participants are randomly assigned to the groups) are very rarely undertaken in integrative medical centres. In cases where they have been done properly, no benefits of the alternative treatment have been demonstrated.[174, 175]

The case of integrative acupuncture research

Using the example of acupuncture and the theory of *Qi* energy, research into this would seem to at the very least merit an exploration of the nature of the energy involved, and the physiological structures and mechanisms that support transport of these life-forces, with attempts to identify and measure them. Nevertheless, whilst it is notable that every human transport and communication system ever discovered in the human body has related anatomical and physiological structures, none have ever been demonstrated for the flow of *Qi* energy. Some researchers have asserted that such structures exist, but these claims remain unverified. Probably the most widely publicised was the work of the North Korean scientist Kim Bong-Han who proposed that he had found meridians in 1962, arguing that microtubular structures existed inside and outside of blood vessels and lymphatic vessels, as well as on the surface of internal organs and under the dermis, and even in plants. He concluded they were the communication system of meridians and called them Bonghan ducts or channels, after his research. These are now referred to as the primo vascular system (PVS) by supporters. It is even claimed that injecting dye at acupuncture points reveals the path of the meridians.[176] The problem is, as former Air Force physician Dr Harriet Hall points out, even though South Korean researchers published a protocol for finding them in mice in 2015, no other anatomists, scientists or researchers outside of the alternative medicine community have ever found them.[177, 178]

You will certainly find websites proclaiming that 'Science finally proves meridians exist!'[179] but as scientists have been using electron microscopes since 1933, if the PVS actually existed in animals and plants as claimed, why have other researchers not found them? Their discovery would also have been an astonishing event of Nobel Prize-worthy significance. However, as Kim Bong-Han disappeared in North Korea in 1966, and no other scientists outside of South Korea have found any evidence of the PVS, these claims seem like those found in the *Fortean Times* rather than in science journals. Other studies have been reported over the years that have attempted to demonstrate that meridians exist, but all have adopted ambiguous methods, usually with pseudoscientific rationales, and have always been performed by acupuncture advocates. For example, apparently, Professor Fei Lun of Shanghai Fudan University claimed that the stomach meridian transmitted infrared light along it by using proton accelerators and electron microscopes, which is odd given that infrared light is easily detectable by simpler optical devices (and even smartphone cameras).[180] In another reported study in an alternative medicine journal, researchers claimed that photoluminescent bioceramics could detect light travelling down meridians.[181] None of these explained what structures the light was actually travelling along, and why these structures (described as interstitial microscopic fluid channels) have no observable coherent anatomical structures. Overall, this work demonstrates a clear lack of rigour in the theoretical constructs, methodological approach, flawed development and testing of instruments, and all of it remains independently unsubstantiated and unreplicated. These approaches are often argued as examples of deceptive 'quantum woo' by physicists (see page 154).

Overall, virtually no base scientific research of this sort is undertaken by North American integrative medical research units, which overwhelmingly publish studies that focus on add-on alternative therapeutic interventions in various scenarios, and almost invariably these studies report positive results.

Overwhelmingly positive outcomes

We also know that any medical study that offers additional treatments (compared with single treatments) usually results in positive patient reported outcomes. Where alternative therapeutics are used as add-ons or complementary therapies, there is a strong bias towards reporting positive outcomes about the alternative therapeutic add-on in the resulting research; more is better. Also, with these studies it becomes very difficult to differentiate any benefits arising from either of the therapies.[182] For example, if faith-healers are combined with physicians in a cancer clinic and patients are treated by both, then if the faith-healers state it was obviously their healing that led to a patient's cancer remission, how could we dispute this? So, unless we simply wish to validate pre-existing beliefs, this sort of approach is fairly useless in establishing the value of any alternative therapy. This sort of research puts the conclusion before the hypothesis and involves a high risk of deception.

Unfortunately, reviewing the output of integrative medical research frequently reveals badly designed studies published in alternative medicine journals with poorly controlled researcher bias – in essence, bad science. One independent review of integrative health research found that only a small number of RCTs were evident, using small numbers of patients and lack of adequate control groups.[183] In 2016, UK alternative medicine researcher Professor Edzard Ernst examined abstracts from the International Congress on Integrative Medicine & Health (ICIMH, Green Valley Ranch Resort, Las Vegas, Nevada, USA, 17–20 May) and found that, out of 387 abstracts, for every negative result expressed there were 52 positive ones. This would be a very unusual finding at a medical conference despite the bias for submitting positive results to learned journals. A recent review of integrative medicine clinical guidelines in China in 2017 also found the quality was low.[184]

Scientific or entrepreneurial revolution?

Overall, the growth of integrative medicine seems to represent more of a populist and consumer-driven trend in healthcare than a revolution in scientific research, although most integrative centres still rely on substantial private donors to fund them. Nevertheless, a rapid expansion of integrative medicine in public healthcare is now occurring, with alternative medicine therapeutics being provided in many public hospitals, including the Royal London in the UK[185] and hospitals affiliated with Yale, Duke and Johns Hopkins in the US,[186] although corresponding improvements in clinical outcomes have yet to be demonstrated. The problem is, this integrative approach will likely erode confidence in science-based medicine and give people false hope in faith-based therapeutics. Yale University neurologist Stephen Novella suggests this is possibly the most insidious form of harm to healthcare, with erosion of standards within the medical profession. Most actively promote additional alternative medicine services, which are seen as increasing their business opportunities and reputation. Mixing good scientific work with faith-based practices that support magical-thinking may well be good for business, but as it currently exists it is more likely to result in more deceptive healthcare practice, rather than improved health outcomes. If I suggest reiki might work in addition to your chemotherapy, I am actually suggesting magical thinking is as reasonable to apply to patient treatment as scientific biomedicine. Unfortunately, that is a recipe for deception to thrive.

Alternative medicine and health claims

In order to explore alternative practices, it is important to understand the differences between them and conventional biomedical practice. Modern biomedicine involves healthcare practices which have evolved under the influence of biomedical science supported by modern evidence–based practice approaches and which currently receive broad international acceptance in most of the economically developed world. In contrast, as discussed above, alternative healthcare is marked by the acceptance of different traditions and a wide diversity and lack of standardisation.

A popular approach to the classification of alternative medicine organises alternative approaches into five broad systems of practice, which are described as follows:

1. Alternative health belief systems
2. Physical manipulative interventions
3. Herbal and nutritional interventions
4. Mind-body interventions
5. Energy interventions (Table 1).

However, there are literally hundreds of alternative therapies, from homeopathy to beer spas, and many of them have practices that overlap. For example, homeopathy is usually described as an alternative health belief system, and yet characterises illness as disturbances in the body's vital energy or life force, so it is also an energy-based approach.

Table 1: Categories and examples of complementary and alternative therapies

Categories	Activities
Alternative health belief systems	Chinese traditional medicine (including acupuncture), homeopathy, naturopathy, Ayurvedic medicine, spiritual and traditional medicine systems
Physical manipulative interventions	Massage, chiropractic, reflexology, hydrotherapy, craniosacral therapy
Herbal and nutritional interventions	Herbal remedies, vitamins, dietary supplements, diets, aromatherapy, detoxification therapies
Mind-body interventions	Meditation, guided imagery, hypnotherapy, music therapy, bio- or neurofeedback, yoga, tai chi, qigong, dance
Energy interventions	Reiki, therapeutic touch, magnetic field therapy, faith-healing

It is beyond the scope of this book to explore all of the different forms of alternative health practice, and new ones frequently arise. Nonetheless, it is useful to explore the most common ones that people are likely to encounter, in terms of deceptive practices, and so these are explored in some detail over the next few chapters.

Chapter 12

Alternative health belief systems

Therapies in this category are characterised by complete systems of beliefs about health that do not use biomedical explanations. There are many, including traditional spiritual belief systems, although in North America the main ones you will most likely encounter are traditional Chinese medicine (TCM), homeopathy, naturopathy and Ayurvedic medicine.

Traditional Chinese medicine

Aspects of TCM have been around for several thousand years, but it was first advanced as a national approach to Chinese health by Chairman Mao Zedong as a part of the communist Cultural Revolution in China during the 1960s and '70s, and continues to be promoted by the Chinese government today.[187, 188, 189, 190] Mao's rationale for the development of TCM in the 1950s was that it would help address the shortage of primary care in China, provide healthcare to underserved populations and offer people better choice in their healthcare.

TCM is based on a wide-ranging collection of different philosophies and therapeutics, from acupuncture to demonology. The theoretical framework includes the notion of complementary yet opposing *yin* and *yang* life forces of cosmic duality and the balance and harmony of a vital energy, or life force, that flows through the body, known as *Qi*. Other theoretical aspects include the concept of wind and its direction (one of the six excesses in TCM which include wind, cold, heat, dryness, moisture and the heat of summer), which are also believed to affect health. Additionally, shamanistic medical beliefs from the Shang dynasty (1600–1046 BCE) are integrated, which suggest that illness may result from the upsetting of ancestors, being cursed, or demons entering the body.[175] Curing here involves pacifying ancestors by suitable rituals or asking spiritual help to expel the demon.[191] Although some of these ideas are clearly based in religious beliefs, many herbal TCM remedies do in fact work, and TCM should not be regarded as a wholly supernatural framework. Nonetheless, the acceptance of TCM risks conflating the possible value of traditional remedies with the metaphysical beliefs attached to them.

A Nobel Prize for Chinese Medicine

One notable success in the world of TCM was the award of the Nobel Prize in Physiology or Medicine to Tu Youyou in 2015. After studies of traditional herbal medicines, Tu Youyou developed a method of extracting a substance, artemisinin, from the plant *Artemisia annua*, which inhibits the malaria parasite. Drugs based on artemisinin have led to the survival and improved health of millions of people with malaria. This was the first time China had won a Nobel Prize in a scientific discipline. However, Liu Changhua, a professor of history at the Academy of Chinese Medical Sciences in Beijing, whilst happy that the drug had saved lives, criticised Dr Tu's methods as being little different from those used by western drug companies exploring traditional medicines to look for new drugs. In TCM, multiple herbs and medicines are prescribed together by the practitioner, and a formula may contain anywhere up to 20 herbs that each have different actions, organ focus and functions. Professor

Changhua suggested that the Nobel award was disrespectful of the TCM tradition. However, other Chinese scientists, such as He Zuoxiu (a member of the Chinese Academy of Sciences) suggested that the ancient pharmacopoeia should be mined and the magical theories of TCM associated with it discarded: 'I think for the future development of Chinese medicine, people should abandon its medical theory and focus more on researching the value of herbs with a modern scientific approach.'[192]

Quality concerns with Chinese medical research

Because TCM was devised as a nationalistic response to health issues in China, any critique of it in China is a highly sensitive issue. Given its current political support, there are also concerns about the quality of Chinese TCM research. A 2013 review of bias risk and outcome-reporting concluded that selective outcome reporting was widespread in Chinese TCM studies, and study conclusions should be interpreted with caution.[193] In 2014, Chinese researchers explored all the RCTs of acupuncture published in Chinese academic journals. A total of 840 RCTs were included, and 99.8% (838) of them reported positive results. Only two trials (0.2%) reported negative results. In scientific terms that represents a significant problem, as there are always some erroneous results to be expected. Reasonably the authors concluded: 'Publication bias might be a major issue in RCTs on acupuncture published in Chinese journals ... which is related to high risk of bias.'[194]

In 2015, the China Food and Drug Administration (CFDA) carried out a year-long review evaluating data from 1622 clinical trial programmes of drugs awaiting approval by the regulator and concluded that most of the results were fabricated. Much of the data was found to be incomplete or untraceable. The report led to claims in the *British Medical Journal* and other media that up to 80% of China's clinical trial data was fraudulent. CFDA officials admitted to serious quality problems in laboratory and clinical research, and in 2017 issued a circular setting out penalties for clinical trial data integrity violations, including intentional data falsification, incomplete and non-compliant data and other data defects.[195]

Acupuncture: A global success story?

Acupuncture, one aspect of TCM, has become one of the most common alternative therapies used in modern medical centres, and is often regarded as the poster child for alternative medicine in that it is argued as a therapeutic practice based outside of biomedical science that has been shown to work. It is suggested to have developed in ancient China. Theoretically, as described earlier, acupuncture points mapped across the body are theorised to correspond to flows of life-force energy, or *Qi*. As previously noted, these pathways are known as meridians in the body. Acupuncture involves stimulating these energy points on the body using needles penetrating the skin to alleviate pain or to treat various health conditions. There are various forms of this needling, and even electro-acupuncture using electrical stimulation.

Studies conducted by scientists across Europe and North America have demonstrated that acupuncture can be useful in helping treat pain and nausea and it is available at most North American pain clinics. However, as previously noted, outside of this work there is, as yet, no scientific evidence that the meridians or acupuncture points exist, or evidence that acupuncture can treat any condition. More recently, the suggested nature of the phenomenon has also become questioned. Although the practice is a reported 2000 years old, and there are numerous studies to suggest that acupuncture needling works for pain and nausea, it is only relatively recently that high-quality scientific studies have been undertaken using sham acupuncture devices as a placebo (that is, using fake non-penetrating needles), or needling at non-acupuncture points to test it.[185–190, 196, 197, 198, 199, 200, 201] The results of a German well-controlled study of acupuncture for back pain in 2007 (and updated in 2015) found that both acupuncture and sham acupuncture appeared to work better than conventional drugs, physical therapy and exercise alone, but that acupuncture worked no better than sham acupuncture.[196] So, clearly there was some effect but most likely placebo. Acupuncture had now failed to prove effective in well-designed scientific tests. Following further studies, the National Institute for Clinical Excellence (NICE) in the UK no longer supports the use of acupuncture for low back pain. The evidence now suggests that acupuncture may actually work more as a powerful distraction or simply, as many scientists, including David Colquhoun and Steven Novella, suggest, simply as an elaborate theatrical placebo.[202]

This is not as strange as it at first may sound, as it well established that pain perception is hugely impacted by psychological factors. Other powerful distraction therapies, like virtual reality, are now showing similar results in pain studies, and the more we understand about the nature of pain, the more we know much of it can be psychologically mediated. For example, most sufferers of chronic pain report that although they may have multiple pain sites in their body, if they are focused upon one, the others are not so apparent. Also, when the chronic pain associated with endometriosis was explored, those women with the worst disease pathology were not necessarily those reporting the highest amounts of pain.[203] Researchers are now beginning to suggest neurochemistry may better explain the effects of acupuncture on pain and nausea, and it probably is not a coincidence that the suggested *Qi* meridians generally follow the pathways of the peripheral nervous system. However, this is not a popular view in the wider public domain, or that promoted by the Chinese authorities.

A TCM conference experience

A few years back I found myself as a guest speaker at a Chinese integrative medical conference in Shanghai, China. I got an email invitation as a guest speaker through a Chinese colleague who asked me at short notice if I was interested in speaking at such a conference, all expenses paid. The idea was to present some of our exploratory work on virtual reality (VR) as a distraction therapy in pain management. My colleague needed a quick answer, so I thought 'why not', as I was available and it was a great opportunity to publicise our work; it was only for a few days and I had never visited China before. A few weeks before I was set to go, I finally received the official conference literature which was in the Chinese language. Using Google Translate I discovered the conference was actually entitled the '2016 Design and Implementation of Clinical Trials in Integrative Medicine Conference'. I was somewhat surprised to find it was an integrative medicine conference as I had publicly expressed my concerns with this in writing and in presentations on several occasions. I could have pulled out at this stage, but decided against this as they had graciously invited me, and I could also discuss research techniques to develop the best evidence-based practices. Also, I must admit I was somewhat curious as to what this sort of conference would look like. Consequently, despite my misgivings, I decided to attend, and vowed to do my best to give the conference a fair shake, so to speak.

My hosts were very hospitable, and a day after I arrived, I found myself sitting in the front row of the Lecture Room in Shuhang Hospital, Shanghai University of Traditional Chinese Medicine, ready to deliver my talk. I got a tour of some of the hospital beforehand, and had asked several nurses, physicians and other staff how they used TCM there. I was surprised to find they all looked a little uncomfortable discussing it, and several noted that actually all of the hospitals offered science-based biomedicine with the usual pharmaceutical and surgical treatments found in the west, as the primary healthcare interventions. TCM, I found, was mainly used as a complementary therapy in most urban centres, but more widely practised in rural China. A few of the doctors and nurses also openly admitted that TCM was actually not so highly regarded by the public now, and it was seen as more of a politically sensitive issue by most of the health professionals I spoke to.

Immediately before my presentation there was one on the use of electro-acupuncture for vagal nerve stimulation by Dr Luis Ulloa of the US Rutgers University. He described its possible value to improve outcomes in the treatment of sepsis by reducing the inflammatory response. It was a well-delivered presentation of scientific work. However, this work's relationship to acupuncture and TCM was also rather superficial. The work involved the electrical stimulation of a nerve in mice through a needle inserted in an identified acupuncture point (I am not sure how you identify acupuncture points in mice – but that is another matter!) but one that also corresponded with the location of the vagus nerve. It used established scientific knowledge of anatomy and neurophysiology, and at no point ever did Dr Ulloa use any reference to meridians to manipulate the flow of life energy (*Qi*) or any other TCM explanations of acupuncture. In effect, what was presented was a study that demonstrated if you stimulate the vagus nerve in mice electrically, you can initiate an immunological reaction. This probably doesn't sound quite so ground-breaking as a claim that acupuncture can help stimulate the immune system, particularly as the vagus nerve innervates the adrenal glands (which produce cortisol, a steroid hormone that regulates a wide range of processes throughout the body, including the immune response). Additionally, providing any penetrating injury through needling is likely to promote some measurable immune response in any mammal. Nevertheless, at least this was some basic-scientific work, but alas, things went rapidly downhill from this point onwards.

The Acupuncture as anaesthesia mythology
The other presentations stretched credibility beyond belief and involved highly questionable medical ethics. Firstly, the Director of the University spoke proudly of how the first open-heart surgery operation in 1975 had been performed using acupuncture for anaesthesia, and then to thunderous applause a guest speaker who was one of the original anaesthetists in that surgery came on stage to say how they pioneered these techniques. These were even commemorated on a Chinese postage stamp at the time.

The hapless patient involved here was a 15-year-old girl, and the reality that later came to light was that, in addition to acupuncture, she was also given powerful sedatives and analgesic drugs (midazolam, fentanyl and droperidol) and local anaesthetics injected into various areas of her chest. The patient had also been taught abdominal breathing exercises for days before the procedure to maintain ventilation, but the surgical team also maintained an endotracheal tube for emergency use in case she became hypoxic.

This episode added to the mythology surrounding the effectiveness of acupuncture as anaesthesia in the west, building on a 1972 story when journalist James Reston wrote about his emergency appendectomy during American President Nixon's trip to China. He was initially reported as having been 'anaesthetised' by acupuncture, but again, it soon became established that he had actually had conventional anaesthesia, and acupuncture afterwards to help pain control in the recovery period. For a more authentic first-hand account of the experience of acupuncture anaesthesia I highly recommend the Chinese ballet dancer Li Cunxin's autobiography, who experienced it as a young man. Suffice to say he was not a fan.

The presentation went on describing how the local hospitals now regularly employed acupuncture anaesthesia for open heart surgery as it was shown to save costs considerably in terms of both anaesthetics and recovery. They also cited a 2011 paper that claimed that during the operation, patients kept on spontaneously breathing.[204] Given my own clinical experience, my suspicions were aroused as the presentation progressed, as what was presented included some science but mixed with half-truths (see page 285) and a large dose of pure propaganda. I have no doubt it is possible to do thoracic surgery with minimal conventional anaesthesia and additional pain control measures, but that doesn't mean it is necessarily a good idea.

Pain is a multifactorial, complex neurophysiological and psychosocial phenomenon, and placebo and distractive effects can be very powerful. In all likelihood, a range of alternative placebos together with pharmaceuticals would probably have had similar effects to those claimed for acupuncture here. However, experimenting with these during major surgical procedures is completely immoral by modern medical ethical standards. Some may deconstruct this as an external view of a very different culture, but to suggest it is reasonable to use low doses of established anaesthetic drugs with acupuncture and keep a patient conscious to save money seems indefensible by any compassionate standard, and this hardly reflects patient-centred medicine. As a nurse who has seen a number of open chest surgical procedures, I would have to say that anyone who has witnessed such surgery and thinks it is good for the patient to be conscious during the procedure is either a sadist or has no respect for human suffering. I'll leave it to your imagination to think what it sounds and feels like as the surgeon saws through the sternum.

Of course, there is a 'What if there is no alternative?' argument, but here there are good alternatives available, and many better proven anaesthetic and pain-control measures that could be used rather than acupuncture. Acupuncture for open-heart surgery falls far short of the 'do no harm' principle. Even one of the Chinese doctors attending, whom I spoke with, thought the whole thing was politically-driven nonsense. By mixing ancient Chinese magical theories of *Qi* energy, meridians and needles with doses of modern sedatives, local anaesthetics and narcotic analgesics, it is impossible to determine what effect the actual acupuncture was having compared with the drugs, let alone any placebo effect. This was extremely poor science by any standard.

In other papers presented on acupuncture-based anaesthesia at the conference, the use of sham acupuncture was cited as being inferior, and all contained copious statistical analysis with positive outcomes. In fact, I have never seen so many large positive results presented in a single medical conference. However, in all of these presentations it was clearly a case of garbage in, garbage out, and overt confirmation bias. The design of the studies virtually guaranteed positive outcomes. If the findings claimed here were actually true and replicable, anaesthetists all over the world would be throwing out their Boyle's anaesthetic machines and embracing acupuncture as the technique of choice. This has been studied outside of China where independent work suggests that acupuncture does not reduce volatile anaesthetic requirements by a clinically important amount.[205]

Unfortunately, good evidence on the basic theory and science of acupuncture simply doesn't exist, and although needling may have a physical and psychological effect, by using underdetermined theoretical suggestions for mode of action, and adding multiple confounding variables into clinical studies, the real value of the procedure as a therapeutic tool becomes obscured.

So, what can we conclude from all this? Far from being the success story of alternative medicine, acupuncture remains a popular therapy but with a large and very poor quality evidence-base for both mechanism of action and effectiveness, and good potential to be exploited by deceptive practitioners. Chinese medical studies that are of doubtful quality make up the majority of the research work in this area, as well as numerous studies of acupuncture with very poor study designs. For pain and nausea, it may be useful for some (most likely due to combined stimulation, distractive and placebo effects) but its value compared with other therapies must also be considered. For the vast majority of conditions, there is currently no strong evidence that acupuncture works any better than placebo, and for conditions such as infertility, heart disease or other significant diseases, no clinical value has yet to be established. Nevertheless, I would hazard a guess, at the time of writing if you explore local clinics offering acupuncture and TCM in your area, you will find TCM practitioners claiming to offer help with immunological conditions (including asthma), IBS, colitis, infertility, neuropathy, arthritis, heart disease and possibly even cancer, using what can only be described as deceptive claims of effectiveness.

Homeopathy and naturopathy

Two other well-established alternative health belief systems you are likely to encounter on the high street are those of homeopathy and naturopathy. Although separate disciplines, they may be considered together as they have distinct similarities. Both involve belief in 'vitalism', and both also have shared a substantial growth in popularity over the last few decades.

Homeopathy

Homeopathy is based upon the philosophy of vitalism that interprets diseases and sickness as caused by disturbances in the body's vital energy or life force. It represents a form of alternative medicine where practitioners treat patients using highly diluted preparations of substances believed to cause their symptoms. The German physician Samuel Hahnemann (1755–1843), as discussed in the last chapter, first elaborated the basic principles of homeopathy in 1796, invoking ideas of curing 'like with like'.[206] The theoretical basis is that a substance that in large doses produces symptoms of a specific disease will, in extremely small doses, cure it. Hahnemann originally experimented with cinchona tree bark that is used as a traditional remedy for malaria; it contains large amounts of quinine. He found that he experienced symptoms similar to malaria when he ingested it, and so concluded that he could treat diseases by using small amounts of substances that caused similar symptoms. This thinking also embodies earlier medieval beliefs in metaphysical rather than physical links between the cause and cure of an illness or injury.[102] Nevertheless, homeopathy has many supporters and Prince Charles has been a prominent advocate of the therapy.

Nosode and sarcode remedies

Homeopathic remedies are prepared from plants, animals and minerals and known as either 'sarcodes' (from healthy organisms) or 'nosodes' (from pathological substances). They are listed in a professional *Homeopathic Materia Medica*, and include substances like belladonna, wolfsbane, lithium, silver, tree cancers and even the livers of rabbits with anthrax. However, there appears to be no global standard because the contents of this database change around the world. If the substance is soluble, it is cut up and one part diluted with distilled water or alcohol and shaken vigorously by banging a vial of the mixture with 10 firm strokes of the arm on a book or board (known as 'succussion'). Today, this is generally done mechanically. If the substance is insoluble, it is ground up and mixed with powdered lactose (known as 'trituration'). At a certain point it is then put into solution and one part then further diluted 99 times. The process is repeated until the desired concentration is reached. Finally drops of the final diluted form are dropped onto sugar pills and dried, ready to be sold. Dilutions of 1 to 10 are designated by the Roman numeral X ($1X = 1/10$, $3X = 1/1000$, $6X = 1/1,000,000$). Similarly, dilutions of 1 to 100 are designated by the Roman numeral C ($1C = 1/100$, $3C = 1/1,000,000$, and so on). Most remedies today range from 6X to 30X, but products of 30C or more are also sold.

A significant problem with the basis for homeopathy is that the actual concentrations are not measured with scientific accuracy, and the remedies used contain virtually (or actually) none of the original substance. The principles of chemistry indicate that there is a limit to the dilution that can be made without losing the original substance altogether. For example, a typical homeopathic dilution of 30C is equal to one part of the ingredient in 10^{60} parts water. However, these dilution factors are hard to understand in practical terms, so here are some analogies to help clarify. A 3C dilution is a one in a million dilution. This is roughly the amount of fluoride in treated drinking water. However, as Dr Ben Goldacre once noted, an example of the more commonly used 30C dilution is that, if we imagine a sphere of water with a diameter of 90 million miles (the distance from the earth to the sun), one molecule of the substance in it is a 30C dilution.[31] At a 200C dilution (and higher dilutions are actually used by homeopaths), things become even weirder, because the dilution is actually more than one in all the atoms in the universe.

It's quantum, Baby!

Homeopaths have argued a theory of 'the memory of water' or 'quantum electrodynamics' to rationalise this issue, providing a scientific explanation for the theoretical model of 'information transfer' from the substance to the water solution, and suggesting that a memory of the molecular structure is retained. This effect was even reported by the French immunologist Jacques Benveniste in a set of antibody experiments published in the journal *Nature* in 1988, creating quite a controversy.[207] The paper caused a sensation, and several news outlets claimed 'Homeopathy finds scientific support!' However, no one, including Benveniste, was able to provide any answers to how this memory of water effect could be produced. Repeat studies in other laboratories detected no effect, which also gave rise to some suspicion of the original results.[208] No other scientists have been able to demonstrate any such memory characteristic. Furthermore, research published in 2005 on molecular water dynamics demonstrated that '…water essentially loses the memory of persistent correlations in its structure within 50 millionths of a nanosecond'.[209]

Later supporters of homeopathy have suggested quantum physics as an explanation, in that they claim there is a subatomic wave field that is carried by the water or sugar in the remedy and interacts with the subatomic fields underlying the physical matter of the patient.[210, 211] This is used as a theoretical basis by modern homeopaths to explain how objects can be influenced, or energy may be drawn from them, at a distance. However, those who are proposing these ideas are not physicists, and offer incorrect interpretations of quantum entanglement. One problem is that these quantum effects average out as more particles come together and scale increases. This is referred to as 'decoherence', and makes any practical physical effects of quantum entanglement proposed by homeopaths highly unlikely. In any case, no observable, experimentally verifiable connection between quantum theory and the alleged therapeutic effect of homeopathy has ever been demonstrated. Most physicists regard this as the justification of beliefs with unscientific references to quantum physics, also known as 'quantum woo'.[212]

Homeopathic magical thinking

Even if one accepts these explanations, they still don't explain why water doesn't react to other impurities in it, or why those don't have unintended effects. Issues with the irrationality of the theoretical basis notwithstanding, another major problem with homeopathy is that numerous well-publicised studies have found no effect any better than placebo with homeopathy, and most homeopathic trials have been identified as very poor quality studies. Despite its popularity, the large body of literature and evidence demonstrating that homeopathy is bunk is comprehensive, and it remains impossible to explain it without resorting to magical explanations.[202, 203, 204, 205, 206, 213, 214, 215, 216, 217] Many homeopathic remedies also embody magical thinking in their nature, such as the notions that diluted ultrasound waves, bits of the Berlin Wall or light from Venus can have clinically significant effects.

In 2017, the UK National Health Service (NHS) stopped funding homeopathic therapies in the UK. This led to a well-publicised legal challenge against the NHS brought by the British Homeopathic Association (BHA) in 2018, which failed (the BHA also had to pay the NHS's legal costs).[218] Overall, homeopathy is best considered a faith-based practice, and is generally harmless if used as an adjunctive therapy, because the preparations contain no active ingredients. However, some do include alcohol, so they can be toxic to people who have liver failure.

Naturopathic medicine

Naturopathy is a related and somewhat confusing field, as definitions of what it actually is, and levels of education, vary widely. In the UK, there are around 2000 Registered Naturopaths, and 2400 or so here in Canada, and the profession has gained in popularity. Overall, it may be considered a form of alternative medicine based on a belief in natural health with a basis in vitalism (see page 151). and beliefs similar to those expressed by homeopaths. Like TCM practitioners, they use arguments of holistic medicine to explain their approach to healthcare.[219] Many also endorse aspects of Ayurvedic and TCM.

Naturopathy has its roots in the 19th-century natural health movement of Europe, which arose in part as a reaction to the ineffectiveness and harsh nature of medical treatments of the time. In Scotland in the 1880s, the physician Thomas Allinson started advocating what he called 'hygienic medicine', promoting a natural diet and exercise with avoidance of tobacco and overwork. He is probably best known for his advocacy of wholemeal bread.

Indeed, many of these ideas are sound principles and are found in modern healthcare today. Such ideas were further developed, and the term 'naturopathy' was coined in 1895 by the German homeopath John Scheel, and adopted by Benedict Lust, a German hydrotherapist and osteopath (therapists that externally manipulates tissues), whom naturopaths consider to be the father of modern naturopathy in North America. The American School of Naturopathy was founded by Dr Lust in New York in 1901. Graduating naturopathic practitioners then formed the Naturopathic Society of America in 1919 and established other colleges and health centres throughout the USA. By 1920, naturopathic practice was well established in Canada. Laws regulating it were enacted in Ontario by 1925, British Columbia in 1936, Manitoba in 1943, and Saskatchewan in 1952.

Lust was a curious character, and was arrested at least 15 times by New York authorities and several times by federal agents for practising as an unqualified doctor, promoting bogus treatments and libel during his career.[220] Much of this was as a result of the reorganisation of medical education and practice in the USA following the publication of a review of this in the USA by the educator Abraham Flexner. *The Flexner Report* (also called *Carnegie Foundation Bulletin Number Four*) of 1910 called on American medical schools to enact higher admission and graduation standards, and to adhere strictly to the protocols of mainstream science in their teaching and research. The *Report* was significant because it succeeded in creating a single model of medical education, characterised by a philosophy that has largely survived to this day. Lust controversially opposed this approach to medicine. He advocated opposition to the germ theory of disease and to vaccination, calling these ideas the most gigantic hoax of modern times. He shunned the use of pharmaceutical drugs and believed that all diseases, including cancer, could be cured by natural processes.

Modern naturopathy holds many similar ideas and, generally,

naturopathy supports prevention of disease through healthy living, positive mind-body-spirit strength, and therapeutics to enhance the body's healing processes.[219] It attributes illness to the violation of natural laws, suggesting that standard medical practices merely treat or suppress symptoms (described as allopathic or salutogenic). However, unlike biomedicine, most of the natural/traditional interventions that naturopaths support today are based on unsubstantiated theories and a collection of faith-based practices, such as homeopathy, nutritional supplementation, detoxification, the use of essential oils and even faith-healing. Some, such as herbalism, rely on treatments that have been superseded by more effective approaches. Naturopaths emphasise homeopathic practice rather than pharmacological science, and their educational preparation reflects this.

Naturopathic medicine regulation and education

In the UK, naturopathy remains a legally unregulated health profession, although practitioners can register with the General Naturopathic Council. However, here across the pond things are quite different. Naturopaths are legally recognised as doctorate-prepared practitioners (naturopathic doctors: NDs) and regulated as a legal health profession in much of North America, including Alberta, British Columbia, Nova Scotia and Ontario here in Canada. In British Columbia, naturopathic medicine is recognised as a self-regulated health profession and has been legally regulated since 1936. British Columbia, Ontario and Alberta currently allow NDs to prescribe pharmaceuticals and perform minor surgeries. There are two private naturopathic colleges in Canada, and neither currently is affiliated with any Canadian public university. Although in the past the UK's University of Westminster offered a naturopathy course, UK universities have generally dropped alternative medicine degree programmes and courses, due to ongoing academic criticism and falling enrolment.

Naturopaths marketing boutique therapies
Today's naturopaths bear little resemblance to the natural health advocates who started the movement in opposition to medicine over a century ago and now offer a wide range of dubious therapeutics. These range from homeopathy, infra-red saunas, detox baths, tonics, nutritional supplements, coffee enemas and even intravenous mega-doses of vitamins. The claims of effectiveness used in the marketing of these various treatments are usually based on very poor quality evidence (such as testimonials), and most represent boutique therapies marketed to people who wish to try experimental therapies unavailable in mainstream medicine. Many naturopathic therapies are based on pseudoscience and are belief-based, although many claim they are science-based practitioners.[102, 221]

The marketing of these treatments inevitably involves some form of deception, mostly by claims of effectiveness in treating a variety of conditions where no such evidence exists. In our 2017 study exploring Internet-based health fraud, out of all the alternative medical scams identified, naturopaths were the largest single professional group promoting them.[21] Most are reasonably harmless, but some, such as colonic irrigation, present distinct risks of serious injury.

One particular growth area of deceptive naturopathic practice that has developed more recently is the use of intravenous (IV) supplement or chelation therapy (an IV infusion of substances intended to remove another, such as iron, lead or calcium, from the body). For example, Vancouver's naturopathic IV Wellness Boutique, run by naturopath Heidi Rootes, will offer to come by and hook you up to an IV vitamin supplement drip at your home or office for about $100 a session. They have reportedly even marketed the mobile service for stag or hen parties as a hangover cure.[222] These designer therapies are marketed by naturopaths at people who want to try experimental things and have the money to do so. That makes for a substantial market, and as Rootes has enthused, they doubled their business within a year of opening![222] However, the benefits claimed are unsubstantiated by health science and these 'treatments' simply represent a new form of commercial exploitational enterprise. Firstly, there is no evidence to support the idea that IV vitamin therapy provides any of the superlative health benefits promised by naturopaths. Moreover, there is no scientific evidence (other than a couple of very old, dubious studies) that bypassing the digestive system for supplementation provides any advantages, unless you have a serious gastrointestinal condition that results in a severe clinical deficiency.[223, 224] As the British Nutrition Foundation suggest, IV supplement therapy consumers are 'wasting their money', as nearly all of the excess vitamins are excreted out in the urine immediately.[225] If a large excess of a substance occurs in the blood, the kidneys rapidly excrete the excess to avoid toxicity. A small amount will be stored in the liver and fatty tissues, but unless you have a bowel disorder, the best way to get your vitamins is in a regular form through the food that you eat.

It is also well established that vitamins and minerals can be harmful in excess; undertaking any form of IV therapy has significant risks attached that need to be justified, and it should only be performed by suitably qualified personnel (see 'Is alternative medicine safe?' on page 205). The use of IV infusions here really is fringe medicine. In 2018, the US Federal Trade Commission made an order to bar a Texas-based firm and owner from making unsupported claims that IV cocktails of vitamins and minerals can treat serious diseases and produce fast, long-lasting results.[226] However, a quick Internet search reveals two local naturopathic businesses offering exactly these: the Vancouver IV Health Centre, and The Drip Lounge in Surrey, BC (which also targets pregnant women). Lastly, the whole idea of why naturopaths would want to perform IV therapy in the first place should raise suspicions. It is the complete antithesis of a natural therapy, and the body has evolved to ensure that the vascular system is protected from external access. The motivation here appears to be financial and exploitative, and I suspect even Benedict Lust would probably spin in his grave at the notion of this being promoted as a natural therapy.

Regulatory pushback against anti-vaccination advocacy

Although naturopathy remains popular, more recently it has experienced many regulatory challenges regarding the promotion of unscientific advice, questionable therapies and exploitational marketing.[227, 228] As a result of the 2019 anti-vaccination crisis, where the World Health Organization declared one of the top 10 threats to global health was the 'reluctance or refusal to vaccinate despite the availability of vaccines', some naturopathic regulators in Canada started reminding their members that they should not advise clients on vaccination.[229, 230] However, recent activity by naturopaths offering counter-vaccination advice has been widespread and indicates that this is still a widely held position. Although many have removed explicit references against immunisation from their websites under direction from their regulatory colleges, many continue to support and practise against Health Canada policy on immunisation.[231] For example, Alberta-based naturopath, Tamara Eriksen, produces and distributes a booklet on colds and influenza that states: 'Unlike immune response to a vaccine, the balanced immunity that develops when you experience illness helps maintain and improve proper immune response to EVERY sort of illness, from infections to chronic disease!', and 'From strictly a HEALTH perspective, the flu vaccine... is not necessarily in your very best long-term interest'. She also promotes other benefits from getting the flu, such as reducing the risk of brain tumours, and curiously suggests treating a fever with ice-cold wet socks worn overnight. A colleague of hers, Paul Theriault (a self-declared world-expert naturopath), suggests that fasting renews the immune system, and that vaccine efficiency is actually similar to that of homeopathic medicines. Neither of those claims is correct. Another naturopath based in Vancouver Island, Anke Zimmermann, surrendered her naturopathic registration in 2019 in BC, as she indicated that she felt that complying with her College's new bylaws and policies on immunisation made it difficult for her to serve her patients with integrity.[232] Apart from the bizarre rhetoric, the health advice offered by these practitioners is hugely inaccurate and clearly against Canadian medical and health policy.

The advice that influenza is not a particularly serious illness for healthy people is a common claim amongst naturopaths and ignores the fact that it kills many people each year. It is also misleading to imply that these were all unhealthy or immunocompromised people. The 1918 global influenza pandemic that killed 50 million people would tend to indicate otherwise. Joe Schwarcz, director of McGill University's Office of Science in Society, suggests the idea that influenza, which kills around 3500 people a year in Canada and hospitalises 12,000 more, can be prevented by homeopathy is absurd.[233] Also, I can confirm treating a fever with ice cold wet socks worn overnight is probably one of the most useless approaches I can think of. Trying to reduce a temperature by applying cold to the extremities overnight would be completely ineffective and uncomfortable. There are far simpler options readily available that work well.

Recently, whistle-blowers from within the naturopathic profession, such as NDs Britt Marie Hermes and Mathew Brignall in the USA, have started to publicly highlight the significant problems with both naturopathic educational and business practices, and these remain an area of concern for many science-based health professionals (see 'Is your doctor really a doctor?' on page 217).[234] Although naturopaths may offer some good advice on healthy lifestyles and nutrition, the majority of naturopathic therapeutics remain nonsense and are mostly faith-based interventions unsupported by any quality scientific evidence. Many of their health promotion practices (such as coffee-enema cleanses and expensive megadose IV vitamins to boost immunity) also run counter to UK and Health Canada recommendations, and simply represent the commercial exploitation of health anxieties.[238]

Ayurvedic medicine

Ayurveda evolved in India several thousand years ago. Two ancient Sanskrit texts are considered to be the basis of the practice and identify eight branches of ayurvedic medicine: internal medicine; surgery; treatment of head and neck disease; gynaecology/obstetrics; paediatrics; toxicology; care of the elderly and rejuvenation; and sexual vitality.

Ayurveda utilises herbs, massage and diets, based upon the 'seasons of life' (stages of the lifespan) and treatment of three mind-body (Prakriti) types. These are 'vata' (said to govern all movement in the mind and body, blood flow, elimination, breathing and the movement of thoughts), 'pitta' (said to govern heat, metabolism, digestion, transformation in the mind and body, sensory perceptions and morality) and 'kapha' (said to govern all structure and lubrication in the mind and body, weight, growth, joints and lungs, and the formation of all tissues). These are called the 'doshas' and their balance is seen to result in health, while imbalance is seen to result in disease.[235]

The goals of Ayurveda are seen as the treatment of disease, prevention of disease, and the improvement of a person's quality of life, by balancing the body, mind and spirit. Basic premises include the beliefs that all living and non-living things in the universe are joined together and that good health is achieved when one's mind and body are in harmony. Ayurvedic supplements can be made either of herbs only or a combination of herbs, metals and minerals. Treatment practices aim to eliminate impurities, decrease symptoms, increase resistance to disease, reduce worry and promote harmony. Interestingly, a 2020 claim on *The Tribune Indian News* site, assured us Union Minister of State for AYUSH (the Indian ministry responsible for traditional medicine), Shripad Naik, had informed them that the British Crown Prince Charles had been '101 per cent' cured of COVID-19 using Ayurveda and homeopathic treatments. They suggested the reason why the Prince's office might have denied acknowledging this cure was because England does not formally recognise Ayurveda as a medical science.[236]

False cancer treatment claims

Although widely used in India, and popularised by the celebrity author Deepak Chopra in North America, currently no health authority in the UK or North America licenses Ayurvedic practitioners. Some practitioners have drawn attention by claiming to be able to treat cancer with their approach. However, Cancer Research UK and the Canadian Cancer Society note there is no good scientific evidence for any effectiveness of Ayurveda in the treatment of cancer. Certain approaches used in it may be helpful as complementary therapies in cancer – for example, yoga and meditation can help relieve stress and anxiety – but that's about it. Reviews of Ayurveda for other conditions (such as for diabetes mellitus) by the Cochrane Library have found that no conclusions can be drawn about its efficacy, due to weak methods and small number of participants in the evaluated studies.[237] Unfortunately, however, there remain many unscrupulous practitioners making deceptive claims for its ability to cure cancer.

Chapter 13

Physical manipulative interventions

Physical manipulative interventions involve manual treatments that are designed to resolve health issues. There are a number of them, including osteopathy, chiropractic, reflexology (massage used to treat illness, based on the theory that there are reflex points on the feet, hands and head that are linked to every part of the body) and craniosacral therapy (that uses manipulations of the skull believed to harmonise a natural rhythm in the central nervous system). Hydrotherapy, or water therapy, is another common form, where water at various temperatures, or as ice or steam, is used to relieve discomfort and promote physical wellbeing, and is very commonly used as a relaxation therapy.

Osteopathy

Despite some differences, osteopaths are similar to chiropractors, at least from the patient's perspective, in that they support the treatment of disease through external joint manipulation. However, in the USA they do have a much higher level of general medical preparation. Nevertheless, in the USA their ranks have also provided some of the most controversial practitioners, such as Joseph Mercola and Sherri Tenpenny, both major anti-vaccination activists who have promoted COVID-19 scepticism.

Osteopathy is based on the principle that the wellbeing of an individual depends on their bones, muscles, ligaments and connective tissue functioning smoothly together. They use physical manipulation, stretching and massage and aim to increase joint mobility, relieve muscle tension and, more controversially, enhance the blood supply to tissues to accelerate healing. Some suggest that they can locate and resolve somatic (body framework) dysfunction using a holistic approach. There's currently no quality body of evidence that osteopathy is effective as a treatment for any health conditions unrelated to the musculoskeletal system, yet some osteopaths have promoted this idea. In one study (similar to chiropractors – see below) osteopath researchers claimed they could detect subtle alterations of texture, tone and alignment indicative of the overall physiologic state in premature infants, and treat them, leading to earlier discharge.[226] However, this was a single poorly blinded study with a vaguely described intervention, where the control group received 'no touch' compared with the treatment group, so not really a fair test of the therapy. However, osteopaths mostly rank low with concerns of deceptive practice, and in the UK and North America they generally have a very good track record of professional practice.

Chiropractic

Another popular form of alternative healthcare practice under this category is chiropractic, which is well established in the UK, Europe and North America, where practitioners are legally regulated. There are over 3000 chiropractors registered in the UK, whilst the American Chiropractic Association estimates that there are roughly 77,000 in the US, and the Canadian Chiropractic Association identifies 9000 in Canada. Chiropractic represents a system of medicine that is based on the diagnosis and manipulative treatment of the vertebrae, which are believed

to cause disorders by affecting the nerves, muscles and organs. The theory of chiropractic rests on three theoretical assumptions:
1. spinal vertebrae become displaced
2. this displacement interferes with nerve action, and
3. manipulating the spine to realign the vertebrae removes the nerve interference, improving the flow of nervous stimulation (or the flow of a vitalistic life force – see page 141) to restore health.

Most chiropractors gain their doctor of chiropractic (DC) qualification from private chiropractic colleges, although some public North American and South African universities accredit chiropractic degrees.

Historically, chiropractic is around 125 years old. On 18 September 1895, the spiritualist and magnetic healer Daniel David Palmer performed the first chiropractic adjustment on a janitor named Harvey Lillard in Iowa to treat his deafness. After manually adjusting his spine, his deafness was reportedly cured. Palmer actually claimed the original idea and basic principles of chiropractic treatment were passed along to him during a seance by the spirit of the deceased doctor Jim Atkinson. He proposed that vertebral misalignments or 'subluxations' impede the flow of vital life force, causing ill health. Palmer's work was continued by his son BJ Palmer after his death, and the field of chiropractic medicine developed further, and has today become a $15-billion business globally.[239]

A profession divided

Currently, chiropractic professionals are divided into two factions. Firstly, there are those who support the original chiropractic theory of vertebral 'subluxation' proposed by Palmer and his son. These are sometimes referred to as 'straight' chiropractors, and follow Palmer's principles. Secondly, there are those who split from Palmer's founding principles (sometimes called 'mixers'). They have moved away from the metaphysical claims of the theory of subluxation to incorporate other biomedical ideas into their practice. These are chiropractors who treat a variety of aches and pains using chiropractic techniques and claim to align more with scientific medicine. Some have also stopped using the term subluxation altogether, and use the term 'misalignment'. Modern chiropractors in this camp also tend to eschew the term 'mixer' and prefer to claim they are simply evidence-based practitioners.

At this point, it is worth noting that the medical diagnosis of 'orthopaedic subluxation' exists, where vertebral misalignment or mechanical joint dysfunction affecting spinal function is identified. This is not the same as the chiropractic subluxations, that are seen as tiny vertebral misalignments claimed to cause illness by interfering with nerves. However, at this time, these have yet to be demonstrated. Chiropractors say they can detect them through manual examination, X-rays, thermography (mapping the temperature of the spinal column externally) or other techniques, such as surface electromyography (SEMG). Nevertheless, they remain undetectable on medical imaging by doctors or radiographers, and SEMG and thermography are not accepted as useful spinal diagnostic techniques in medicine. For straight chiropractic, there is currently no evidence to support the contention that nerve interference originating in the tiny misalignments of a spinal segment causes disease elsewhere in the body.[240, 241] For conditions such as asthma, infantile colic, neck pain, bed-wetting, period pain and carpal-tunnel syndrome, a number of systematic reviews of the published research have identified either no effect, insufficient evidence and/or significant bias in the reported research. A 2018 review of chiropractic studies noted no evidence that chiropractic treatment was effective as either primary or secondary prevention for disease through subluxation.[242]

Today's 'mixed' (for want of a better term) chiropractors maintain they are 'doctorly prepared diagnostic practitioners' and can help treat a variety of musculoskeletal conditions, including whiplash injuries, sciatica, herniated discs, chronic pain (also migraines) or improve function/performance. There is some evidence that when people have back pain or a crick in their neck, manipulating or exercising it may help relieve the pain and discomfort. Nevertheless, as with acupuncture, although there is a significant body of literature and studies that support the use of chiropractic spinal manipulative therapy (SMT) for pain-related issues (notably low back pain), little quality research exploring the nature of the mechanism exists. Whether chiropractic works more effectively than other techniques, such as exercise and physiotherapy, is currently also debatable. A 2011 substantial systematic review of SMT for low back pain identified that: 'High quality evidence suggests that there is no clinically relevant difference between SMT and other interventions for reducing pain and improving function in patients with chronic low-back pain.'[231, 243] Another 2020 study concluded the same for chronic low-back pain in young adults.[244] Overall, chiropractic has a much more problematic history with deceptive practices.

Chiropractors sue Simon Singh

In their 2008 book, *Trick or Treatment*, UK science authors Simon Singh and Edzard Ernst reviewed the evidence for chiropractic and summited that whilst: 'Chiropractors... might compete with physiotherapists in terms of treating some back problems, but all their other claims are beyond belief and can carry a range of significant risks.'[245] One problem with the therapy is that chiropractic adjustments involve quite forceful manipulations and sometimes these can be damaging if not performed carefully (see page 210). In fact, following Singh's criticism of the value of chiropractic for illnesses like asthma in children in *The Guardian* newspaper in the UK in 2008, the British Chiropractic Association (BCA) brought a lawsuit for libel against him. An initial hearing ruled that Singh's use of the phrase '...happily promotes bogus treatments' was stating, as a matter of fact (rather than as personal opinion or metaphor), that the BCA was being consciously dishonest in promoting chiropractic for treating children's conditions. Singh appealed, and the charity Sense About Science launched a lobbying campaign to draw attention to the case. The publicity produced by the libel action led to a significant public backlash, with numerous formal complaints of false advertising arising against individual chiropractors in the UK. In April 2010, the Royal Courts of Justice allowed Singh's appeal to move ahead, ruling that the original judge had '...erred in his approach in the original ruling'. The BCA withdrew their libel action shortly after this and the case eventually sparked a legal review of libel laws in the UK, resulting in the passing of a reformed Defamation Act by the British Parliament in April 2013 to help prevent cases of frivolous libel lawsuits for defamation of character by clarifying the legal definition.[246, 247, 248]

Paediatric and anti-vaccination chiropractic issues

In both Europe and North America, there has also been significant criticism of chiropractic over the last few years regarding two issues. Firstly, the growth and promotion of paediatric chiropractic, and secondly, the role chiropractors have in the ongoing anti-vaccination crisis. Infant chiropractic has developed as a trend where chiropractors advertise to treat new-born babies and children on the basis that they can correct misalignments of the spine caused during childbirth or normal growth. Here is an example of an advertisement from a US chiropractic clinic in Long beach, California:[249]

Dr. Tammy Portolese of Portolese Family Chiropractic says, 'When there is a misalignment of the spine, the nerves that flow out to all of the organs are compromised, so when we do an adjustment, we're simply taking pressure, nerve stress, off the spine, so the body can express itself'.

Portolese also suggests that the pressure used on a baby is gentle similar to that used to check fruit for ripeness, and that chiropractic care has also proven safer and more effective than prescription medications and antibiotics. The advertisement also claims that regular chiropractic care in babies can help alleviate:

- breastfeeding feeding and latching issues,
- ear infections and ear aches,
- colic and acid reflux,
- fussiness.

Another Canadian clinic offered similar advice (which has since been removed):

The spine develops rapidly in the first 10 years of life. It is highly affected by the falls and injuries common in those years and the repetitive movements that occur [in] the following eight years (backpacks, increased computer usage and poor posture).

The first trauma we all go through is the birth process; it can cause stress to the infant's spine and may impair nerve function which can contribute to dysfunction. As babies grow, they begin to crawl, sit and walk by using their spine.

Another example of dubious chiropractic claims is research suggesting that chiropractic helps improve cognitive function in children.[250]

None of these claims is supported by independent scientific evidence, and some are completely inaccurate. With infants and children under 18, bones are still in a phase of growth, development and remodelling, and the vertebral end plate growth is incomplete. In younger children, the cartilaginous growth areas in the bones are immature and potentially vulnerable to injury if subjected to manipulation. Additionally, back pain in children is rare and when it does occur, it is potentially a more serious problem and should always be brought to the attention of a paediatrician rather than a chiropractor.

A 2002 paper from the Canadian Paediatric Society reported that there were no satisfactory studies of chiropractic treatments for back pain in children. Some studies had suggested that chiropractic manipulation of the neck could provide short-term relief of neck pain in children, but its value hadn't been compared with other therapies.[251]

In 2008, two chiropractors published a review of chiropractic manipulation in paediatric health conditions, indicating that chiropractic as a healthcare intervention for children's medical conditions continued to be supported by very poor scientific evidence.[252, 253] However, such criticism of infant chiropractic has met significant resistance from the profession, and the practice has expanded. In March 2019, the regulatory body for chiropractors in British Columbia (the College of Chiropractors of British Columbia – CCBC) confirmed that they would undertake a thorough review of the scientific evidence and also banned chiropractors from claiming to effectively treat various childhood conditions where evidence of efficacy was not available, including autism, ear infections and cancer and even prevention of Alzheimer's disease.

Many chiropractors have also expressed opposition to public vaccination policy based on their belief that infectious diseases are a result of spinal issues reducing natural immunity, and that, therefore, vaccines are unnecessary.[254] In 2016, the disgraced UK doctor Andrew Wakefield (best known for a fraudulent 1998 study and being struck off – see page 261) was a keynote speaker at the annual conference of the International Chiropractors' Association on chiropractic and paediatrics in

Maui, Hawaii. Here in British Columbia, the CCBC policy from 1991 specifically prohibits chiropractors from providing advice about immunisation, but in 2018, its vice-chair was reported for creating a Facebook video suggesting that smoothies were more effective than the flu shot for preventing flu. After a Canadian Broadcasting Corporation investigation revealed this, the vice-chair immediately resigned from the board.[255]

These issues illustrate the ongoing divisions within the profession, a significant problem being that chiropractic is a fragmented profession with widely differing belief systems that lack a solid empirical theoretical basis for its practice. Although many people report success with back pain treatment by chiropractors, we still cannot confirm if it is an effective therapy compared with other approaches, or even how or if it works. The truth is, a spinal manipulation for pain may give some short-term relief, and many people find this helpful, but the ongoing benefits are not well evidenced, and as far as treating other health issues go, the claims made by chiropractors are often wishful hyperbole. More recent evidence suggests that physiotherapy and exercise may be more beneficial than external spinal manipulation, and for other conditions, the evidence for any efficacy is extremely poor in quality. Some chiropractic procedures do hold significant risks (see page 210). Nevertheless, the profession has established its popularity as a commonly used alternative therapy and, like acupuncture and TCM although the profession is well established, it has a worrying history of deceptive practitioners. This has not gone unnoticed by the public, and a 2016 Gallup Poll found that chiropractic rated lowest among health professions with regard to public perceptions of ethics and honesty.[256]

Massage therapy

Massage therapy is generally used for the treatment of body stress or pain and involves the physical manipulation of soft tissues by touch. The title 'massage therapist' has been recognised for those who have been professionally trained to give therapeutic massage. In the UK, the profession is not legally regulated but, similar to naturopaths, there is a voluntary process for massage therapists to apply for membership of the Complementary and Natural Healthcare Council (CNHC) or the General Regulatory Council for Complementary Therapies (GRCCT), which are independent organisations. Since there are no laws to protect the public from the incompetence of massage therapists, becoming a member of one of these regulatory bodies helps the massage therapist demonstrate some professional commitment. In Canada, the profession is regulated in five provinces (under the title Registered Massage Therapist), but in most of the USA it is not.

Massage therapy is an increasingly popular healthcare option across Canada.[151] According to a 2018 survey, massage therapy is the most utilised paramedical extended health benefit, behind only dental and vision care, with 53% of people using it to treat a diagnosed condition or injury.[257] It remains one of the less controversial alternative health strategies and there is some evidence (although not high-quality) that it can help with relaxation, relieve stress and anxiety, and help support rehabilitation and pain reduction in some circumstances. This is mainly through muscle relaxation, increasing perfusion to tissues and possibly helping endorphin release.[258] Due to its widespread acceptance, it is regarded less as an alternative treatment and simply as a useful adjunctive therapy. However, like other alternative strategies, it has a weak theoretical base, and some claims of the efficacy of massage for specific conditions that have been made (such as its efficacy in treating lymphoedema or tendonitis) remain highly suspect.[259, 260] As such, its role as an additional health promotion therapy may be useful to help reduce stress, depression and anxiety in clients, but other than that, there is no significant evidence that supports its use for other conditions. In the UK, a significantly thornier issue is the lack of regulation of qualifications and training standards in this area, which can lead to a wide variety in skills and competence.

Chapter 14

Herbal, nutritional and mind-body interventions

Herbal remedies, vitamins, dietary supplements and specialist diets are some of the oldest forms of alternative medicine, and also represent a major sector of modern healthcare business. This category includes the use of natural herbs, vitamins, minerals, probiotics and also aromatherapy and detoxification therapies and nutritional counselling. The principle of these approaches is either that the particular herb or substance has curative properties (such as garlic for asthma), that there is a dietary deficit of the substance (such as vitamins), or that there is an overabundance of a substance which is toxic (e.g. mercury or polychlorinated biphenyls).

Botanical and herbal remedies

Botanical remedies were inventoried in great detail in ancient Egyptian, Chinese and Indian cultures, and in the Middle Ages in Europe. Herbal therapy is the use of herbs to treat specific conditions or to enhance the function of various body systems, such as claims of boosting the immune system, treating allergies or preventing a cold. Herbal medicines may act on the body like prescription drugs (and most drugs are simply attenuated forms of plant-based substances, such as aspirin being derived from willow bark). The usefulness of various herbal and botanical remedies varies, and many do have positive effects; however, their success is often lower than with established pharmaceutical products that have been developed for specific conditions. There are hundreds of these remedies, and because such herbal supplements may interact with prescription medication, it is important that these are advertised both informatively and accurately. This is often not the case, and inflated claims of efficacy are common, as with dietary supplements.[261]

Dietary supplements and interventions

Multiple studies have demonstrated the effectiveness of nutritional interventions, vitamins and therapeutic diets, such as low potassium and protein diets in renal failure to help stabilise biochemistry, or nutritional interventions for those undergoing chemotherapy to help maintain weight and muscle mass and improve survival.[262, 263] However, these are accepted medical interventions, and most hospitals have highly qualified registered dietitians on staff to provide dietary advice for a range of conditions. Probiotic supplements – live micro-organisms found in the human digestive tract, and often called 'friendly bacteria' – are another example here. They are taken to enhance the digestive system either as a supplement or in natural forms, such as in yoghurt or other fermented foods.

However, the singling out of miraculous wellness diets or 'superfoods', is usually an indicator of deception and ignores the complexity of nutrition and other lifestyle factors that affect personal health. Nevertheless, fad diets identifying the latest super-nutrient appear very frequently. The antioxidant craze is a good example, and nutritional advice focused on antioxidant intake, ageing and cancer health continues to be popular in the media despite a lack of evidence for their effectiveness.

Antioxidants

In 1956, Dr Denham Harman suggested in a famous geron-
tological journal paper that cellular damage (resulting in ageing,
but also in cancer and other diseases) primarily occurred
through the action of free radicals in the body.[264] Free radicals are
chemical compounds (such as hydroxyl) with atoms or groups
of atoms with an odd number of electrons that are formed in
normal metabolic processes in the body. These substances form a
useful part of our immune system, as they can help break down
damaged cellular components (such as DNA, cell organelles
or membranes). However, if there are an excess of them in the
body, the theory is that they can cause more widespread damage
to cells and tissues. In his paper, Harman suggested ageing
occurs because cells accumulate free radical damage over time.
However, antioxidants are molecules that can safely interact
with free radicals and terminate their action, and so Harman and
others postulated that increasing one's intake of antioxidants
might help slow the effects of ageing and disease processes.
Sadly, despite some initial promising research, numerous studies
have now demonstrated no good effect from increasing dietary
antioxidants. After years of work with antioxidant supplements,
Harman himself concluded that exogenous antioxidants don't
enter the mitochondria of cells, and overall are not likely to be
helpful in preventing tissue damage or increasing lifespan.[265]
Some research has also suggested that increasing antioxidant
intake can even be harmful in certain circumstances.[266] This
has not stopped alternative practitioners touting the value of
antioxidant superfoods such as goji berries and kale smoothies,
and if you search the Internet for antioxidant diet books, you will
get over 11,000,000 results.

Much of the output of dietary health-promotional advice is
from nutritionists (whose qualifications vary considerably). In
the UK nutritionists (or nutritional therapists as they may be

known) can register with the British Association for Applied Nutrition and Nutritional Therapy (BANT). This does involve passing an assessment of qualifications, character and insurance status. However, this is far less rigorous than becoming a registered nutritionist or dietician (which requires degree-level professional qualifications). In 2012, a number of problematic nutritional therapists highlighted by the *Which* consumer advocacy magazine for offering dangerous advice were BANT members.[267] Practices include electrical food intolerance testing and a reported £60 sale of a one month's supply of recommended supplements (on top of a £60 consultation fee). After an investigative journalist gave a set of bowel cancer symptoms, one nutritionist advised that muscle testing would identify the cause of the problems. This simply consisted of the nutritionist pushing against the forearms to measure resistance as she read out a list of possible physical and emotional problems. Interestingly, at the time of writing, the UK Universities Central Admission Service (UCAS) no longer lists any BSc/MSc degrees in 'Nutritional therapy' or 'Nutritional medicine'.

Another well-known UK TV 'holistic' nutritionist who used a doctoral title to promote her diet books and herbal sex pills on TV shows is 'Dr' Gillian McKeith, who had an infamous spat with UK physician, Dr Ben Goldacre, regarding her qualifications between 2008 and 2010.[268] McKeith was a popular media nutritionist whose book *You Are What You Eat* (2006) sold over two million copies, despite promoting some dubious dietary practices. McKeith has advocated the increased consumption of chlorophyll to increase blood oxygenation (there is no evidence that this will have any effect on blood oxygen levels) and, worse still, the consumption of wild blue-green algae, which contains cyanobacteria that are able to produce a range of powerful toxins.[269] McKeith was challenged in 2007 by the UK Advertising Standards Authority, and highlighted by Ben Goldacre in his 2008 book, for using the prefix of 'Doctor' in her publicity, when it was evidently a qualification obtained through a distance course from a (now obsolete) non-accredited American college.[31] The adverse publicity does not seem to have significantly dented her public popularity and her website remains active, advertising a range of questionable products and services, even though the nutritional ideas she promotes are a mix of science and pseudoscience. She was still appearing on celebrity reality and daytime TV chat shows recently (most notably in 2018–2019 for flashing her knickers), and runs social media accounts. However, she no longer promotes herself as 'Dr' Gillian McKeith.

Often such nutritionists (and even some actual doctors) will claim that specific foods or specific supplements can improve general health and wellbeing or, in the most extreme examples, can cure serious diseases such as cancer, and many also promote fashionable diets such as alkaline water (see page 286), juice diets or the paleo or keto diet, and they have become remarkably prevalent in popular culture despite the lack of any good scientific foundation.[270] Exploring the scientific evidence for all of these fad diets could easily become a book in itself, but the vast majority make deceptive promises of health benefits based on mistaken notions or pseudoscience.

Aromatherapy

Aromatherapy, also known as essential oil therapy, is the use of extracted oils from plants that are claimed to balance, harmonise and promote the health of body, mind and spirit via inhalation, external application or sometimes ingestion. Like many alternative therapists, the levels and training of aromatherapists are not standardised and the discipline is unregulated in both Europe and North America. There is currently no quality evidence that aromatherapy can either prevent, treat or cure any disease, and scientific studies are difficult to design because the point of most aromatherapy is the smell of the agent rather than any chemical properties.[271] There is some evidence that it may be effective in combating postoperative nausea and vomiting, and it remains popular, but like many of the therapies discussed here, its marketing is often misleading and mainly based upon faith rather than scientific evidence.[272, 273]

Mind-body interventions

Mind and body interventions are rather a wide categorisation of alternative healthcare based on therapies that are focused on the body and mind and how they interact. They include various methods of body movement, meditation and mindfulness. Movement-based therapies (such as yoga and tai chi), meditation or mindfulness for progressive relaxation, guided imagery and hypnotherapy are the most popular alternative health promotional therapies in this category.[151, 274]

Movement-based therapies

Movement therapies use movement and body work to promote physical, mental, emotional and spiritual wellbeing. Practices such as yoga, tai chi and qigong involve gentle exercise and are helpful as health promotional activities where they have some well-evidenced benefits, and for improving general health, pain management, psychological state (reducing depression, stress and anxiety) and for improving mobility. The physical benefits observed also include increasing flexibility, function and strength.[274, 275, 276, 277, 278] Outside of these health promotional benefits, there is however, less quality evidence of specific efficacy for other common medical conditions, such as diabetes or renal failure, and the positive effects are most likely due to the demonstrated health benefits of engaging in gentle, social exercise and relaxation.[279, 280, 281]

Yoga is a meditative movement practice that originated in India as a form of spiritual activity and helps flexibility, agility, balance and relaxation. Qigong is part of TCM, combining relaxed movements with a meditative aspect and controlled breathing. Tai chi began as a Chinese martial art and combines physical movement, breath control and meditation in a dance-like sequence of poses based on the movements of animals. All involve moment-to-moment-based sequences of physical activity that are designed to produce a positive, relaxed and meditative state.

Dance therapy is another movement-based mind-body modality that uses dance to allow the body and mind to move freely in response to music. This, too, has some evidence of effectiveness as a health promotional activity.[282, 283] Nevertheless, even these movement therapies must be undertaken with care. In a recent study by Professor Evangelos Pappas, of Sydney University, yoga was seen to cause musculoskeletal pain (mostly in the arms) in more than one in 10 participants. The researchers also found that the practice worsened over a fifth of existing injuries, and the injury rate was up to 10 times higher than had previously been reported.[284]

Additionally, the deceptive marketing of yoga with expensive add-ons such as oxygen-yoga (with higher O_2 concentrations) or 'goat yoga' (yes, that is practising yoga with goats) has become commonplace. For example, www.goatyoga.net claims 'Goat Yoga Improves the Functioning of the Endocrine System' and can help you with your hormonal balance.[285] This is, of course, hyperbole, and there is no evidence of significant health benefits to doing yoga with goats rather than doing yoga alone, apart from possibly having more fun.

Meditation, mindfulness and hypnotherapy

Meditation is a method of focusing attention to increase relaxation, quiet the mind and reduce stress. It is a part of several religious cultures (including Zen Buddhism) and can be practised while one is still or active, such as during walking. Like massage, different types of meditation have a variety of purposes and techniques. 'Breath meditation' is a simple example that involves the person emptying their mind and focusing all of their attention on their breathing. 'Centring' is another technique that involves focusing on a chosen word. 'Mindfulness meditation' is a way of paying attention to, or being mindful of, a variety of topics, such as thoughts, actions or the environment. 'Walking meditation' is another form of mindfulness, because the individual is mindful of the interaction of the inner body, the external body and the environment with each step. There is some compelling evidence that such activities and other cognitive behavioural therapies can have some health promotional benefits, such as helping people to quit smoking, and helping people maintain a more positive mental state for dealing with stress, anxiety and depression.[286, 287, 288, 289]

Hypnotherapy is another form of guided deep relaxation that focuses the attention of the unconscious mind. It has also been used with some reported success as a health promotion activity for such things as behavioural change (e.g. quitting smoking or dealing with phobias), memory recall of suppressed events and improving self-esteem.[290, 291, 292] Currently, the mechanisms involved and the benefits compared to other approaches remain somewhat unclear. Sometimes practitioners in these fields do make unrealistic claims for the benefits; they are legally unregulated in the UK and training varies considerably. For example, hypnotherapists in the UK can undertake a one-year diploma and register with the UK College of Hypnosis and Hypnotherapy, or with the British Institute of Hypnotherapy & NLP, as qualified hypnotherapists, or after doing a 15-20-day certificate course for around £3000. For that, no prior qualifications are needed except being over 18 and having a good understanding of written and spoken English.

The scientific evidence on the value of hypnotherapy is far from clear. A good source of the state of the art of most healthcare interventions is the Cochrane Reviews, freely available from the Cochrane Library on the Web (www.cochranelibrary.com/). A Cochrane review is a systematic, rigorous and independent review of all research published on a particular healthcare intervention. These reviews are therefore valuable sources of information for those receiving and providing care, as well as for decision-makers and researchers. A recent Cochrane review of hypnotherapy to stop smoking found insufficient evidence to determine whether hypnotherapy was more effective for smoking cessation than other forms of behavioural support.[293] These therapies may help some people, but they are expensive, and because of the lack of educational standards, regulatory control and nature of placing people in relaxed highly-suggestible states, treatment may put clients in vulnerable positions. For example, in 2015 a Lincolnshire hypnotherapist, Gary Nairado, was jailed for 10 years after sexually assaulting a number of female clients during treatment sessions.[294]

Energy therapies

In North America, there has been significant interest in proposed human energy field (HEF)-based therapies over the last 40 years; these include Reiki and Therapeutic Touch (TT). They represent modern interpretations of a number of traditional faith-based therapeutic interventions and beliefs around the existence and flow of invisible (to conventional science) spiritual or life energies in the body. Neither TT nor Reiki have a good scientific basis or evidence of value, other than as a general form of relaxation. However, that is not what you will find in their marketing materials.

Therapeutic Touch

Dora Kunz (a psychic) and Dolores Krieger (a nurse educator at New York University) developed TT in the 1980s. Kunz suggested that it had origins in ancient Sanskrit yogic texts, described as a 'pranic' healing method (another belief in a vital, life-sustaining force in living beings (see page 141)). The technique is now taught in approximately 80 colleges and universities in the USA and in many other countries, including here in British Columbia.[295,] [296] TT practitioners claim to be able to detect and manipulate a proposed human energy field by passing their hands over the patient and smoothing this out. It does not normally involve any physical contact. Practitioners claim to be able to reduce pain and anxiety and even accelerate healing.

There have been several attempts to establish scientific evidence for TT over the years.[297] The most controversial attempt was carried out by a US schoolgirl, Emily Rosa, who became the youngest person ever to have a research paper published in a peer-reviewed medical journal. At the age of 9, she completed a scientific study of TT that was published in the *Journal of the American Medical Association* in 1998.[298] She had watched a video outlining the benefits of TT, which claimed that practitioners could detect others' HEF. With encouragement from her family and a doctor, she carried out a simple experiment for her Grade 4 science fair to see if trained TT practitioners could detect a HEF, as claimed. It involved two experiments, the first with 15 practitioners in 1996 for her science fair project, and the second in 1997 with an additional 13 practitioners, which led to the publication. The experiments required the TT practitioners to sit at a table and put their hands through a screen. On the other side of the screen, she randomly selected which one of the TT practitioner's hands she would hold her hand over. The TT practitioners were then asked to say when they detected Rosa's HEF. Practitioners correctly located Rosa's hand an average of only 4.4 times out of 10 attempts.

The openness of the TT practitioners to taking part in this trial should be acknowledged, and there are questions of ethical conduct and potential bias (by both *JAMA* and the researchers) in the study that remain unresolved. It appears that no ethical review had been undertaken prior to the study and consent from the first set of tests was on the basis that it was for a science fair, not for publication. Therefore, this was not the best example of good quality science. Nevertheless, no other experimental study has reported different findings.

Some theoretical suggestions have been made as to how the energies identified by TT practitioners could be occurring and be measured.[299] However, empirical methods for measuring them have not been taken up by the TT community, and none of the work has been independently validated. Hence, despite numerous low-quality and small-scale studies exploring TT, there is currently no good quality scientific evidence that HEFs exist, or that TT interventions work any better than placebo. Repeated reviews of research for benefits for healing or anxiety or pain reduction identify that there are insufficient data to demonstrate that these are effective therapies, and higher quality studies indicate no effect. Some of the original more uncertain Cochrane scientific reviews of TT have now been withdrawn over concerns of quality of the studies included.[300, 301, 302] In the study I and colleagues published in 2021, all the recent TT research studies covering a range of clinical issues over the previous decade were reviewed, including 1302 patients. Seventeen of the 21 studies examined reported very positive outcomes, but only four of them exhibited a low risk of bias. All others had serious methodological flaws and significant bias issues, were statistically flawed and were identified as low-quality studies. No quality evidence for any of the claimed benefits of TT was found in the work. Therefore, as an alternative therapeutic strategy, TT currently remains practically indistinguishable from faith healing, and yet most practitioners still claim it has a scientific basis.

Faith-healing

One last area of practice that is briefly worth exploring here is the odd world of faith healing. Practitioners assert that the healing of a person can be brought about by spiritual faith through prayer or through other rituals that stimulate mystical energies or a divine presence that remedies disease and promotes healing. Although most people would probably think this is fairly rare in this day and age, numerous examples of the practice still exist, and it has even been researched with multi-million-dollar studies. Technically, it is also difficult to separate energy therapists such as Reiki and TT practitioners, from faith healers, as they involve the same principles, of a practitioner personally channelling spiritual energies and even the ritualised practices of the moving of hands in supernatural ways to influence a healing outcome. As previously noted, there are unfortunately insufficient data to demonstrate that any therapies based on human energy fields provide effective treatments that are any better than placebo.

In Christian churches, the practice of 'the laying on of hands' is another approach involving of faith as a symbolic and formal method of invoking the Holy Spirit, primarily during baptisms and confirmations. Although primarily a Christian practice, forms are also practised in other religions, and intentional healing by the laying on of hands remains a popular complementary therapy. This could also be considered as a form of therapeutic touch, although in this context the energies are regarded as divine. The actual organised system of belief may be different from more established religions, but they all represent forms of spirituality and manipulation of divine forces. One Dutch study claimed to have detected a physical effect of some sort of HEF, with the laying on of hands using biosensors to detect photon emissions during healing sessions. This was a single small study of 36 participants, but the researcher gave no indication of the theoretical position of the healer and no other confirmatory repeat studies have ever been demonstrated, so, like the Korean studies reporting the physical organs of meridians, these findings remain highly suspect.[303] To date, there is no scientific evidence of any practical effect as a therapeutic intervention to treat specific illnesses. Proponents will often argue that faith healing represents a valid alternative way of providing care and we should simply consider this a different way of constructing the body, treating the body as a site for the performance of religion.[304] Whilst certainly an interesting intellectual argument, the effects of faith healing remain unsupported by any quality evidence. Despite what practitioners argue, there is currently no scientific basis for it, and it remains a purely unempirical practice, and one fraught with a history of deception. Although there are currently no well-conducted systematic reviews of faith healing available, there is actually a fair amount of discussion of the subject and even some experimental work in the literature.

Intercessory prayer (praying for the benefit of another) and the laying on of hands have been two areas most widely publicised, particularly Christian intercessory prayer. The intercessor is one who pleads another's case, and is an aspect of religious beliefs found in many different religions. Several well-publicised studies have conducted quasi-scientific inquiries into the value of prayer to help clients get pregnant, to recover more quickly from surgery or infections, or to reduce disruptive behaviour in dementia. Most have reported positive outcomes.[305, 306, 307, 308, 309, 310] Even a few reviews of the research in this area have been undertaken. One found no effect, although another claimed to have identified a significant positive effect of intercessory prayer.[311, 312] On closer inspection, the work exemplifies the problems with a poor understanding of the methods of scientific research. Even in the positive review, the author openly acknowledged that no attempt had been made to assess the validity of the various arguments in deciding which studies to include and which to leave out. A crucial problem with the majority of these studies is they lack any substantive theoretical framework, robust methodology and/or, most importantly, a falsifiable hypothesis; in essence, exemplifying bad science.

It has been argued by both doctors and nurses that intercessory prayer is a valid area for scientific research.[311, 313, 314] However, this also demonstrates a rather poor understanding of scientific philosophy by some health professionals and academics. I often use this as an example for debate with my graduate students, asking them how they would design a scientific experiment to test the effects of prayer on health. It's actually a complex question, as a meaningful experiment of this nature is practically impossible to do. Science can answer questions of comparison with clearly identified and falsifiable hypotheses (i.e. a proposition that can clearly be demonstrated to be true or false), but it is impossible to do so when the hypothesis is a subjective statement based on vaguely defined notions with multiple possible confounding factors. For example, as Ben Goldacre noted, to construct a testable hypothesis here, we would need to consider and state precisely which deity the prayer was directed at, exactly how much prayer, at what time, what sort of prayer, what form, how was it carried out, when was it undertaken, who was praying (relative, friend, stranger), what was the status of the person praying and the patient (a minister, believer, infidel or sinner, or whether in good standing with the deity), was the prayer conducted in a place of worship or not, etc.[31] The confounding variables here are limitless and even researchers interested in this field have pointed out these issues.[314] It is also a hypothesis that is impossible to disprove, as there is no empirical way to ascertain if a hypothesis such as 'Does intercessory prayer speed up wound healing?' is false, as no amount of negative results can ever disprove it. Philosophically, this then presents the 'argument from ignorance' problem – arguing a proposition could be true because it has not yet been proven false. If we cannot disprove that prayer speeds up healing, that does not mean it is true. This argument was classically demonstrated in Bertrand Russell's cosmic teapot argument: Russell wrote that if he were to assert, without offering proof, that a teapot, too small to be seen by telescopes, orbited the Sun somewhere in space between the Earth and Mars, he could not expect anyone to believe him solely because his assertion could not be proven wrong.

The whole raft of subjective baggage attached to research on the effects of prayer makes it scientifically meaningless. In essence, it is the same as trying to scientifically answer the question: 'Does god exist?' and humanity has not produced a definitive answer to that question in over 5000 years of scientific inquiry.

Worse still, the resources being invested in this area have been huge. One large study by Benson et al, exploring the value of prayer to speed up healing following cardiac bypass surgery, cost a reported $2.4 million USD (mainly funded by Christian groups), and a number of physicians in North America supported the work.[306] However, many professionals, science writers and laypersons critically responded following the publication of these papers. Simply put, we cannot prove or disprove the effects of intercessory prayer through scientific inquiry. A pragmatic approach would be that as an intervention the believer should be free to use it, if it is with the patient's wishes, as there is nothing to suggest it does any harm, and it costs nothing. Spending millions of dollars trying to prove it works as a therapeutic intervention with science is quite simply nonsensical.

To illustrate the ongoing popular appeal of faith healing (as discussed in Section IV), there was a local faith healer based here in Vancouver who called himself the 'Dreamhealer' and ran a faith-healing business here for a number of years. Adam

McLeod set up his website and business when he was a high-school student back in 2003, initially selling a book on his remote healing powers, and then progressing to offering distance-healing, workshops and DVDs. At his Dreamhealer workshops (costing hundreds of dollars to attend) he claimed to perform 'group energy treatments'. He has said he became aware of his gift as a teenager, when he could see people's auras which he could use to his advantage in games of hide-and-seek, and in basketball at school. Apparently, other children used to accuse him of cheating at hide-and-seek because he could see their auras shining out from the objects they were hiding behind. As a self-described energy healer, his gift was said to be being able to visualise and manipulate people's energies for health benefits whilst he was in a trance, or to teach them to do it themselves. He also claimed he cured his mother of multiple sclerosis when he was 14, and that his healing methods were connected to his First Nations heritage from the Penobscot band in Maine, where his father's grandmother's family included a Penobscot shaman.

In 2004, his website described these requirements for providing a distance-healing consultation:

> In order for a long-distance treatment to be possible you will need to provide me with a clear colour face photo and a brief description of your illness. A description of any medication you are on and mention of any scans you have had or plan to have. This is useful to plan the treatments around the scheduled medical scans. You might say, 'I thought he could tell me what's wrong.' Well, I can. But I am not here to prove to anyone that I have this ability. I have gone well beyond that. The more information I have, the easier it is to focus in on the problem area. After all, the purpose of this is to get your body on the road to recovery. I conduct most of my healing sessions at long distance. I need to be in email contact to follow-up on the healing process. The client must be relaxed, with their feet on the floor (if possible) for about ½ hour

*while the treatment is being administered. It would be beneficial,
but not essential, if you concentrate on the area being healed.
Before follow-up treatments can be carried out, I need an email
explaining any sensations you may have felt and any changes
in your condition. If you don't take time to communicate then I
won't take time to heal. Some people feel nausea; dizziness; tired,
and tingling throughout their body or in the area being healed.
Care must be taken that you are not in a situation where you
require concentration or balance at the time of healing.*

He has also appeared in the media and on national TV
in 2007, in the popular news show *On the Hour with George
Stroumboulopoulos*, discussing his faith-healing abilities.[315] He
offered endorsements of his powers from the astronaut Edgar
Mitchell and rockabilly musician Ronnie Hawkins. It seems
that his faith-healing career proved less profitable as a source of
income, as he then went on to qualify as a naturopath operating
out of the Yaletown Vancouver Naturopath Clinic, where he
was pictured among the staff on their website in 2018, complete
with stethoscope. In 2018, his own Dreamhealer website still
proclaimed him to be an 'internationally renowned energy
healer and best-selling author' citing he 'shared the stage'
with luminaries such as Deepak Chopra and David Suzuki,
and advertised a fee-based workshops in Toronto and British
Columbia. Today his website has closed and now simply links
to the Yaletown Naturopath Clinic website, and oddly he is also
no longer practising as an ND after a brief four-year career in the
field.

As with most healers of this nature, when you unpack these
claims further, all is not quite what it seems, whilst some seem
highly inflated and leave many unanswered questions. His claims
of a First Nations heritage do not appear to be endorsed by any
members of the Penobscot Nation, his internationally best-selling
books are actually self-published (despite mentions of Penguin

as the publisher), and his claim to be attending 'medical school' on his website was actually attending a private naturopath training college. In his workshops where he claimed 'he bridges his innate healing abilities with naturopathic knowledge to teach others how to access their own healing abilities', cameras or recording devices are not allowed, so exactly what he was doing is unverified.

Such faith-healing shows or 'workshops' are a fairly staple feature of those claiming to have such innate mystical gifts, as they offer far more remuneration than individual healing sessions, and allow for the effects of group psychology to influence people. These are the same tactics that have been used by time-share sales people and scam artists for years. A key example is Christian evangelist Peter Popoff, who claimed to heal sick people on stage in front of an audience and was exposed by the magician James Randi as a fraud back in 1986. Popoff pretended to know private details about participants' lives by receiving radio transmissions in an earpiece from his wife who was off-stage and had gathered information from audience members prior to the show. Despite being unmasked as a fraud, the following bankruptcy and collapse of his ministry due to financial mismanagement, Peter Popoff is still selling 'Miraculous Alabaster Oil' and prayer on Vision TV and the web today.

McLeod's claims of being a 'co-main' presenter with Deepak Chopra at a healing event were also inflated, and actually involved him being one of six presenters. Like many in this line of work, all of the narrative surrounding his healing powers relies on self-promotion, showmanship (at which he is particularly skilled) and testimonials, rather than evidence. These are not normally the skills one associates with a healthcare professional (other than the Dr Oz variety). If there were hundreds of people healed by a faith-healer's supernatural gifts, it would be reasonable to expect a mass of evidence supporting this, but there are only ever a few testimonials. Nevertheless, if a cancer patient who is being treated with chemotherapy goes and sees a faith healer and then gets better, they will often accredit this to the faith healer rather than the medicine. In the case of the Dreamhealer, perhaps it could be that a young boy, troubled by his mother's chronic suffering, tried to help and as he saw her improve, was convinced (or was convinced by others) that he had a special gift, which he subsequently found he could make money out of. Whether McLeod truly believes he has mystical gifts or is simply capitalising on people's credulity is difficult to determine. He seems very genuine and convincing, and may truly believe in his powers. In any case, technically he has done nothing illegal and, generally, people prefer not to directly and too closely question the claims of individuals who have a history of family suffering and claim to have mystical healing abilities, preferring instead to give them the benefit of the doubt.

Regrettably, faith healers have a terrible reputation for scams, preying on the vulnerable going back over a century, and new examples of such fraudsters continue to arise almost annually. In Leicester in the UK, in 2015, Mohammed Ashrafi, a self-professed spiritual healer was sentenced to nine years in prison, with six years for fraud and attempted fraud and three for blackmail. He claimed he could help with health and financial problems, and had previously been active in Canada (where he was also wanted by the police), operating a lottery fraud where victims say he told them his prayers could deliver a big win – for a price. Bizarrely, the trick he used there involved cracking open a boiled egg to reveal the winning lottery numbers inside![316]

Chapter 15

Magical health machines

Blinded with pseudoscience

Another alternative health business sector that has developed significantly is the sale of devices that are said to have a positive effect on health in some way or as diagnostic tools. Indeed, it is sometimes difficult here to differentiate those devices based on scientific evidence from those not.

TENS machines for pain control

One well-known example is the use of transcutaneous electronic nerve stimulation (TENS) devices to combat pain; these were widely used in maternity units, and do have a physiological theoretical basis. The electrical pulses are believed to stimulate nerve pathways in the spinal cord, which block the transmission of pain. These devices became very popular in the late 1980s and 1990s, and I recall it was offered to my wife by midwives during the birth of both our children (for a fee). The devices themselves appear very high-tech with a flashing LED, threshold control and electrodes applied to the skin. They are also significantly costly. However, despite the scientific basis for the way that TENS works, the theory remains largely a matter of conjecture and a 2009 review of 17 studies (with a total of 1466 women) demonstrated that pain scores were similar in women using

TENS and those in control groups.[317] Another 2017 review of TENS to assist in chronic pain also found no difference between those using TENS and a sham TENS machine, implying any effect was likely placebo based.[318] This indicates another common trend with many alternative therapies: many do seem to work, but often very weakly, or no better than a placebo. There is certainly no harm in people using TENS as an additional therapeutic pain intervention, but the current scientific evidence is still rather sparse to support its value. Nevertheless, if you search the Internet for 'TENS and pain relief', the claims of its effectiveness you find in the results (outside of the scientific literature) appear somewhat inflated.

The wonder of radionics

On the other hand, there are many devices that have absolutely no scientific theoretical basis or, worse, are completely based on pseudoscience. Radionics is one of the oldest and most interesting examples. Radionics practitioners claim to be able to diagnose illnesses from a patient sample remotely. It involves the use of tissue specimens (e.g. skin, hair or blood) as a diagnostic and therapeutic sample. The ideas were devised by Albert Abrams (1864 – 1924), who became a millionaire by leasing the radionics machines which he had designed. Abrams claimed to be able to detect special energy frequencies and cure illness by matching these frequencies with his machines. He even claimed them to be so sensitive that he could tell someone's religion by looking at a drop of their blood. The American Medical Association described him as a 'quack' and in 1924 *Scientific American* ran numerous trials on his devices and found them to be non-functional.[319] In the United States, the commercial practice of radionics is banned but there remains interest in the UK (with the UK Radionics Association) and in Canada (through the Radionics and Dowsing Institute of Canada). At the time of writing, both will sell you equipment ranging from budget-minded diagnostic pendants for a few dollars, to the electronic Zenith Device for $355 CAD (which is purported to shift time, space and gravity), and the even more awesome Atlantis Superconductor for $599 (which resembles a plastic bowl).[320] There are no systematic reviews of these therapies, and evidence of any efficacy is virtually non-existent.

Electro-diagnostic machines

Electro-acupuncture devices

For those who are interested in acupuncture but do not wish to undertake the training involved in learning the meridians and acupuncture points, there are currently devices on sale on Amazon that claim to be able to identify flows of *Qi* energy and light up at acupuncture points. For example, the 'Point-O-Select acupuncture point finder with automatic and manual point search and integrated [sic] electrostimulator'. The name is straight out of 1950s' advertising, a time when Cessna advertised 'Land-O-Matic' for its new tricycle landing gear on its aircraft. These devices retail for around £60–£120, and the use of such devices to detect and monitor acupuncture points has a long and chequered history. The first claims for the electrical detection of acupuncture points date to the 1950s, with claims by Reinhard Voll in Germany in 1953. He, and several other researchers, concluded that skin points with unique electrical characteristics were identifiable that resembled traditional acupuncture points. However, the validity and reproducibility of these studies have been long debated and they are viewed with considerable scepticism in the medical community.

They actually seem to measure galvanic skin response (GSR) or skin conductance (SC), now more commonly called electrodermal activity (EDA). This is a measure of the variations in the electrical conductance of the skin. This may be caused by the variation through changes in sweating, for example, and has nothing to do with acupuncture points or flows of *Qi*. The measurement of EDA is very prone to influence by a variety of environmental factors, and even pressing on the device more firmly can change the results. Few people (even in the acupuncture world) seem to take these devices particularly seriously, and there is no scientific evidence they work. A 2007 paper examining them suggested that the extent to which acupuncture points are truly associated with unique electrical measurements remains a contested issue and should be systematically reviewed, whilst a 2012 researcher found they were inaccurate and unreliable.[321, 322] Nevertheless, I have met several people who have seen them used and believe this provides solid evidence that acupuncture points and their associated meridians exist.

The miraculous ZYTO machine

Following on from Reinhard Voll's ideas of the 1950s and the identification of EDA (electrodermal activity), a number of other so-called 'electrodiagnostic' (EDA) devices have been marketed. Many retailers state the devices are able to help determine the cause of a disease, allergies, deficiencies in vitamins, what homeopathic remedies should be prescribed, or even if a disease is present. Unsurprisingly, many manufacturers have also been sued over such claims. For example, one of the best known is the ZYTO company (based in Dublin, Ireland and Utah, USA) which sells such devices and claims 'a simple galvanic skin response scan can help inform your wellness decisions by providing accurate readings directly from your body'. These devices are popular with naturopaths and chiropractors (many endorse ZYTO on the company website) and their products have even have been used by some US dentists in the past. Their devices use a hand sensor that relays EDA to a computer that runs ZYTO's exclusive software. ZYTO claims that the data are correlated and compared with 'virtual items' in its software database, and each 'virtual item' is said to represent a different physical item or biomarker of interest. Anyone with any knowledge of information science will immediately suspect this is meaningless technobabble.

In the USA the devices cost from $88 for the basic compass model to $13,150 for their Elite model. This is also in addition to a $35–$45 monthly subscription fee! The technology involved is pure nonsense in terms of established diagnostic value, and uses EDA and computer algorithms (that have no demonstrated clinical significance) to produce practically meaningless print-outs of health items. Dr Stephen Barrett of the Device Watch Organization tested one of their products in 2016, and found, 'My basic scan results were so inconsistent that they could not possibly be clinically meaningful. In addition to being inconsistent, my food-category bio surveys recommended excluding so many foods that the resultant diets could be extremely unhealthful.'[323]

What the devices actually do is identify specific alternative medicine products from the company's associated essential oil and nutritional supplement vendors (e.g. doTERRA, Nature's Sunshine, Youngevity and Young Living). The ZYTO software claims to be able to identify personalised products for the client available from these company's product lines. The idea is clearly to increase sales for alternative practitioners and natural health store owners, and they even state so in their ZTYO marketing literature: 'Help others make better wellness decisions and watch your business grow.' This is certainly ingenious advertising. It represents a good example of marketing that remains within the law by making very vague statements of actual benefits, but implying significant gains in wellbeing. ZYTO even notes that its devices' results are not reproducible, or of diagnostic value, on its website FAQ pages, so they have covered their legal liability. Overall, the theoretical and scientific basis for this device is the equivalent of buying a digital electrical multimeter and measuring your skin resistance to get a number, and then finding a product in the local pharmacy that has the same number in the bar code. There is no established scientific diagnostic value. Its real value lies in its ability to generate income for ZYTO, and as an income generation strategy this is surely a scammer's dream come true.

The company has had some legal challenges over the years, although as they market their machines through practitioners, they have mainly avoided direct legal challenges. For example, Dr Barrett identified that between 2008 and 2010, ZYTO Corporation was included as a defendant in four lawsuits filed by people who had been tested by a ZYTO device during their treatment at the South Coast Center for New Medicine in California. A ZYTO filing with the Securities and Exchange Commission indicates that ZYTO settled its portion of these suits in 2011 with agreements under which the company admitted no fault but paid a total of $10,000.[324] Several state regulators have acted against practitioners who employed ZYTO devices as diagnostic tools. In 2015, the Arizona State Board of Chiropractic Examiners ordered chiropractor Michael E Bean to pay a $250 fine and be placed on probation for six months and to cease and desist the use of ZYTO Bioscan technology.[325] The US Food and Drug Administration (FDA) warned ZYTO in a 2015 letter that the company should desist from any marketing claims that its devices could diagnose any disease or illness.[326] In 2016, ZYTO was compelled to recall the software used in its devices as a result of FDA action that found the labelling 'false and misleading'.[327] Nevertheless, they appear to have weathered these issues which do not seem to have impacted their profits as they have now expanded their business into Europe. Their current glossy website (www.zyto.com/) claims they are a 'global leader in biocommunication technology' and appears to be doing well, marketing their current product lines.

Ionisation bracelets

Another more commonly seen example of mystical health machines are fairly low-tech ionised bracelets. These devices generally claim to be based upon the idea of meridians (the lines of bio-energy flow) and energy fields from TCM that I described earlier. The manufacturers suggest that they can help correct imbalances in *yin* and *yang* energies in the body, achieving a state of balance of *Qi* (or *Chi*) energy. Currently, advertisements for Q-Ray bracelets appear on television in North America regularly, and you can order one of these for around $70–200 USD from the manufacturer's website, or by mail order. There are also lesser-known brands, such as Balance, Bio-Ray, IRenew and Rayma, that can all be considered to be part of the ionised bracelet family. Although they are not advocated for any specific health problems today, between 1995 and 2003, Q-Ray bracelets were purported to give relief from arthritis and joint pain. A well-publicised 2003 RCT revealed no evidence of their effectiveness for joint pain control compared with placebo.[328] Following this, a case was brought to the US Federal Trade Commission, which was unable to find any basis for claims related to TCM and concluded that it was 'part of a scheme devised to defraud consumers'. Q-Ray appealed the finding, but lost this appeal in 2011 when the court ordered them to return $11.8 million to customers.[316, 329] Today, the Q-Ray company sales literature simply claims the devices give greater clarity, performance at a higher level and more positive feelings. The current scientific evidence for these bio-energy fields is inconclusive at best, and again there is little evidence they actually work. Nevertheless, sales of these devices appear to remain healthy (and the Q-Ray company profitable despite its multi-million-dollar losses in the 2003/2011 law suit). Notwithstanding the dubious history of the products, I frequently come across health professionals wearing these bracelets and advocating for their efficacy.

An infinite variety of imaginative remedies

There are numerous other forms of alternative medicines and therapies we could explore, such as crystal healing, psychic surgery, DNA healing, rolfing, cryogenics, biofield tuning, Bowen technique, rebirthing, ozone anti-ageing, etc. More seem to be invented every day, such as the case of William Edwin Grey in California, a doctor who is currently involved in a disciplinary action for selling homeopathic sound wave remedies for diseases (including Ebola).[330] Many use deception and pseudoscience to market their products, but in any case purchasing such therapeutics involves the use of faith, intuitive and personal knowledge and emotive rationales, rather than the use of scientific evidence. We could go on and debunk more of these in terms of science, but that is not really our purpose here, and there are many other books and media exploring this subject in detail. Often, the counter-argument from those supporting alternative medicine and healthcare is to ask, where is the harm with using them as they might work and are perfectly safe, especially when compared with scientific medicine? Unfortunately, though, this isn't always the case either.

Chapter 16

Is alternative medicine safe?

Although alternative medicine is usually regarded as 'mostly harmless', the implications of engaging with it are not always clear, and serious injuries and deaths do occur just as with conventional medicine. The most obvious form of harm is that of direct damage resulting from the use of an alternative therapy, but there are other forms of harm to consider too.

Using alternative remedies instead of medicine

One issue is favouring alternative medicine over conventional medicine and then putting off seeing a doctor or nurse, resulting in serious health problems or even death. Unfortunately, this is not as rare as one might suspect, and only the most serious cases tend to get reported in the media.[331] In 2019, a British mother with breast cancer died after she shunned freely available medical treatment and used laser, magnet and natural remedies and a vegan diet instead.[332] The cancer had been treatable when diagnosed three years earlier. Another recent case here in Canada involved an Alberta couple whose son died of meningitis after being treated with natural remedies from a naturopath and who had delayed seeking medical advice from a physician.[28] Another Calgary couple were jailed for 32 months for criminal negligence after their 14-month-old son died of a treatable Staphylococcal infection and was not taken to a physician until too late, whilst the parents searched the Internet for natural remedies. There is also some research documenting this phenomenon, and a large-scale 2019 Yale Cancer Center study exploring cancer patients who had used alternative therapies found that those who used complementary medicine were more likely to refuse other conventional cancer treatments and had a two times greater risk of death compared with patients who used no complementary medicine.[333]

Some alternative therapeutics also present significant risks of harm if used instead of conventional medicines as we know they simply do not work.[19, 334, 335] A particularly problematic case here is the use of homeopathy, which seems harmless enough but is frequently promoted in place of actual medicines, giving rise to false hope and unnecessary health risks when marketed as a replacement for established medicines that are effective. For example, in 2006, an investigation by the BBC in the UK found 10 homeopathic clinics and pharmacies went against government guidelines by recommending unproven remedies for malaria and other tropical diseases such as typhoid, dengue fever and yellow fever. Homeopathy is unregulated by law in the UK, and the General Pharmaceutical Council's case against the pharmacists involved was later dropped, as they did not consider that the pharmacists' fitness for registration was impaired such that it ought to be removed or restricted.[336, 337] London-based Ainsworths (a chemist which has two Royal Warrants for supplying homeopathic products to the Royal family) was told to stop advertising homeopathic vaccines in 2013 by the UK medicines regulator after an investigation by the BBC. The products found on sale included vials of homeopathic remedies labelled 'Meningitis Vac Hib', 'Measles Vaccine', 'Rubella Vaccine', 'Pertussin' and 'Pertussis [whooping cough] Vaccine'.[338] This seems to be an ongoing issue, as even in 2019 Ainsworths was reported to be selling an anti-vaccination book, stating vaccine-preventable infections could be treated homeopathically.[339]

Another example is the Amma Resonance Healing Foundation in Ethiopia, which was brought to the attention of the WHO in 2009 for offering homeopathy as 'an ideal alternative and complement for the treatment of HIV/AIDS in developing countries'. The Foundation, established in the Netherlands, was run by the British homeopath Peter Chappell. He and his colleague Harry van der Zee claimed that their homeopathic remedies could reverse AIDS. In 2014, a German homeopathic journal published an article stating that a team of homeopaths had travelled to Liberia to cure Ebola, and claimed their remedies could work in serious epidemics of the infectious disease. This provoked understandable criticism from scientists noting that there was no evidence that homeopathic remedies had any effect on the body, or Ebola, and that even to instigate clinical trials would be unethical.[340, 341] Despite these concerns, the US-based National Center for Homeopathy charity states on its website that: 'The good news is that a small international team of experienced and heroic homeopaths have arrived in West Africa, and are currently on the ground working hard to examine patients, work out the "genus epidemicus", and initiate clinical trials.'

In another 2015 case, a group of Canadian homeopaths claimed they could detect, prevent and treat the tropical disease chagas (American trypanosomiasis – a serious infection that can cause heart failure). They even obtained Canadian public funding, with Quebec-based charity Terre Sans Frontières (TSF) acquiring the sum of $350,000 to send homeopaths to Honduras to treat people with chagras.[172] After a Canadian Broadcasting Corporation (CBC) news story, and many health professionals complaining that there is currently no evidence that homeopathy is anything more than a placebo for treating dangerous tropical infections, the government withdrew funding in 2019.[342] The more recent promotion of homeopathic immunisation instead of vaccines by homeopaths and naturopaths is another example. In 2018, Health Canada warned that homeopathic remedies were not an alternative to vaccines.[343] A good-quality randomised, blinded, placebo-controlled trial of homeopathic vaccines undertaken in 2017 revealed absolutely no antibody response to either the homeopathic remedies or placebos, compared with a robust response to the vaccines.[344] However, in 2019 a CBC investigation revealed four local homeopaths who were promoting homeoprophylaxis, implying homeopathic remedies could protect children from infections as an alternative form of vaccination.[343, 345] In 2019, the BC College of Naturopaths commenced disciplinary action against three naturopaths for anti-vaccination activity.[229]

Using alternative remedies in combination with other drugs without notifying your physician

Another issue is people not informing their physician that they are taking supplemental alternative remedies that could interact with their medical prescription drugs. This has led to serious health issues due to their combined effects. A problem here is people often feel uncomfortable in telling their doctor or nurse they are using alternative healthcare products, or simply think they are perfectly harmless as they are natural so do not need to. A 2002 scientific review identified that elderly patients frequently suffered harm from alternative therapies, and herbal treatments were associated with serious adverse events through unwanted drug interactions with patients' prescribed medicines as well as direct toxicity.[26, 98] Issues of people not informing their doctor that they are taking supplements that could interact with their prescription drugs is another area that has led to serious health issues due to the unanticipated combined effects of alternative and medical remedies.

Misdiagnosis

Then there is also the potential harm of misdiagnosis through incompetence or through the use of bogus diagnostic tools (such as the devices mentioned above). The case of Canadian naturopath Anke Zimmermnan in 2018 provides a fascinating example.[29] After much adverse publicity, she gave up her naturopath's licence in 2018 after diagnosing a young boy's aggressive behavioural issues as being because he was in 'a slightly rabid dog state' resulting from a dog bite when younger. She even prescribed a homeopathic treatment based on the saliva of a rabid dog.[29, 346] At a minimum, misdiagnosis will lead to expenses for useless therapies to treat the misdiagnosed disease, and at worst the misdiagnosis of and failure to treat an actual serious illness. Another example is the frequent use of chronic Lyme disease (CLD) as a diagnosis by chiropractors and naturopaths.[347] This is a controversial diagnosis amongst physicians, and relates to the attribution of various uncharacteristic symptoms to a prolonged bacterial infection with *Borrelia burgdorferi*. The claimed symptoms of CLD are atypical in their lack of well-recognised clinical abnormalities that are found in actual Lyme disease, and in many cases, the absence of any laboratory evidence of infection, and an absence of plausible exposure to the infection. The mere name CLD is in itself a source of confusion as a chronic form of the disease has yet to be identified or agreed upon in the medical world. The problems usually diagnosed as CLD include chronic pain, fatigue and neurocognitive and behavioural symptoms, as well as various neurologic and rheumatologic diseases. These represent a wide range of possible problems. Nevertheless, despite this complexity and controversy CLD is frequently misdiagnosed and treated by alternative medicine practitioners.[347, 348]

Additionally, psychological harm has also been recognised as a problem, where alternative therapies have been employed unnecessarily for behavioural or other non-medical issues, such as in the case of 'conversion therapy', where religiously-based therapeutic interventions are employed under the incorrect assumption homosexuality is a treatable illness.[22, 23] Another recent example was in 2020 where UK homeopaths were forbidden (once again) from promoting a fake cure for autism by the government watchdog, the Professional Standards Authority (PSA).[349] Neither autism nor homosexuality are illnesses.

Direct harm resulting from alternative healthcare

Of course, there are also many documented cases of patients using alternative remedies that have caused direct harm as well. In the UK, a TCM practitioner, Ying Wu, prescribed high doses of extracts from the Aristolochia plant to treat acne in a 58-year-old woman for several years, reassuring her that the pills were 'as safe as Coca-Cola'. As a result of the medication, the woman lost both kidneys, developed urinary tract cancer and had a heart attack. Wu was taken to court in 2010 and given a two-year conditional discharge, as the judge decided to be lenient considering he did not know the pills were dangerous, and because the practice of TCM was unregulated in the UK.[20, 31, 350] In another example, in 2006 the US FTC in the USA cracked down on the advertising of IV megadose vitamin therapy by naturopaths, citing safety concerns.[338, 351] Nevertheless, in 2017 30-year old Jade Erick died as a result of IV treatment with curcumin (turmeric extract) provided by naturopath Kim Kelly in California. The treatment was given for eczema, a skin condition which is difficult to treat but which has a number of approved medical treatments (none of which being IV curcumin). Unfortunately, in reality the naturopath provided a lethal turmeric injection.[338]

Serious injuries with alternative physical therapies such as chiropractic and even acupuncture are also well documented. Stroke and paralysis following neck (cervical) manipulation with chiropractic are one example.[24, 25, 352, 353, 354, 355] The actual incidence of stroke following chiropractic cervical manipulation remains controversial, and chiropractors continue to maintain that its incidence following such neck adjustments is extremely low.[356] However, a 1999 study identified 10 patients who had experienced a stroke due to arterial damage through chiropractic neck manipulations. None had pre-existing symptoms and the neurological deficits were severe in nine of them (one was in a persistent vegetative state and one in persistent locked-in syndrome).[357] Astonishingly, it was also found that only one of them had formally consented to the procedure. This is not uncommon, and I and several colleagues I know have had cervical manipulations from chiropractors in the past. None of us were ever warned of potential risks or asked to sign consent documents.

In 2017, retired bank manager John Lawler attended a chiropractor in York for treatment of leg-ache, and suffered a fractured cervical vertebra following a manipulation which resulted in his death.[358] The family reported that the chiropractor, Arleen Scholten, had diagnosed a 'vertebral subluxation complex' which she aimed to treat by manipulating his neck. Mr Lawler had a long history of spinal disease, which was apparently known to the chiropractor. The manipulation involved using a drop table, a device which allows for sudden thrust to a person's spinal or pelvic area, while simultaneously dropping a section of the table a small distance.[359] An inquest into his death found he had died as a result of a broken neck.

The treatment had resulted in a torn and dislocated C4/C5 intervertebral disc, paralysing him from the neck down. Following the manipulation, he became symptomatic, and his wife claimed she heard him shout 'You're hurting me!' and 'I can't feel my arms'. Scholten decided to turn him over and then manoeuvre him into a chair next to the treatment table and described him as like a 'rag doll', a classic symptom (bilateral paralysis) with a cervical spinal injury. She reportedly said at the time she thought it might have been a stroke, but that would have given rise to a one-sided paralysis, not bilateral.

For a possible cervical injury risk, medical professionals would normally apply a cervical collar, and log-roll or slide patients onto a stretcher or spinal board for caution until an X-ray examination could be undertaken to rule out a fracture and possible damage to the spinal cord. One would never sit a suspected neck-trauma patient up in a chair without support, as this would be highly likely to compound the severity of such an injury. So why a person claiming significant musculo-skeletal and spinal expertise did so is quite unfathomable. When the ambulance arrived, the patient's family reported she provided an inaccurate and misleading history to the paramedics, leading them to believe the incident was a medical one rather than a traumatic incident, and so they transported John downstairs to the ambulance without stabilising his neck.[359] If given the correct history, they would have likely stabilised his neck in situ, which would also have increased his chances of survival. Arleen Scholten was initially arrested for manslaughter but later released, as the criminal investigation into his death ruled out any charges. The investigating committee of the General Chiropractic Council, the regulator which reviewed the case, decided to allow her to continue to practise.[360]

In 2002, researchers from the Canadian Stroke Consortium reported on 98 cases in which external trauma had triggered strokes (blood clots forming in arteries supplying blood to the brain). Chiropractic cervical manipulation was the apparent cause of 38 of the cases, with 30 involving vertebral artery dissection (tearing of the lining of the vertebral artery) and the remainder by carotid artery dissection. Canadian researchers have suggested the incidence of ischaemic strokes in patients under 45 is around 750 a year, and researchers believe that the data suggests around 20% are due to neck manipulation, so there may be gross underreporting of chiropractic manipulation as a cause of stroke.[361, 362] A 2016 study by a chiropractor-led research team indicated that the rate of strokes was around six per 1000 patients in those aged over 66.[356] However, this is not representative of the age of those seeking treatment for neck-related pain issues, who are often younger. Even if the incidence is low and stroke following chiropractic neck manipulation is rare, one must consider these figures in the terms of risk of a severe neurological impairment as a result of a treatment for a non-life-threatening condition, where other safe treatments are readily available.

As discussed earlier, the chiropractic treatment of infants and children is another area of controversy. This is a rapidly growing area where chiropractors are now offering spine and neck manipulations as a form of lifestyle medicine rather than for the treatment of illnesses. Although cases of serious injury have rarely been recorded, there is not currently a good sense of how widespread such injuries are. A seven-year-old boy was reported with cranial nerve damage in one paper, where it was reported that cervical spine stretching during chiropractic manoeuvres might have led to clot formation and subsequent blockage of the basilar artery to the brain.[363] Another US report described a case of quadriplegia following a chiropractic manipulation of an infant.[364] More recently, an Australian infant reportedly suffered a broken neck from a chiropractic manipulation.[365] The fact is we do not really know how much of a risk infant and children's chiropractic poses, and as there is no evidence of effectiveness for any paediatric condition, that should be reason enough not to do it.[366]

Although there are few reports on injuries sustained through acupuncture, there is also some evidence that these do sometime occur. A 2010 review revealed a total of 479 cases of acupuncture-related adverse events, including sub-arachnoid haemorrhage (bleeding on the surface of the brain), pneumothorax (lung collapse into the cavity between the chest wall and lung), nerve damage, bleeding and haematoma (a large blood clot in the body), perforated gall bladder and bowels, and serious infections. The patients involved ranged in age from two to 73 years and some died as a result of their injuries.[367] Although rare, around 100 fatalities have been reported after acupuncture in the medical literature.[368, 369, 370, 371] Of the 87 articles reporting traumatic injuries in the 2010 study, around 70% were authored not by the acupuncturists themselves but by the physicians who treated the injuries. This represents a common problem with alternative medicine practitioners, in that as damage arises often in single-practitioner interactions, adverse events are infrequently documented.

Dangerous advice

Harm may not simply be caused through the prescription of alternative remedies; it may also simply occur as the result of dangerous advice. In 2015, in Australia a naturopath advised a breastfeeding mother to take a liquid-only diet that nearly starved her eight-month-old baby to death. The former nurse recommended a raw-food diet and, eventually, a water-only diet to the woman who was exclusively breastfeeding the infant at the time. Marilyn Pauline Bodnar pleaded guilty to aiding and abetting the mother in failing to provide for the boy in a 2018 court case over the issue and agreed never to work with children again.[372]

Relative risk

Overall, it may certainly be true that alternative medicine is not as risk-laden as conventional medical treatment, but that should be expected given that conventional biomedical care deals with serious acute and life-threatening illnesses and conditions that require highly invasive and sometimes aggressive interventions in people across the whole socio-economic spectrum. Other than for childbirth, people are rarely admitted into hospitals nowadays unless they are seriously ill, whereas in Europe and North America alternative medicine is generally performed on relatively wealthy people who mainly have minor or chronic health issues, and who are treated in expensive private clinics or offices. Therefore, even though alternative practitioners often cite modern medicine as being fraught with risk and harmful, comparing the relative risks is difficult as its clientele are fundamentally different. It is not simply a case of alternative medicine offering everything to gain and nothing to lose, as there are risks involved as with any form of healthcare. The ancient medical principle *Primum non nocere* – first, do no harm – applies just as much to alternative as to conventional medicine, but regulation is less stringent in the alternative health sector, and the risks involved are often far less obvious.[373]

Chapter 17

Regulation and education

In terms of deception, as previously discussed a key problem is that much of the alternative medicine industry is very poorly regulated. Its regulation varies considerably across the world, and this has led to huge opportunities for scammers and deceptive practitioners to operate fairly unimpeded by the laws that govern science-based health professionals. In a 2017 study on Internet health scams, alternative medicine accounted for 21% of the suspected scams identified.[21] A clear pattern emerges of alternative practitioners making claims far beyond those supported by the evidence, and using emotional appeals to sell products and services. Although many honest alternative practitioners exist who will openly state the faith-based nature of their therapies and give an honest appraisal of their ability to help a health problem, inevitably many others make inflated claims of efficacy of their treatments for various diseases, and lay claim to a sound scientific basis for their work where none actually exists. It is difficult to discriminate the practitioners here who actually believe in what they are selling from the crooked individuals who simply want to make fast cash. However, the results for the consumers are the same, and these may be worse than simply a financial loss.

Is your doctor really a doctor?

One serious problem here concerns the nature of alternative healthcare qualifications. In Europe and North America, public universities offering health professional programmes must be accredited by a variety of internal and external bodies to ensure academic and professional standards and credibility. Clinical health professional qualifications (such as a medical doctorate, or a nursing degree) normally mean there are entry gates involving an initial degree with a significant science component, a lengthy programme of advanced-level studies across the age span and across a broad range of disciplines and therapies, a research component and (possibly most importantly) a wide range of rigorously assessed clinical practice. In the shadowy world of alternative medicine this is not necessarily the case, and a qualification can mean virtually anything you want it to. Even with the regulated professions there are issues. Unfortunately, the reality is there is no meaningful quality control or standard of educational preparation, even for some legally accredited and regulated practitioners in many areas. Let us take a closer look at the educational preparation of two mainstream alternative healthcare practices that use the tile of 'doctor' here in North America (and in many other countries) chiropractic and naturopathy.

Chiropractic doctors

Chiropractic is a regulated health profession in the UK, Canada and the USA and practitioners will frequently argue they are the equivalent of physicians in their expertise and focus on primary health care in the community. In the UK and Canada, chiropractors gain a Doctor of Chiropractic (DC) qualification over a four-year postgraduate programme, and must pass a National Board of Chiropractic Examiners certification examination. They must also be licensed in the area where they practise. This would, on the face of it, seem a high standard. In the UK many of these are taught in newer universities and, in Canada, all but one of the colleges that teach chiropractic are private colleges (the exception being in Quebec). Overall, the award of a doctorate by these institutions is not necessarily commensurate with the standards required for the level of an MD or PhD qualification in research-based public universities in the UK or in Canada. Even where programmes exist that are accredited through publicly funded universities, this is not necessarily a good indicator of academic or clinical expertise. Although some public institutions now accredit or offer chiropractic education (e.g. Teeside University, London South Bank University, the University of South Wales, the University of Central Lancashire in the UK, the Université du Québec à Trois-Rivières in Canada and the University of Johannesburg in South Africa), this trend reflects a move to market more commercially oriented programmes in addition to established academic programmes. This has been largely driven by the increasing competition in the higher-education sector. For example, in 1975 around 10% of people aged 15 and over were educated to degree level in the UK, 12% in the USA and 13% in Canada. Today those figures are, 28% in both the UK and USA, and 39% in Canada.[374] This has led to intense competition between institutions for students, especially within newer colleges, and unfortunately the growth in higher education does not necessarily reflect the academic or clinical merits of newer disciplines.

During my academic career, I have seen this at first hand in several institutions where the main driver for development of a new academic programme has been financial interest, and where the naming of programmes as 'science' rather than 'arts' degrees has been based upon market research rather than scientific or arts-based content; science degrees generally sell better. Another indicator of this trend is the number of international students enrolled in post-secondary institutions, which has been steadily rising for over two decades in both the UK and Canada, with their numbers increasing at a higher rate than that for domestic students. International students in Canada totalled 245,895 in 2017, representing 12.0% of overall enrolments.[375] All of this has made the expansion into new programmes, such as chiropractic, more of a business decision than a reflection of societal needs and academic advancement. Indeed, the recognition of 'doctorly prepared' healthcare practitioner by legislators in various provinces in Europe and North America has generally been granted upon consideration of the number of credits and length of the programme, rather than level and nature of substantive content, academic merits or even the level of clinical preparation. The drive to accept new health professions such as chiropractic and naturopathy into legislative frameworks has been more based upon their populist appeal and substantial political lobbying from those professions rather than the emergence of new, coherent disciplines exhibiting innovative evidence-based practices and professional standards.

For example, the Palmer College of Chiropractic in Iowa, USA charges a yearly tuition fee of around $34,000 USD, apparently with a student acceptance rate of 100% for those with first degrees.[376] It teaches anatomy, physiology, embryology, biochemistry, microbiology, nutrition, philosophy and even evidence-based practice. On the other hand, it also teaches faith-based theories of illness, and considerable practice on how to detect and treat vertebral subluxations by hand (as it acknowledges they cannot be seen on X-rays... although it also teaches diagnostic imaging). Overall, 64.4% of Palmer College of Chiropractic-Davenport students are reported to graduate within six years.[377] This preparation is argued to be the appropriate basis for preparing chiropractors to be 'doctorly-prepared primary healthcare practitioners' able to diagnose, treat or refer all patients. The adequacy of this preparation for primary healthcare practice is highly questionable at best. There is minimal content on interpreting or even undertaking health research, exploring specialist populations or conditions, and the overall practice experience is focused on treating every condition with a single therapeutic approach (SMT).

When one contrasts this with the work of doctors, nurse practitioners/specialists or physiotherapists, who have training and education to treat a wide range of conditions with multiple therapeutics, the award of a doctoral qualification for chiropractic makes little sense, apart from marketability. Physiotherapists, who have a broad range of clinical skills and are an essential part of healthcare teams in hospital intensive care units, only require a Master's level qualification. In many of Canada's states and provinces, chiropractors are not even permitted to order X-rays (DCs in Alberta, Ontario and Newfoundland currently have authority to order X-rays and certain diagnostic imaging in varying degrees). Additionally, chiropractors do not undertake extensive practice in a wide range of clinical settings, including acute care or hospitals. Therefore, they do not gain the experience with a wide population-base or any significant acute or emergency care that medical students and nurses will encounter in their supervised hospital-based experiences before graduating. Chiropractic clinical experience is gained in the school, or by watching and taking part in clinical practice in private chiropractic offices and clinics, almost exclusively with relatively wealthy and healthy walk-in clients.

In attempts to align the chiropractic profession with a more rigorous preparation, and move away from the straight chiropractic model, some chiropractic colleges are now requiring students to pass an 'objective structured clinical examination' (OSCE), a practical examination of differential diagnostic skills (as required by medical students and nurse practitioners). However, the chiropractic version is administered and assessed by chiropractors with its own professional focus and with no independent accreditation. It simply involves taking a medical history, forming a diagnosis and demonstrating a variety of physical examinations. On the other hand, medical and nurse practitioner students undertaking OSCEs may encounter any potential condition in their exam, are required to perform a full physical (and where appropriate psychological) assessment of the client, and make a differential diagnosis and treatment/referral plan. Overall, in terms of clinical preparation, the chiropractic standard is nowhere near comparable to that for physicians, nurse practitioners or physiotherapists, who get to experience the whole spectrum of healthcare issues across the age span in highly varied populations before qualifying.

Naturopathic doctors

Currently, in the UK, naturopaths qualify with a degree or diploma-level qualification, although postgraduate quali-fications, such as iridology (a discredited form of diagnosis based on colour of the iris), are available. However, in North America things are quite different, and they are legally permitted to call themselves doctors in many states and provinces; in British Columbia (BC), two private colleges of naturopathy education offer doctoral qualifications (ND) – the Boucher Institute of Naturopathic Medicine in BC and the Canadian College of Naturopathic Medicine in Ottawa. Both do so under accreditation from the Council on Naturopathic Medical Education and the Association of Accredited Naturopathic Medical Colleges (both privately-funded US bodies). Despite very different educational and accreditation standards compared to other health professionals, and accreditation from unimpressive bodies, many US state health regulators and the BC Health Professions Council have accepted the ND title as a doctoral qualification, again ostensibly on the basis of the entry requirements (a bachelor's degree), length of the programme and credit requirements.

It is worthy of note that the Boucher Institute teaches vitalism, homeopathy, herbalism, acupuncture, electrotherapeutic stimulation, hydrotherapy (including detoxification by colonic irrigation), SMT, craniosacral therapy, the five elements theory of health (wood, fire, water, metal and earth), energy healing and nutritional supplementation. Despite this, it claims to have 'a unique biomedicine-oriented curriculum' with a 95% success rate on licensing exams. More worryingly it also teaches a course on emergency medicine, despite its instructors having no clinical medical experience in this field whatsoever.

Naturopaths receive no clinical experience in acute care, the emergency room or any hospitals during their education. Like chiropractors, naturopaths undertake all of their clinical training in labs or private clinics, and under the mentorship of other naturopaths, and so have minimal exposure to acute care or diverse patient populations. Despite the highly dubious educational and accreditation standards for a doctoral qualification, and the wide range of non-science therapeutics taught, the BC Health Professions Council and other jurisdictions have accepted the ND title as a valid doctoral qualification, and naturopaths like chiropractors may legally use the title 'doctor'.

Naturopathic whistle blowers

Former naturopath Britt Hermes, and former naturopath instructor Mathew Brignall of the US private alternative medicine college, Bastyr University, have raised numerous concerns with the quality of the educational preparation of naturopaths. Hermes has noted: 'The requirements for matriculating into naturopathic school are extremely lax. A bachelor's degree may be required. There are usually low or no GPA minimums. A graduate exam, such as the GRE, and the medical school entrance exam, MCAT, is not required.' She also affirms that naturopathic training involves significantly less clinical training than is experienced by medical students, and that the curriculum 'emphasises branches of alternative medicine that have been debunked (i.e. homeopathy, energy healing), are unproven (i.e. botanical therapies), or even dangerous (i.e. ozone therapy)'. Having experienced both alternative and conventional university graduate education, she has confirmed that the basic science courses taught in naturopathic schools are entry-level courses and not on a par with the rigorous science-based courses taught in medical schools.[378]

Hermes began to question naturopathy after her experiences working in an Arizona Clinic in 2014 where she was treating cancer patients with a herbal supplement called Ukrain (an extract of the herb, greater celandine – *Chelidonium majus*). Shipments of the drug regularly arrived at the clinic and, oddly, cancer patients would pay for their treatments in cash. One day the shipment had not arrived and Hermes brought the matter to the attention of the senior naturopath at the clinic. He informed her that he suspected the FDA had confiscated the shipment, and she became suspicious that she was working in a practice that was illegally importing and injecting cancer patients with a drug not approved by the FDA. Upon researching this, she confirmed that Ukrain was not FDA-approved, and realised that it was potentially a federal crime to administer such a drug to cancer patients. 'Once I realised that, everything changed virtually overnight,' she says. She spent much of the weekend on the Internet reading critiques of her own profession. 'By Monday morning I had hired a lawyer and I quit the practice.'[379] Like Simon Singh, after her criticism of naturopathy and of Bastyr University, Hermes received a cease-and-desist letter over claimed defamatory remarks from their lawyer in 2017. She was also sued for defamation by the Arizona naturopath Colleen Huber over opinions expressed about the dubious treatments and human subjects research at her cancer clinic in Arizona and over suspicions that Huber was cybersquatting the domains BMHermes.com and BrittHermes.com in order to redirect them to naturopathic websites. Huber lost the case, which she had brought in a German court to take advantage of German defamation laws in 2019.[380] Hermes was joint winner of the 2018 John Maddox Prize, awarded by the organisation Sense about Science in recognition of her advocacy and writing on evidence-based medicine. Judge Colin Blakemore stated that: 'Hermes's story is one of exceptional courage.'

I asked long-experienced naturopath and former Bastyr University faculty member, Mathew Brignall, what his thoughts were on the current state of the naturopathic profession. He said:

As a naturopathic doctor and educator, I have had the unique experience of having a front row seat as alternative medicine went from a small group working largely within the structure of the health care system to becoming a full-blown counter-culture of stuff and nonsense. I used to teach at a school that gave degrees in alternative medicine at some $450 per credit hour, but can reveal the secrets for much less. Health gurus broke my field of study and turned it from an optimistic and vibrant field into a laughing stock and a menace to public health.

The physician KC Atwood concluded that the training of naturopathic doctors in North America amounted to a small fraction of that of medical doctors who practise primary care. They undertake no hospital-based supervised training, and he concluded that their literature '…is replete with pseudoscientific, ineffective, unethical and potentially dangerous practices'.[241]

There are also other routes to naturopathic qualifications. For those not wishing to engage in such lengthy and costly preparation to be a naturopath, L'Institut de Formation Naturopathique (IFN) is an online college that offers online naturopathy certification (although not an ND) for $1200 and graduates are able to become practising members of the ÉducoSanté Society (a Montreal-based alternative medicine society) as well as the International Association of Naturopathy Hygionomists (AINH), which also seems to be affiliated with the institute. This was the certification gained by Brittany Auerbach, aka Montreal Healthy Girl, an infamous YouTube video blogger with no other professional health qualifications, who in 2018 advised cancer patients to forego conventional medicine to try her alternative nutritional therapies. She has also posted anti-vaccination blogs. Amongst other incorrect nonsense, she also posted material claiming that viruses in vaccines inflame brain tissue, and that children with autism may have parasites 'longer than their bodies' that are expelled when they do cleanses.[270, 381, 382]

The alternative-diploma mill

In fact, the online alternative medicine qualification industry is a thriving business. You can gain accreditation in a variety of health disciplines very easily. Currently, you can earn a Doctor of Naturopathic Medicine, Advanced Diploma, or a Reiki Master qualification for $12.99 in a six-hour online course at www.udemy.com. You can add a Crystal Reiki Master or an Animal Reiki practitioner for another $12.99 each. Alternatively, an online Natural Nutrition certificate is available from the Canadian School of Natural Nutrition for around $800, or their more advanced diploma for $5725 CAD. Entry simply requires a high-school diploma *or* to be 19 years of age or older.

None of these qualifications has any recognition by public educational or health institutions, but they do allow deceptive practitioners to post diploma-mill qualifications on their walls, and appear knowledgeable. For those with more disposable income it is also possible to acquire a two-year online PhD in something quite esoteric such as 'Transformative Studies' from the California Institute of Integral Studies for around $50,000 USD (a New-Age private college which had its accreditation of its psychology doctorate revoked in 2011 by the American Psychological Association). You can even present such eminent academic qualifications for recognition as a doctoral professional to teach in a local college. The founder of a local college Therapeutic Touch programme did so for a number of years before retiring. The Langara College based here in BC offers a Therapeutic Touch Practitioner certificate, costing around $2500 to acquire. When I enquired some years back of their rationale for teaching unscientific therapeutics in a publicly-funded college (in what appears to be a course preparing people to be professional faith healers), I was advised by their head of department that it was because there was good demand and it was profitable. Their dean also defended the practice on business grounds. It seems some schools simply don't corroborate international qualifications, or are happy to accept them at face value if it means they can run profitable programmes.

I have had the debate with several alternative practitioners over the years, who claim they are doctorly-prepared primary healthcare practitioners, one of whom described arguments about the quality of their education as 'fantasy'. A significant problem here is if you have spent $140,000 USD on tuition for your chiropractic qualification, for example, any critique of its validity and quality is likely to offend and be met with firm resistance. After all, any agreement with such arguments is likely to impact both credibility and income. This is another significant issue and as alternative medicine colleges are not transparent in sharing their curricula or examination methods, and what they are teaching is not independently accredited, the actual level of practice and content being taught is very difficult to determine. Many colleges also market their alternative programmes, promoting totally unrealistic salaries for graduates after they have completed them. All this has left us in a confused state of affairs as far as what qualifications actually mean, and has left students at the mercy of colleges offering expensive qualifications that may be practically useless without resorting to deceptive practices to build up clientele once qualified.

Overall, there is a whole spectrum of qualifications available in the sector with widely varying costs, standards and accreditation associated with them. This is a major problem for the public when attempting to establish the credibility of any alternative medicine practitioner or teacher. It is very difficult to tell if the qualifications are actually worth anything, and even where 'accredited', this may not have any clinical value. Practically these qualifications may have little or no value. You can study levitation in a four-year accredited doctoral programme, but the likelihood you will actually be able to ascend to the skies unaided at the end of it is zero.

Despite the attempts of some alternative medicine professions to align themselves more with scientific biomedicine in their education (such as in the case of chiropractic) and the rise of integrative medical centres, the world of alternative medical qualifications remains a morass of dubious practices. Even though there are many examples of people who are not what they appear to be in the conventional medical world, you are much more likely to encounter deceptive qualifications and outright fake qualifications in the world of alternative medicine.

Chapter 18

It's science, but not as we know it

Another problem for people considering alternative healthcare is understanding the claims of scientific evidence often asserted by these providers. Scientific research is not always simple to understand, and whilst many alternative medicine practitioners will state their practices are beyond conventional science, many more claim scientific support for their work when in fact there is none or, if any research does exist, it is highly suspect. Advertisers have long known that claiming your product or service is scientific makes it far more marketable. One only has to look at the preponderance of sexy scientific claims accompanying cosmetic advertisements on the television, with images of scientists in white coats in glossy high-tech labs, to observe this. Another example is the almost universal use of the stethoscope in medical marketing imagery. However, much of alternative medicine research also relies on very bad science and pseudoscience.

Gross exaggerations of evidence

It is often falsely claimed that a therapy is 'evidence-based' or it is an effective intervention for a condition where in reality there is no evidence of effectiveness. To do so represents a form of deception, and practitioners should not be making such claims under current advertising standards in both Europe and North America. Such misleading claims are regularly highlighted by scientists on social media. For example, Clifford Hardick, the past president and current member of the regulatory board that oversees more than 5000 chiropractors in Ontario, Canada, delivered a speech to his colleagues at a conference in Atlanta in 2017 in which he claimed success in treating children with developmental problems such as autism.[383] There is no evidence that chiropractic can help autism, or even any clearly defined theoretical mechanism how it might do so; this is pure marketing hyperbole.

Another chiropractic researcher, Greg Kawchuk of the University of Alberta, claims that 'his team has proven that manipulation does work for patients with acute low back pain – a significant discovery that reinforces the validity of a primary chiropractic technique'. However, at the time of writing he has published no studies conclusively demonstrating this, and no independent scientific work supports that assertion. Unfortunately, there are innumerable other cases of the exaggeration of positive effects in alternative healthcare, and studies that demonstrate what we call confirmation bias – the tendency to search for, interpret, favour, and use information in a way that confirms or supports one's prior beliefs or values. This is, of course, also seen in biomedical science, but due to well-established rigorous controls of study design, ethical approval, independent validation, confirmation, replication and dissemination processes, is less of a problem there. Alternative healthcare is more of a closed shop, where we often see studies undertaken by those with a particular stake in a treatment, designing or performing them in such a way that positive outcomes are much more likely, and with no external independent validation.

Two Therapeutic Touch therapy (TT) outfits here in British Columbia (BC) were found culpable of misleading advertising on the grounds of inaccuracy, and misleading scientific claims following complaints to Advertising Standards Canada (ASC) in 2016. These were the BC Therapeutic Touch Network Society (the organisation promoting TT in BC), and a clinic in Delta, BC, who had a TT practitioner making unsubstantiated health benefit claims in a local newspaper advertisement. They had claimed TT would help people heal and recover faster, hasten post-operative recovery, balance emotions, relieve depression, assist cancer patients to deal with the side-effects of therapy, boost the immune system, assist in recovery from addictions, assist in pre- and postnatal care and calm anxiety and aggression in patients suffering from various forms of dementia. The BCTTNS appealed the finding and claimed that: 'Over 50 doctoral and 20 post-doctoral studies are available through the (BC Therapeutic Touch) Network, which have proven the effectiveness of Therapeutic Touch.'

I and some colleagues explored this evidence and found that there were indeed plenty of studies and dissertations available, but all were of very poor quality, mostly from private diploma-mill colleges, and all those which made positive claims of effectiveness exhibited a high risk of bias. Most of the studies were published with very small sample sizes in self-interest, low-impact journals (such as the *Journal of Alternative and Complementary Medicine*) or had very poor experimental design that was virtually guaranteed to provide a positive result. Some were opinion pieces, and others simply nonsensical postmodern theoretical ramblings. There was no high-quality, independently verified or replicated work, and in fact the higher-quality studies that BCTTNS cited were ones that actually concluded TT had no effect. I asked Dr Edzard Ernst, a well-known alternative medicine researcher I have cited earlier, to take a look at the work, and he too concurred it was very poor quality. The ASC found against BCTTNS and upheld the complaint, finding that:

The efficacy claims regarding Therapeutic Touch therapy were medical treatment outcomes for serious diseases and conditions that readers of the advertisement would associate, in whole or part, with conventional medicine practices and procedures. However, Council found that the studies and research provided by the advertiser were insufficient to support such claims. It concerned Council that the claims and statements could cause readers to believe that Therapeutic Touch therapy was an alternative to medical treatment for some of the identified conditions.

A growing phenomenon

There is no doubt the alternative medicine universe is expanding. As published scientific studies continue to show alternative medicine to be generally ineffective, contrariwise more North Americans are using them than ever. Alternative medicine is even being adopted more widely in mainstream institutions as integrative medicine as a response to popular demand. The fact is people like the positive, more personal approach employed in this industry. Part of the reason for this growth is undoubtedly the historical failure of modern medicine to provide a positive and inclusive experience to patients. This is rapidly changing, and the move away from the old paternalistic medical approach is well underway. There is still a long way to go, and for most of us our GP surgeries and waiting rooms still look as institutional as they did in the 1950s. Nevertheless, although a (usually rushed) visit to the doctors or hospital is never likely to be seen as an enjoyable experience, making it less unpleasant and a more positive patient-centred experience; is certainly possible and something nurses have been attempting to provide in the system for some time.

In an attempt to be seen as less politically divisive, and more inclusive, even the World Health Organization (WHO) and Pan American Health Organization in its 2014–2023 strategy, encouraged the integration of traditional medicine and complementary medicine (including homeopathy) into national health systems. However, after a backlash to this from many international scientific quarters, the WHO then clarified that it didn't support things like homeopathy to treat infectious diseases such as tuberculosis, malaria, influenza or infant diarrhoea. Nevertheless, given the evidence put forward for alternative medicine on the larger scale and its growing popularity, this raises the question of why alternative medicine is still 'alternative'.

If TCM or homoeopathy were more effective than conventional medicine, one might reasonably expect China and India (where homeopathy is widespread) to have established excellent control of common illnesses through their extensive use. Unfortunately, this is not the case: chronic obstructive pulmonary disease (COPD) is increasing massively in China, with 8.6% of the country's adult population (almost 100 million people) now suffering from this chronic lung disease, and India remains the country with the highest burden of tuberculosis. Of course, there are multiple socio-economic factors behind these statistics, but the claims that low-cost and easily available natural alternative medicines can easily treat these conditions are not supported by public health figures or scientific research.

Given the ancient roots claimed for many of these therapies, and their asserted effectiveness it would seem odd that these are not now the dominant forms of healthcare across the globe. Nevertheless, amongst proponents, this point usually provokes the Big-Pharma/medicine suppression of alternative medicine conspiracy argument (see page 89). In North America, people spend the same amount of money on pharmaceutical products as they do on unregulated nutritional supplements, vitamins and other herbal or natural remedies, and as we have seen, the alternative healthcare industry has become a multi-billion-dollar business in itself.[97, 98]

Additionally, social media in our age of instant mass-communication has supported the growth of many conspiracy theories from alternative healthcare proponents, and with them an increasing distrust of scientific medicine. This has undoubtedly helped support the growth of the alternative healthcare industry. The latest COVID-19 pandemic scepticism and denial theories going around provide key examples. Unfortunately, this has brought with it a rise in deceptive health practices and the return of quackery, fake-medicine and health scams in volumes probably unwitnessed since the turn of the last century. Regrettably, we are living through a new heyday for snake-oil sales and the alternative medicine business has become a major player here. Many of these remedies are also promoted by self-styled celebrity health gurus who have seized the opportunity to expand their influence, and we will explore this further in the next section.

Section V

Health, fame and fortune

Chapter 19

Success and irrationality

The deluge of daft health advice from the rich and famous seems to be an increasing social phenomenon. There are numerous examples of sensationalist claims of health interventions by the rich and famous and the promotion of mysterious health practices by otherwise rational, intelligent and talented individuals. These often include the promotion of novel miraculous foods or products, and the characterisation of established scientific healthcare as flawed, blinkered, corrupt, frozen or even conspiratorial. You only have to pick up a lifestyle magazine to find examples, with Oprah Winfrey and Dr Oz championing the latest nutritional fads, Jessica Biel and Jenny McCarthy arguing anti-vaccination rhetoric, or Deepak Chopra suggesting health is all a state of mind and nothing objectively exists outside of our consciousness. All these examples illustrate the appeal of celebrity and tend to provide simple solutions to complex health problems. However, these folks do hold great social influence. Oprah Winfrey has 42 million followers on Twitter, more than the population of Canada. So, what drives these bizarre behaviours, and why do so many people look to social gurus and celebrities to guide their health practices rather than to health professionals?

The Nobel disease

Many people are surprised to learn that a number of Nobel Prize winners have gone on to act completely senselessly after receiving the award. The Nobel Prize is perhaps the most notable recognition of scientific achievement and is awarded to scientists who have advanced their fields in ground-breaking ways. However, having received the prize, some of these influential laureates have gone off the rails. In fact, this has happened so frequently it has become known as 'Nobel disease', the tendency of Nobel Prize-winning scientists to endorse or perform research in pseudoscientific areas in their later years. There are numerous examples. The following are a few of the most well known. These are a mixture of unfounded 'magical thinking' and refusal to accept scientific evidence (both forms of self-deception) and in only one case, apparent deliberate deception. However, because of the eminence of the individuals expressing these beliefs their ideas have gained far more credence than would otherwise have been the case.

The French surgeon **Alexis Carrel** (1873–1944) won the Nobel Prize in Physiology or Medicine in 1912. His Nobel biography references his pioneering vascular surgical techniques, academic achievements and distinguished service in World War I, and his several famous books. However, he also had a fervent belief in telepathy, mysticism and clairvoyance, and even expressed a desire to move to South America to become a dictator at one time! Carrel argued passionately in favour of eugenics and praised Germany for its 'energetic measures against the propagation of the defective, the mentally diseased, and the criminal'. He also insisted that there was a major error in the US Constitution revolving around the issue of equality: 'The feebleminded and the man of genius should not be equal before the law,' he wrote.

Another example is **William Shockley** who invented the transistor with colleagues John Bardeen and Walter Brattain;

he received the Nobel Prize for this work in 1956. Later, his Shockley Semiconductor Laboratory set up in California became the first establishment to work on semiconductors in what is now known as Silicon Valley. However, later in his career, Shockley proposed the idea that people with low IQs were a social burden and should be paid to undergo voluntary sterilisation. Most of these people, he claimed, were African Americans. He stated: '… the major cause of the American Negros' intellectual and social deficits is hereditary and racially genetic in origin and, thus, not remediable to a major degree by practical improvements in the environment.'

Kary Mullis was the Nobel Laureate for Chemistry in 1993 for his work developing the polymerase chain reaction (PCR) technique as a cheap and effective way to copy large amounts of DNA. Following this he became a denier of the proven link between HIV and AIDS and a climate-change denier, and also argued that astrology should be included in mainstream education. His autobiography also notes that he is '…perhaps the only Nobel laureate to describe a possible encounter with aliens'.[385]

Another more recent example of Nobel disease is the pharmacologist **Louis J Ignarro** who, along with two other researchers (Robert Furchgott and Ferid Murad), won the Nobel Prize in Physiology or Medicine in 1998 for their work on nitric oxide as a signalling substance in the cardiovascular system. This work helped the development of successful new drugs to treat cardiovascular disease. However, Ignarro then went on to work as a paid consultant for a suspect nutritional supplement business called Herbalife. In 2003 he became a member of the company's Scientific Advisory Board, apparently, collaborating on nutritional supplement development for cardiovascular and athletic performance supplements, which is a very grey area of nutritional science. This company has since come under significant criticism from numerous quarters, including from the

New York Post and US Federal Trade Commission (FTC) for being primarily a pyramid marketing scheme. In 2016 it paid a $200 million USD fine as part of a settlement with the FTC.[386] In 2019, the US Securities and Exchange Commission (SEC) announced that Herbalife would pay $20 million USD to settle charges of making false and misleading statements about its business model and operations in China.[387]

Herbalife had reportedly paid Ignarro and his consulting firm over $15 million USD in fees over the years, and yet in 2003 he published a positive study in the *Proceedings of the National Academy of Sciences,* on the value of the ingredients found in their Niteworks product without disclosing his conflict of interest with the company.[388] This prompted the University of California Los Angeles (UCLA) to start their own investigation and, whilst they acknowledged this was unfortunate, no disciplinary action was taken against him. The journal editor, however, admitted that this undisclosed conflict of interest was a mistake and issued a correction to the paper.[389] Ignarro still appears in videos promoting Herbalife products, and is a frequent speaker at their promotional events. At the time of writing, he also remains Professor Emeritus of Pharmacology at the UCLA School of Medicine's Department of Molecular and Medical Pharmacology.

Yet another interesting case is that of the French virologist **Luc Montagnier**, who in 2008 won the Nobel Prize in Physiology or Medicine along with Françoise Barré-Sinoussi for the discovery of the human immunodeficiency virus (HIV). In 2010 he then shocked colleagues at a scientific meeting for Nobel laureates when he suggested a novel method for detecting viral infections that claimed the existence of quantum imprints from teleported DNA that reflected the basic principles of homeopathy (see page 151). He outlined work he had published in a 2009 paper.[390] While homeopaths around the world claimed his research validated homeopathy, scientific colleagues around the world greeted it with severe criticism and disbelief.[391] Biology Professor Paul Z

Myers described the paper as 'unprofessional', and as well as noting numerous significant methodological flaws in the work, criticised the publication process as having an 'unbelievable' turnaround time.[392] The paper was submitted on 3 January 2009, revised on 5 January 2009, and then accepted for publication on 6 January 2009. For any academic, that is an astonishingly quick process, as it normally takes months to get a paper reviewed and published; my last one took a month just to get the editor to assign reviewers! As it turned out, the chairman of the publishing journal's editorial board was actually Luc Montagnier himself.[393]

Whilst Luc Montagnier was praised by Deepak Chopra (see page 252), his work remains unreplicated, and he has since made other bizarre claims unsupported by any quality scientific evidence about electromagnetic waves from bacteria causing autism.[394, 395] This theory is promoted by his latest research group, Chronimed, and claimed as a basis for the long-term antibiotic treatment of autism and chronic Lyme disease. More recently, in 2020 he claimed that the COVID-19 pandemic was man-made in a laboratory as the result of an attempt to create a vaccine for HIV / AIDS. These ideas have been firmly refuted as pseudoscientific and lacking any evidence by researchers in these fields, although seized on by conspiracy theorists like Del Bigtree (see page 241) to support their arguments.

Probably the best-known Nobel winner who then went on to promote unfounded ideas was **Linus Pauling** (1901–1994), the only person ever to win two unshared Nobel Prizes. He received these awards for chemistry in 1954 and for peace in 1962. Pauling contributed hugely to the development of chemical theories, and was one of the founders of the fields of quantum chemistry and molecular biology. His impact in healthcare, however, has been more problematic. In his later life Pauling was largely responsible for the unproven theory that megadose vitamin C is effective against colds and other illnesses, including cancer. This is a theory still championed by naturopaths and even some physicians to this day. However, Lining's original ideas have now been fairly conclusively demonstrated as incorrect and his results based on flawed studies. Vitamin C has not proved to be a magic bullet for cancer after 60 years of research, although many integrative physicians, naturopaths and nutritionists continue to argue for the efficacy of mega doses of vitamin C against cancer.[396, 397, 398]

In 1968, Pauling advanced the idea that people needed nutrients in much greater amounts than the existing recommended dietary allowances (RDAs). He also suggested that large doses of certain vitamins and minerals might well be appropriate to treat some forms of mental illness. He termed this approach 'orthomolecular' (creating the optimal molecular environment for body cells through the introduction of natural substances). After that, he expanded the list of illnesses he believed could be influenced by his orthomolecular therapy, and in 1970 announced that taking 1000 mg of vitamin C daily would reduce the incidence of the common cold by 45% for most people. In 1976, Pauling and Dr Ewan Cameron, a Scottish physician, reported that of 100 terminal cancer patients treated with 10,000 mg of vitamin C daily, the majority survived three to four times longer than similar patients who did not receive vitamin C supplements.

The Mayo Clinic conducted three double-blind studies involving a total of 367 patients with advanced cancer to test Pauling and Cameron's ideas. Their studies, performed in 1979, 1983 and 1985, found that patients given 10,000 mg of vitamin C daily actually did no better than those given a placebo. Pauling criticised these studies, suggesting that the chemotherapy treatments the patients had also received had interfered with the effects of vitamin C (even though he had previously stated that vitamin C therapy could be used alongside conventional cancer treatments).[399, 400, 401, 402] At the time Pauling had also struck up a working relationship with a controversial chiropractor named

Irwin Stone who championed some other unconventional nutritional theories, including claiming that scurvy was not a dietary issue.

By 2010 a number of other studies on medical use of megadose vitamin C had been published, and theoretical propositions for the possible effect of megadose vitamin C were being discussed, such as its action as an antioxidant, an agent in collagen and catecholamine synthesis, or as a modulator of immune cell biology. However, these were all postulated from preclinical (in vitro and animal) studies. In 2007, US researchers showed that vitamin C could inhibit the growth of some tumours in mice. However, they also noted that these findings were at an early stage and didn't say how or if they would translate to humans.[403] Despite these initially promising findings, a 2010 review of all the clinical research to date with some 1609 cancer patients concluded that '...we still do not know whether vitamin C has any clinically significant antitumor activity. Nor do we know which histological types of cancers, if any, are susceptible to this agent. Finally, we don't know what the recommended dose of vitamin C is, if there is indeed such a dose, that can produce an anti-tumour response.'[399]

Although Pauling's megadose vitamin claims lacked convincing evidence and appeared to be based on an inadequate statistical analysis of data from a case series, there is still a strong belief that megadose vitamin C is a sound cancer treatment, even though we actually know no such thing. This seems to be mainly a result of his eminence as a scientist, rather than a theoretical breakthrough. The impact of this is that the clinical value of vitamin C continues to be explored in scientific experiments today, but currently with no good work demonstrating efficacy.[18, 404, 405, 406, 407] We also know that megadose vitamin C can produce kidney stones and damage,[373] and interfere with radiotherapy and chemotherapy treatments. Some studies have even suggested that vitamin C might accelerate cancer growth. Currently, there is ongoing clinical work, but the hopes for vitamin C as a cancer cure remain unfulfilled, and the results of research are very mixed. The current state of research does not support the clinical use of megadose vitamin C for cancer. Currently the National Health Service (NHS UK) and Cancer Research UK do not approve the use of high-dose vitamin C as a treatment for cancer, and neither does Health Canada or the US FDA. Nevertheless, many naturopaths and some medical clinics still sell megadose vitamin C therapy (often administered intravenously) to cancer patients.

Pauling also contributed to the health food industry's successful campaign to weaken FDA consumer protection laws for nutritional supplements. Today, Pauling's unfounded advice about vitamin supplements continues to be problematical, and a good example of how 'eminence-based medicine' (rather than evidence-based medicine) can affect modern healthcare practice.[18, 374, 408]

The curious case of the 'inventor of email'

One recent example of an intelligent and talented person acting rather irrationally is that of Dr Shiva Ayyadurai, a Massachusetts Institute of Technology (MIT) graduate with an engineering Master's degree and a PhD in Biological Engineering. He has suggested in public media that the UK doctor Andrew Wakefield (see page 261) was actually persecuted for his work trying to link autism to vaccination. He has also claimed links between genetically modified organisms (GMOs) and autism, none of which has been demonstrated. In 2015 he also published a widely discredited study claiming that there were high levels of formaldehyde in GMO soy. More recently he has become notable for his controversial claim to be the 'inventor of email', which he even cites in his Twitter account tagline. He certainly did work to develop an early office email system at the end of the 1970s, which he patented in 1982 under the name EMAIL. However, it is pretty much universally accepted that Ray Tomlinson is credited as the inventor of email as part of a programme for ARPANET in 1971, and by 1978 (when Ayyadurai was working on it) most of the things we take for granted in modern email systems were already in use (e.g. headers and even attachments). Thomas Haigh, a historian of information technology at the University of Wisconsin, noted that: 'Ayyadurai is, to the best of my knowledge, the only person to have claimed for him or herself the title "inventor of email".' Whilst EMAIL was very impressive for a teenager's work, it contained no features that were not present in previous electronic mail systems and seems to have had no obvious influence on later systems.[384] Electronic mail services were widely used and were even commercially available long before 1980. Intriguingly, he also only started making this claim about 30 years after his EMAIL programme was developed.

Chapter 20

Health and celebrity

There are also plenty of examples of celebrities making highly speculative health claims, and the ability to build commercial success from celebrity health-guru status has proved very lucrative for many. The following are probably some of the best-known examples.

Oprah Winfrey

Oprah Winfrey is undoubtedly a talented actor and business-woman; she is also one of the most famous people in the world. After she delivered an epic Golden Globes speech in 2018 there was even discussion of her running for US President in 2020. Glitterati from Ivanka Trump to Ron Howard have praised her inspiring oratory, whilst other celebrities like Lady Gaga said they would vote for her if she were to run. Even some political observers agreed she would be a serious contender. However, she has also endorsed and supported much dubious health advice over the years, and also helped create some dubious health celebrities.

In 2004, she introduced Dr Oz in his first appearance on the *Oprah Winfrey Show*, where he was denoted as 'America's Doctor' (a moniker which he has since trademarked). Oprah's approval helped Oz get his own TV show by 2009. As a regular medical expert appearing on 'Oprah', he has used the platform to back a range of weird and wonderful health practices (including faith healing) and promote his own brand (see page 249). Her instincts about his celebrity potential have certainly proved correct in that he has become immensely popular, and his multi-million-dollar media empire now extends to books, magazines, radio, websites and television.

Another celebrity doctor whom she helped create was 'Dr Phil' Phil McGraw (who holds a PhD in clinical psychology, and is no longer licensed as a psychologist in his home state of Texas, or in any other state in the USA). He also got his start on Oprah's show, after meeting the TV star in 1995. By the late 1990s he had started appearing on her show as a life coach, and in 2002 he launched his own eponymous show. Like Dr Oz, McGraw has been reprimanded for using his celebrity status to enable ethically debateable practices. In January 2008, McGraw visited pop star Britney Spears in hospital, apparently in an attempt at getting Spears and her parents to take part in an 'intervention' on the Dr Phil television show. Immediately afterwards, he issued public statements about Spears that were rapidly condemned as a violation of their trust by her family. In 2016, he was criticised for marketing diabetes pharmaceuticals through paid sponsors that were presented as friendly advice about the disease from a trusted source. A 2018 investigation by the *Boston Globe* also uncovered some unethical practices from his show, including giving vodka to a guest who was battling alcoholism.

Oprah also presented shows promoting faith healing with the discredited Brazilian faith-healer and psychic surgeon, João Teixeira de Faria, known as 'John of God', in 2010 and 2013. This faith healer promoted magical healing activities ranging from putting forceps in the nose and random cutting of the flesh, to scraping of the eyeball to cure infections and other problems. Despite having been demonstrated as a complete fraud by the magician James Randi (who provided explanations for his activities as simple parlour tricks in 2005), he also became the subject of what is considered probably the largest sexual-abuse scandal in Brazil in 2018. Twelve women alleged that Faria abused them, which was then followed by more than 300 other complaints of abuse when the story reached the media. He was arrested in December 2018. Unsurprisingly, at the time of writing the relevant Oprah episodes (and nearly all media making references to John of God) have been removed from Oprah's website. However, one video clip still remains, entitled 'Lisa's Search for a Cure' from a 2010 show where a guest describes a nasal probe procedure (forceps inserted into the nose) that he performed on her to cure her health issues.[409]

There are numerous other times when Oprah has promoted dubious health practices on her shows, in a sensationalist daytime reality TV format, rather than any attempt to provide a critical appraisal of novel therapies. These include anti-vaccination activist Jenny McCarthy (see page 255), the actor Suzanne Somers sharing her unusual secrets to staying young (oestrogen cream and huge doses of vitamins), and New-Age doctors such as Dr Christiane Northrup, a gynaecologist who advocated using Qigong (the Chinese alternative medicine practice) to increase 'energy flow' to the vagina and cure female ills, and Dr David L Katz, a defender of homeopathy, who has suggested anecdotes are a good source of medical knowledge. These guests may increase viewing figures as entertainment, but probably do little to help people with real health issues. However, presenting these guests are knowledgeable experts in a populist media format is problematic; promoting unfounded health advice has the potential to do serious harm.

Mehmet Oz

Arguably, one of Oprah Winfrey's most successful health celebrity creations (he has made more than 60 appearances on her show) is

Dr Mehmet Oz, the Turkish-American cardiovascular surgeon. Oz remains a board-certified physician and has been a professor at the Department of Surgery at Columbia University since 2001. He also directs the Cardiovascular Institute and Complementary Medicine programme at New York Presbyterian Hospital (an integrative medicine programme). Despite his earlier successful medical career, Dr Oz embarked on a second career as a health celebrity from 2003 onwards, when he started recommending and promoting a range of bizarre and New-Age remedies and diets in the media, from folk-medicine to astrology. Since 2009 he has had his own TV show and developed a substantial media empire with his website, books, magazines and newspaper columns. As a practising physician he has achieved notable success in this area, and become the king of sensationalist health claims, even though much of his health advice is absurd.

Dr Oz has backed numerous cures which he has said can help people lose weight, from coffee bean extract to the extract of a Southeast Asian fruit named *Garcinia cambogia*, which have been demonstrated as ineffective by numerous nutritional researchers. Based on the results of one poor-quality study on the bean he had read, he declared in a 2012 show that 'You may think magic is make-believe, but this little bean has scientists saying they've found the magic weight-loss cure for every body type'. Criticism of his show was swift after it was subsequently revealed the product was peddled by supplement marketer and frequent show guest Lindsey Duncan, who had a financial stake in the companies making the extract. A class-action lawsuit was filed against Dr Oz (and related corporate entities) in February 2016, alleging that he promoted products such as Labrada Garcinia Cambogia Dual Action Fat Buster and Labrada Green Coffee Bean Extract Fat Loss Optimizer as a 'magic weight-loss cure' and 'revolutionary fat buster' in his media, without sufficient scientific evidence to back up the claims. Without admitting any liability, the defendants reached a $5.25 million USD settlement deal to the class members in 2018. The defendants also promised not to re-air three episodes of the 'Dr Oz Show' that promoted the products, as well as to remove online clips from all three episodes. The study that Oz had cited was also retracted (due to concerns over the data's validity) and, following an investigation by the Federal Trade Commission (FTC), Lindsey Duncan paid $9 million USD to settle with consumers who had purchased the green coffee dietary product.

Oz also heavily promotes spiritualism (and even astrology) in his work, and has brought several self-proclaimed 'spiritual mediums' on to his TV show, where they've done everything from psychic readings to telling audience members how their loved ones actually died. Oz has even suggested that connecting with the dead can help lower stress levels by helping people make peace with their deceased loved ones. Like Oprah, he also helped support the faith-healer John of God in a 2005 ABC television documentary, where he offered inane justifications for John's supposed psychic surgical practices rather than expose them as simple manipulative tricks. In 2011, he invited the faith-healer Dr Issam Nemeh on to his show where the audience was shown several people who claimed to have been healed by him by the laying on of hands. The episode resembles a faith-healing carnival sensation act rather than a serious investigation of the practices.

A 2014 *British Medical Journal* study examined the health claims showcased on 40 randomly selected episodes of the two most popular internationally syndicated health talk shows, the 'Dr Oz Show' and 'The Doctors'. They found that about half of the recommendations either had no evidence behind them or actually contradicted the best available scientific advice.[410] Nevertheless, Dr Oz has turned his controversial media image into a great commercial success by embracing fame and fortune in promoting sensationalist faith-based remedies and, although his business practices have been called out as highly questionable, he has an estimated net-worth of at least $30 million USD. As a testament to the power of celebrity over science, in May 2018, President Donald Trump appointed Oz to be a member of his Council on Sports, Fitness and Nutrition.

Deepak Chopra

Deepak Chopra is another famous doctor and advocate of alternative medicine. Like Dr Oz, he is also beloved by Oprah Winfrey (who also features in the banner on his website) and has become a controversial New-Age guru, and one of the best known and wealthiest figures in alternative medicine. One of the earliest proponents of the meditation trend, his millions of fans regard him as a spiritual leader, a prophet of mindfulness and a New-Age sage. To others, he's a charlatan and pseudoscientist, and a prime exponent of bullshit.

Chopra originally studied medicine in India before emigrating to the United States in 1970 where he completed residencies in internal medicine and endocrinology. As a licensed physician, he was obviously talented and became chief of staff at the New England Memorial Hospital in 1980. After he met the Indian spiritual leader Maharishi Mahesh Yogi in 1985, he resigned his position there and became involved in the Transcendental Meditation movement. Since then, he has written numerous books, and become a promoter of Ayurvedic medicine, the Indian traditional medicine that utilises herbs, massage and diets, based upon the 'seasons of life'. He also has connections to several US universities, including Northwestern and Columbia. He founded the Chopra Center for Wellbeing in southern California, which offers a range of mind-body services. Chopra's website states that people can go there '...to heal their physical pain, find emotional freedom, empower themselves, and connect to their inner spiritual life', but also that a 60-minute massage will cost you $330 USD.

Chopra frequently debates with scientists about health and philosophy in the media, providing faith-based answers to scientific challenges to his ideas, by which simple trick he avoids answering them (except in the most abstract or metaphorical terms). He is renowned for making ludicrously self-evident and tautological statements beloved of postmodern philosophers, such as: 'Attention and intention are the mechanics of manifestation!' and 'Karma is experience, and experience creates memory, and memory creates imagination and desire, and desire creates karma again'. More concerningly, he also advocates unsound ideas about biological and physical science, challenging even some basic assumptions of science, such as Newtonian physics and the concept of evolution, using spiritual arguments.

Deepak Chopra's most excellent adventure

Chopra asserts a personal explanation of quantum mechanics in his books, in that that there is a 'Newtonian' reality where a wave and particle appear to be distinct entities, but that quantum physics connects the Newtonian regime to a hidden mystical region where space and time are unified. He then asserts that an analogous relationship exists with respect to mind and body, which are unified by this mystical region. You may be forgiven if you think this imaginative narrative sounds surprisingly similar to the plots of the 'Bill & Ted' trilogy of films. However, Chopra is not a physicist and, although this simplistic explanation seems appealing, he confuses wave-particle duality with the quantum measurement problem, which is a completely different issue concerned with the effect of sub-atomic measurement.[411] When challenged to provide more precise statements about his 'quantum' processes with clear scientifically valid arguments, Chopra fails to do so and resorts to his usual mystical pleonasms. Noted physicists such as Lawrence Krauss, Sean Carroll and Brian Cox have all analysed Chopra's quantum assertions, and all agree that Chopra's statements about quantum processes (and health) are not supported by modern physics. These assertions are spiritually based and really represent another good example of 'quantum woo' (see page 153).

Chopra also argues that consciousness not only gave rise to the entire universe but also directs evolution, suggesting we are all evolving towards a higher state of consciousness, which conveniently negates the principle of natural selection (something that has actually been scientifically demonstrated). His brand of relativistic philosophy supports practically any idea you wish, including that (as he Tweeted in 2010) his personal meditation caused an earthquake, that the moon doesn't exist unless a person sees it and that you can manipulate reality by thinking about it. The philosophical nature of these arguments makes them impossible to refute. However, the trouble is this type of rationale is very problematic in healthcare as it supports victimary thinking, with blame and self-reproach for virtually every health problem. It promotes the idea that cancer is all in your mind, or that you can heal yourself through strength of thought or that a person can change their DNA and alter their gene expression by accessing their consciousness. The ill person becomes seen as a victim of their own mind, rather than a person who has contracted an illness.

Chopra has also argued that AIDS can be treated with 'Ayurveda's primordial sound'. Taking issue with this in 2003, University of California Professor of Medical Ethics, Lawrence Schneiderman noted ethical issues with his ideas in that, 'To put it mildly, Dr Chopra proposes a treatment and prevention programme for AIDS that has no supporting empirical data.'[412] Currently, there is no significant scientific evidence to show the effectiveness of Ayurveda for the treatment of anything. Some research demonstrates that certain approaches used in Ayurveda are helpful as complementary therapies (e.g. yoga and meditation can relieve stress and anxiety in people living with cancer), but it remains a faith-based discipline rather than an evidence-based one.

These ideas ignore the clear evidence that a lot of illness is completely beyond our control, as illustrated by the sad death of the extremely talented, and very fit, actor Chadwick Boseman, who died from bowel cancer at the age of 42 recently. However, as philosophical and spiritual positions they are scientifically impossible to refute. Like the other examples here, the development of a carefully fashioned celebrity health authority image has resulted in considerable success for Chopra, which some find at odds with his devotion to being a simple spiritual man. His net worth is currently estimated at around $50 million USD, and he recently purchased an exclusive New York condominium for $14.5 million USD where he now resides. As he noted in one interview, 'Spiritual people should not be ashamed of being wealthy'.

Jenny McCarthy

The ex-model and actor Jenny McCarthy rose to prominence in 2007 in the media after claiming that vaccines gave her son autism, and that she was able to 'cure' him through a special diet and supplements, opinions based upon her beliefs and internet searches rather than actual scientific evidence. McCarthy helped the discredited British doctor Andrew Wakefield (see page 261) achieve a voice in the USA and co-authored an anti-vaccination book with him in 2011, called *Callous Disregard*. Oprah Winfrey first provided McCarthy a massive audience via her 2007 TV show where she praised McCarthy's unwillingness to bow to authority, her faith in herself and her use of the Internet as a tool for bypassing society's conventional sources of medical expertise.[413] During the show she suggested that Google was a prime source of her information.

Following her appearance on Oprah, McCarthy was invited

on *Larry King Live* and *Good Morning America* to further spread her anti-vaccine message. Author Seth Mnookin estimates that between the three shows, she reached around 20 million viewers.[413] The WHO now cites the 2019 vaccination crisis as one of the top 10 threats to global health, whilst Oprah's website currently provides a section for McCarthy's autism claims along with her special dietary and (notably incorrect) vaccination advice without any correction or acknowledgment of the problems or inaccuracy of this content.[230, 414]

Gwyneth Paltrow

Of course, no contemporary discussion on health celebrities would be complete without considering Gwyneth Paltrow. Oscar and Golden Globe winning actor and business woman, Gwyneth Paltrow also dived into the celebrity health business. In 2008 she launched *goop*, her New-Age natural health and lifestyle company. Goop has developed into the famous web-based brand, goop.com. According to Paltrow, the name came from someone telling her successful Internet companies have double Os in their name! Goop sells a range of lifestyle products and dispenses New-Age and spiritual advice such as, 'eliminate white foods', and 'nourish the inner aspect'. However, goop's promotion of pseudoscientific and dubious health practices has come under fire from numerous academics, physicians and scientists over the years.

Some of Paltrow's more bizarre health claims have included that she rid her body of parasites by subsisting for eight straight days and nights on a diet of raw goat's milk, and that a herbal vaginal mugwort steam-cleanses the uterus and balances female hormone levels. The goop website has met almost global ridicule for selling exclusive designer health items mainly targeted at women – items such as a $15,000 24-karat gold-plated vibrator, or the more accessibly priced $66 vaginal jade eggs claimed to help strengthen pelvic muscles and improve the female orgasm.

A NASA scientist criticised goop in 2017 for claiming that its Body Vibes healing stickers ($120 for a pack of 24) were made with the conductive carbon material NASA used in space suits to monitor astronauts. Mark Shelhamer, former chief scientist at NASA's human research division, noted this claim was false. He said the suits contained synthetic polymers, spandex and other materials, not carbon. His response to the goop claim was: 'Wow. What a load of BS this is.' Later, goop removed the NASA claim from the website and issued a now standard goop disclaimer statement indicating that the opinions expressed by the experts and companies it uses do not necessarily represent the views of goop.

However, goop continues to market the magic healing stickers on its website, claiming that: 'Human bodies operate at an ideal energetic frequency, but everyday stresses and anxiety can throw off our internal balance, depleting our energy reserves and weakening our immune systems. Body Vibes stickers come pre-programmed to an ideal frequency, allowing them to target imbalances. While you're wearing them – close to your heart, on your left shoulder or arm – they'll fill in the deficiencies in your reserves, creating a calming effect, smoothing out both physical tension and anxiety. The founders, both aestheticians, also say they help clear skin by reducing inflammation and boosting cell turnover.'

There is of course, no good scientific evidence for any of those claims, or any physiological mechanisms by which a non-pharmaceutical sticker applied to the skin can reduce inflammation or boost cellular turnover. This is pure pseudoscientific nonsense designed to sell the product. The US comedian Stephen Colbert even did a sketch on the goop stickers on his show.

Two other significant critics of Paltrow's products have been the Canadian health law professor Timothy Caulfield and San Francisco gynaecologist and obstetrician, Dr Jennifer Gunter.

Caulfield published his bestselling book, *Is Gwyneth Paltrow Wrong About Everything?* in 2016, in which he explored the effects of celebrity culture on the public's understanding of science. Professor Caulfield notes: 'Celebrity culture can be dangerous, make no mistake.' He even tried one of goop's recommended two-day cleansing detox diets as a personal experiment and met in Hollywood with its creator, Dr Alejandro Junger. He reported the regimen was very unpleasant and he had no beneficial results from it.

Dr Gunter has frequently explained why leaving a polished piece of mineral in the vagina is not a good idea as it introduces a serious risk of infection and toxic shock syndrome. She has also clarified that a vaginal steam will do nothing for health and might even be harmful. Similarly, Dr Amos Grunebaum, an obstetrician and gynaecologist at New York Presbyterian Hospital, has said that vaginal douching has long ago found to be one of the worst things a woman can do for her health since it disturbs the natural flora of the vagina, and can promote problems such as urinary tract infections and yeast overgrowth.

In response to these criticisms Paltrow retorted by promoting an article on the goop website in 2017 titled, 'Uncensored: A Word from our Contributing Doctors'. The two physicians recruited by goop who made statements in the article were Dr Steven Gundry and Dr Aviva Romm. Paltrow Tweeted a link to it using Michelle Obama's 2016 statement 'When they go low, we go high'. Evidence-based medicine champion Dr David Gorski could not help but notice in his medical science blog that this seemed a little ironic, given Paltrow's statement on the same issues in a *Hollywood Reporter* interview at the time was: 'If You Want to Fuck with Me, Bring Your A Game.'

The article implied that her critics (mainly targeting Dr Gunter) were anti-feminist, and negatively influencing women's rights to control their own sexuality. Dr Gunter had actually challenged the inaccuracy of the marketing claims for some of goop's products and the potential risks to women's health for some of the promoted practices. One goop story that Gunter had criticised suggested that bra-wearing could increase the chance of breast cancer, when research suggests that breast size is associated with breast cancer risk and not the use of brassieres. Goop's concerns here have not stopped them selling a range of designer bras for $84-$740 USD a throw. Furthermore, the majority of goop's products are targeted at affluent younger women using emotional marketing techniques, and goop would seem to be exploiting the fact that this demographic are the main purchasers of alternative health products.[21]

As Dr Gorski observed in his blog, although goop's Dr Gundy was once an academic surgeon, he had abandoned academia to undertake private practice and sell nutritional supplements. Gundy promotes the theory that the plant proteins called lectins (found in grains, beans, nuts, fruits, eggplant, tomatoes, potatoes and dairy) are the cause of many modern illnesses, including obesity, gastrointestinal issues, autoimmune disorders and allergies. Not surprisingly, the evidence for this is slim, and the majority of other nutritional scientists do not concur. Likewise, Dr Aviva Romm (goop's other health expert), a midwife and herbalist who became a physician, now runs a business selling books, supplements and online courses that make vague claims about restoring women's health from a range of symptoms. Most of these she attributes to 'adrenal fatigue', a diagnosis that other medical specialists, including the US Endocrinology Society, do not recognise, and thyroid disease. These goop doctors are, in effect, both fringe-physicians who endorse New-Age beliefs and sell their own products (which are promoted through goop) rather than respected independent scientific authorities.

Goop's standard disclaimer (which looks as if it were crafted by their legal counsel) is now applied to virtually all of their wellness products and web advice pages on the site. In other words, it suggests they are absolving themselves of any responsibility for the validity of the health claims or advice given on their site that might help sell their products. They might as well write 'none of the content on goop may of course be true'.

However, none of this has dented goop's ongoing success as a business. It is now running health workshops or 'summits' as they are hyped to be. At the time of writing, the last three-day 'in goop health' summit in London, UK in June 2019 sold tickets at $1000 a throw for one day, or $4500 for the whole weekend's events (including two nights' accommodation). The most expensive weekend packages reportedly sold out rapidly. In 2020, due to the COVID-19 pandemic, they were offering one online, featuring Ayurvedic, energy healing and Gaga (a form of Israeli dance) experts, and oddly the US actor Laura Dern for some reason. The US content passes priced at $200 a throw also sold out.

Chapter 21

The anti-vaccination crisis and celebrities

One example that illustrates the power of celebrity social influence was the role of celebrity influence in the 2019 vaccination crisis. The Wellcome Trust Global Health Monitor study of 2018 reported that declining confidence in vaccination had become a growing problem in many global regions, whilst as previously noted, the World Health Organization lists vaccine hesitancy as one of the top 10 threats to global health.[17, 415] Vaccines protect billions of people around the world and have completely eradicated some diseases, such as smallpox; immunisation programmes had also been bringing the world close to eliminating others, such as polio. However, other diseases, such as measles, are making a resurgence as people are now avoiding vaccines fuelled by fear and misinformation about their safety.

The anti-vaccine movement and Andrew Wakefield

There has always been some resistance to vaccination policies, but before we explore this further, let us review what we actually know about vaccines and public safety. Vaccines are one of the most successful biotechnologies ever to be invented, and have literally saved millions of lives. A vaccine works by training our immune system to recognise and attack foreign pathogens, either viruses or bacteria, by producing our own antibodies rapidly to protect us from getting infected. To do this, certain parts of the pathogen must be introduced into the body to trigger the immune system to respond. These are called antigens, and the genius of vaccination is that we have devised various methods of training our immune system to recognise and attack the pathogen without us actually having to get the infection itself. There have been numerous ways devised to make vaccines over the years. For example, we can use dead pathogens, where the specific virus or bacteria is inactivated with heat or chemicals and then introduced into the body (e.g. polio). We also have sub-unit and congregate vaccines, where we can isolate a specific substance (usually a protein) from the pathogen that will trigger an immune response and use that (e.g. influenza). Another method is to isolate a form of a toxin secreted by a pathogen, make it safe for the human body and then use that to trigger an immune response (e.g. tetanus). We have newer genetic messaging techniques used to create vaccines. Instead, of injecting foreign parts of the pathogen or toxins, these use DNA or mRNA from the pathogen to teach our own cells how to make a protein (or part of one) to trigger an immune response if the real virus enters our bodies (e.g. a protein found in the SARS-CoV-2 virus). These can usually be made more rapidly than with other approaches, and this is why an early COVID-19 vaccine has been developed using this technique. Lastly, there are recombinant vaccines where scientists are able to take a harmless pathogen, attach the DNA of a more dangerous disease to it, and train the body to recognise and fight both effectively (e.g. rabies).

As we can see, the development of vaccines is a highly technical field, and often some substances such as adjuvants (such as aluminium hydroxide) are added to vaccines in minute quantities (much less than is orally ingested) to make them more effective by causing the immune system to recognise the pathogen more quickly. This avoids people having to have multiple 'booster' vaccinations. Naturally, all this complex biotechnology has made people question how vaccines work, what they contain, why additives are necessary, how they are tested and, most importantly, if they are safe.

The good news is that the UK, Canada and the USA currently have the safest vaccine supplies in history. Longstanding vaccine safety systems developed and improved over the last 50 years ensure that modern vaccines are as safe as possible. Occasionally reactions to vaccines do occur, but in the vast majority of cases these are very minor. If we take the measles vaccine as an example, there were huge health issues with this previously common childhood disease, such as febrile convulsions (2%), pneumonia (10%), clotting problems (1/300 cases), encephalitis (brain swelling – 0.1% or 1/1000 cases) and death in 0.3% (1/3000) cases. In contrast, in terms of risk of taking the vaccine, about 5% of people get a mild fever and general malaise and 5% get swollen glands; transient joint pain occurs in about 25% of post-pubertal women and encephalitis in one in a million cases.[416] This may sound concerning, but compare that to the situation before the measles vaccination programme started in the 1960s, when an estimated three to four million people got measles each year in the USA alone, of which only 500,000 were reported. Among those reported cases, 400 to 500 died, 48,000 were hospitalised and 1000 developed encephalitis from measles. In terms of risk, it is clear that the vaccination risk is minimal compared with the risk of the disease itself.[417] Overall, the dangers one experiences driving to a vaccination appointment are generally far riskier than the vaccination itself, but people still struggle to understand relative risk as it is not an intuitive concept (see relative risk – page 214). This misunderstanding is something anti-vaccination activists frequently use in misinformation campaigns, often with false claims of huge numbers of 'vaccine-injured children' being covered up and millions of injuries being suppressed by the government with conspiracy theories (see page 61).

All in all, researchers have been studying and working with vaccines for decades and we now have excellent data on their safety in use, and new vaccines (including those for COVID-19) have to undergo the same highly rigorous testing as existing vaccines before they are approved for public use. Nevertheless, the complexity of vaccine development and safety monitoring (and the fact that many of the diseases they are for have reduced substantially – see page 261) has meant some people have suggested vaccines are the causative agent for various growing health problems in society (from asthma to autism). As reasonable hypotheses, these have been explored, but none of those has been found to be true. This is a good example of the 'correlation does not equal causation' fallacy. For example, the decrease in pirates on the high seas over the last 300 years is not the cause of global warming, despite there being a demonstrable correlation. Nevertheless, these ideas have taken hold with some people who have anti-science agendas and have led to a modern-day anti-vaccination movement that is highly problematic for public health, and one based almost entirely on the spread of misinformation. As a key example, as I am writing this, Australian anti-vaccination protests are in the news ahead of the roll-out of the COVID-19 vaccination programme there.[418] Much of this concern and mistrust was sparked-off by the dubious research practices of one UK doctor.

The anti-vaccination movement was strongly revitalised following the publication of a paper in *The Lancet* by British doctor and researcher, Andrew Wakefield, in 2008, which proposed a connection between the measles, mumps and rubella (MMR) vaccine and the development of autism in young children. Several studies published later disproved any such causal relationship and a journalistic investigation revealed that there was a conflict of interest with regard to Wakefield's original work, as he had received funding from litigants against vaccine manufacturers (which he did not disclose to either his co-workers or to the medical authorities). By only selecting data that supported their case in the study, Wakefield and colleagues effectively falsified data.[419] For all these reasons, *The Lancet* retracted the study, and its editor declared it 'utterly false'; Wakefield was subsequently struck off the UK Medical Registry for fraud. The verdict declared that he had 'abused his position of trust' and 'brought the medical profession into disrepute' in the studies he carried out.[420] Since then, many large studies have found that vaccines do not cause autism.

Judy Mikovits, the sensational virologist

Another antagonistic figure, who has publicised highly dubious and what appear to be substantially biased claims in this field which have gone viral, is the US virologist Judy Mikovits. She was a largely unknown Research Director at the Whittemore Peterson Institute (WPI), a US private research centre in Nevada, until she co-authored a notorious paper that suggested an obscure agent named xenotropic murine leukaemia virus-related virus (XMRV) caused the condition variously called chronic fatigue syndrome (CFS) or myalgic encephalomyelitis (ME). Other researchers soon questioned the findings, and the paper's claims were found to be incorrect, and it was retracted by the journal that had published it. A further larger scale and more rigorous study confirmed there was no evidence that XMRV was a human pathogen. She eventually left WPI in a very acrimonious parting-of-the-ways involving a lawsuit against her. Since then, she has spread a conspiracy theory, mainly promoted in a sensationalist book she co-authored, *Plague of Corruption: Restoring Faith in the Promise of Science*. She suggested Dr Anthony Fauci (Director of the US National Institute of Allergy and Infectious Diseases – NIAID) directed a cover-up of research work, and 'everybody else' [presumably at WPI] was paid off millions of dollars in funding from him and NIAID.[421] She has also weighed in on the autism debate with controversial theories about causes and treatments and more recently on vaccine safety. Her discredited work and legal issues over the years, like Wakefield, have made her a martyr in the eyes of many anti-vaccine advocates and more recently furthered the spread of misinformation about the COVID-19 vaccine, with unsubstantiated claims regarding its safety. Her latest claims have been made in video clips which YouTube, Facebook, and other platforms have taken down because of inaccuracies.[422]

Celebrity vaccine and infectious disease advice

Despite having no expertise in epidemiology, many celebrities have also joined in support of the anti-vaccination movement and Wakefield, supporting a resurgence of serious infectious diseases that had previously been declining. The list of celebrities and famous people who have publicly expressed concerns over vaccine safety or disparaged vaccination programmes includes Jenny McCarthy (as discussed above), Robert De Niro, Cindy Crawford, Jessica Biel, Jim Carrey, Alicia Silverstone, Charlie Sheen, Kirstie Alley, Juliette Lewis, Kristin Cavallari, Rob Schneider, Bill Maher, Robert F Kennedy Jr and former US President Donald Trump. All of them have made statements indicating significant misunderstanding of the science behind vaccination and vaccine safety testing. Some have also quoted false information promoted by anti-vaccination sites on the web, such as that children receive too many vaccines, overwhelming their immune systems, or that vaccines contain dangerous levels of chemicals such as aluminium, formaldehyde or mercury (which are untrue). As famous people do have significant influence, their impact on the public uptake of vaccination and public health should not be underestimated.

Interestingly, celebrities have been somewhat less forthright in commenting on the current (at time of writing) COVID-19 crisis. Oddly. Gwyneth Paltrow has been notably silent on goop's ability to tackle the issue with their amazing wellness products. 'I've already been in this movie,' she joked recently. 'Stay safe. Don't shake hands. Wash hands frequently.'[423] Paltrow was referring to her role in the 2011 Steven Soderbergh film *Contagion*, where she played a woman who has a fling on her way from a business trip in Hong Kong and catches a highly contagious virus, sparking a pandemic. Her advice seems to fall counter to goop's marketing of numerous immune-boosting supplements and treatments designed to keep you well and prevent infections. However, on the goop webstore it is business as usual, and they are now selling facemasks, a nice Anorak one for $100 CAD, one with a bow for $70 CAD, and a sexy lace-trimmed number for a bargain $60 CAD. Whilst most celebrities, like singers Taylor Swift, Ariana Grande, and actors Tom Hanks and Ryan Reynolds are telling people to take the virus seriously, a minority have taken the stage as COVID sceptics. Dr Drew Pinsky, an American addiction specialist who ran a hit TV and radio advice show called *Loveline*, was flippantly dismissive of the potential threat from COVID-19 in a video interview on social media. He has since apologised for being insensitive. Actor Rob Schneider, the former US TV show *Saturday Night Live* performer, suggested the coronavirus crackdowns were nothing more than political stunts by elected officials seeking the spotlight. The US Fox News host Sean Hannity, also echoed similar comments.[424] These remarks were not well received by the broader media or the public, and most celebrities have probably followed their agent's advice and kept silent on any health issues surrounding the pandemic.

Absolute certainty: Success and tunnel vision

Uncertainty is abundant in our daily lives, and yet one thing that unites all of these famous and celebrity health pundits is their seemingly unshakeable certainty they have found the answer to specific health issues that have somehow eluded science and the general public. In normal life we are uncertain about such things as which restaurant to choose for a meal out, when and if to get married, which school is best for our kids, or who to trust for financial advice. For most of us uncertainty means not knowing something and is a daily part of our lives. In health science, however, uncertainty really means something else, and that is how well something is known. And, therein lies an important difference, especially when trying to understand what is known about healthcare interventions.

Uncertainty in healthcare science

Health is a complex and multifaceted matter and, contrary to media representations, physicians actually cannot advise you with any accuracy exactly how long you have left to live, or if a treatment will work for you or not. We can be certain we will all eventually die, but exactly when is highly unpredictable, even for highly experienced nurses and physicians with a patient who has been diagnosed with a terminal illness. In terms of medicines and surgical interventions we can advise on a likelihood of a successful outcome, but not guarantee it. The problem is in health science there is rarely absolute certainty, but research reduces uncertainty to practical levels where we can judge therapies and medicines to be useful for particular problems or not.

In many cases, theories have been tested and analysed and examined so thoroughly that the chance of them being wrong is minute (such as electromagnetism). This does not mean all aspects of the theory remain completely understood, but if we have a solid theoretical understanding of the mechanisms involved, good quality replicated independent large-scale studies and a well-established history of effective use, we can be fairly certain. At other times, uncertainties linger despite lengthy research and numerous studies (as with acupuncture). Often there is a mass of what we could call 'poor quality' evidence that a treatment works, relying on testimonials, lab or animal studies, and small-scale experiments. Here the use of the therapy remains more based upon faith than science.

In these cases, health professionals make it their job to explain how well something is known or likely to work and when gaps in knowledge exist, and scientists qualify the evidence to ensure others don't form conclusions that go beyond what is known. Science-based health policy-makers use scientific knowledge to avoid making critically wrong choices if the unknowns aren't considered. For instance, public health vaccination policy could risk another epidemic like the Spanish flu of a century ago, if uncertainty in the spread influenza is understated. For these reasons, uncertainty plays a key role in informing public health policy, and generally policy will err on the side of caution, as with the COVID-19 pandemic. Even though it may seem counterintuitive, science-based health professionals like to point out the level of uncertainty. This is because in order to be honest, truthful and valued as trusted health professionals, it is important to be as transparent as possible and it shows how well certain phenomena are understood.

Considering the many sources of scientific understanding, health scientists have sought to provide decision-makers with careful language regarding uncertainty. A 'very likely' outcome, for example, is one that has a greater than 90% chance of occurring. Health data or model projections in which we have 'very high confidence' have at least a nine out of 10 chance of being correct. However, in this culture of transparency where health scientists describe degrees of certainty and confidence in their findings, others (such as fanatics, or those willing to exploit uncertainty for their own benefit) suggest that less than complete certainty is the same as not knowing anything. This is a serious problem in the modern world of the Internet and social media, where self-proclaimed experts with dubious qualifications are ten-a-penny. However, apart from poorly qualified commentators, even well-respected scientists and celebrities are human, and as we have seen, sometimes, they do go off the rails and get things spectacularly wrong. As a ward sister once remarked to me as a junior student nurse: 'Always remember, the hospital is full of highly qualified idiots.'

The Dunning-Kruger effect

One problem is that having gained fame and international celebrity, or established success in one field, there seems a tendency for the human ego to override its normal restraint mechanisms and the person to become convinced of their own infallibility, or that they possess expertise far beyond their actual limits. This type of self-deception takes on a form known by psychologists as the 'Dunning–Kruger effect'. Psychologists Kruger and Dunning tested the psychological theory of illusory superiority in their 1999 cognitive bias study, *Unskilled and Unaware of It*.[425] Here they suggested a cognitive bias exists in which people mistakenly assess their cognitive abilities as being far greater than they actually are. Usually, this term is applied to relatively unqualified people, with no training or expertise who claim expertise in a specific topic they have no education or training in. However, the phenomenon of illusory superiority can also apply to people with personal success in one field who do not recognise their lack of ability or expertise in another. Without self-awareness, such people fail to objectively evaluate their competence or incompetence, and can start to believe in their own mythology, and that only they have superior knowledge to those working in the field.

All of the celebrities examined previously exhibit this behaviour to some degree, promoting outlandish therapies, diets and cures that they are certain work. Possibly, some also believe they are so far above normal human integrity they need not be concerned if their ideas are correct or not (see Harry Frankfurt's ideas on bullshit [see page 39]). In essence, this behaviour represents a form of tunnel vision, and it is likely to be how the Nobel Prize winner Linus Pauling became so fixated on vitamin cures for cancer, or how celebrities like Gwyneth Paltrow, Oprah Winfrey and Dr Oz continue to champion New-Age spiritualist health solutions, going far beyond any evidence of health benefits. They all appear completely certain of their infallibility, and exude a kind of fervent self-confidence that is undoubtedly appealing.

Follow the leader

On the flip side, we have the propensity of people to follow the behaviours of leaders, celebrities and trend-setters. The UK anthropologist Dr Jamie Tehrani has suggested we may even have evolved this way, observing that fame is a powerful cultural magnet. As a social species, we acquire the bulk of our knowledge, ideas and skills by learning from others rather than through individual trial and error. However, we pay far more attention and tend to copy the behaviours demonstrated by famous people more than those of ordinary members of our community.[426] Companies get celebrities to advertise their products because they know that our perceptions of value are actively influenced by fame. He suggests whilst celebrity culture has no doubt been shaped by the modern world, it is rooted in much more basic human instincts, such as social hierarchies based on dominance, and prestige (voluntarily conferred status). The most convincing theory suggests that prestige evolved as part of a raft of psychological adaptations that support cultural learning. For example, our ancestors learned to recognise and reward individuals with superior skills and knowledge (such as in hunting) and learn from them as this was a beneficial behaviour for all. Therefore, we have a socially learned behaviour to follow successful people. Nevertheless, as this strategy is indiscriminate, following modern celebrities' ideas can lead to people adopting all kinds of useless behaviours exhibited by the role model, including ones that actually have nothing to do with their success. In general, certainty is extremely rare in healthcare, and anyone who tells you they are absolutely certain their therapy will cure your health issue should be treated with extreme scepticism. The likelihood is they are either self-deceptive fanatics or simply out to make money through health scams.

Cargo-cult thinking

Many years ago, as an undergraduate student, I studied social anthropology and was fascinated by the phenomenon of cargo cults, which represents a useful metaphor to explain some of these behaviours. The term 'cargo cult' encompasses a diverse range of practices that occur in the wake of contact with the commercial networks of technologically superior colonising societies. The name derives from the belief that various ritualistic acts will lead to a bestowing of material wealth of some kind (the cargo).

The best-known examples are from World War II, where contact with the Japanese and American military in the Pacific brought about a transformation of the Indigenous peoples of Melanesia by building airbases and dropping cargo by parachute to their units. At the end of the war, the military abandoned these airbases. Those technological products that had been seen or become available to the Melanesian islanders through the colonising armies then disappeared or became in short supply. In response, several charismatic leaders arose amongst the remote Melanesian populations and developed cults that promised to restore deliveries of these goods (such as food, arms, radios and vehicles) on their followers. The leaders also suggested that the cargo was really gifts from the gods or ancestors. In attempts to get cargo to fall by parachute or land in planes or ships again, islanders imitated the same practices they had seen the military personnel use. They mimicked the day-to-day activities and dress styles of US soldiers, even performing parade ground drills with wooden or salvaged rifles. In a form of sympathetic magic practice, they also built life-size replicas of aeroplanes out of straw and mock airstrips complete with wooden control towers to encourage aircraft to land. But here is the thing – even though the cargo never arrived, the leaders maintained their cults for years as the social benefits of belonging to the group persisted, and they provided hope for the elusive products in the future. Today, the original cults have almost completely disappeared although some cargo cults were reportedly still active as recently as 2006.[427]

This term represents a useful metaphor to describe an attempt to recreate successful outcomes by replicating circumstances associated with those outcomes. In this way we could argue that those who follow celebrities, or subscribe to goop or *The Oprah Magazine*, are seeking to emulate the success of their idols by recreating their lifestyle choices. However, the circumstances mimicked by them are either unrelated to the causes of those outcomes or insufficient to produce their success by themselves (in the former case, this is also an instance of the *post hoc ergo propter hoc* logical fallacy [since A followed B, event B must have been caused by event A]). Outside of people mimicking celebrities, we can also see this type of activity in the world of pseudoscience publications, in what the physicist Richard Feynman once described as 'cargo-cult science'. Examples include journals that purport to be scientific but are not, and those focused on many of the therapeutic approaches described in Section IV.

A matter of trust

Although health celebrities are frequently shown to be spectacularly wrong, this doesn't seem to dent the appeal of their ideas. In February 2020, the Fox TV presenter Pete Hegseth, surprisingly, stated on air that he hadn't washed his hands in 10 years, noting 'Germs are not a real thing... I can't see them, therefore they're not real'. In their recent book, *The Misinformation Age: How False Beliefs Spread*, Calin O'Connor and James Weatherall (both professors at the University of California Irvine) examine how information spreads, and how social consensus on truth or fallacy occurs. In a recent interview they noted how Hegseth's statement was an excellent example of how people often believe irrational things, and where people pass on knowledge from person to person based on trust where they can't verify things easily for themselves.[428]

Such trust in celebrities has even prompted some fraudsters to use celebrity endorsements when none was ever given. 'The Great British Bake-Off's Mary Berry recently condemned cannabidiol (CBD) adverts using her image and quotes.[429] Mary posted a statement on Facebook, saying that she was 'appalled' to learn companies with which she had no contact had been using her image to advertise CBD oil and face cream online. Similarly, actors Tom Hanks and Clint Eastwood flagged companies using their image to peddle their CBD preparations.[430, 431] A Better Business Bureau study in 2018 found that many of the celebrity endorsements in advertisements for cosmetic and health products were faked. Many celebrity names are used without their knowledge or permission, including those from Oprah Winfrey, Ellen DeGeneres, Tim Allen and Sally Field.[432]

This has become even more prevalent today with the advent of celebrity social media. Now people have powerful tools to shape who they interact with, and how messages are spread. For example, if you are a believer in homeopathy, rather than explore the basis for your belief or discuss it with people who challenge your beliefs, you are simply more likely to go and find people online (particularly famous people) who also believe in it, and engage with them and their followers through social media.

Deceptive health businesses and those celebrities who promote their own brands rely on the fact that they have significant social influence as they are seen as trusted sources, and that few of those who follow them will ever attempt to validate their claims. In the next section we will explore how such modern health businesses capitalise on such behaviour, and use sophisticated psychological marketing techniques to sell you useless health products and service. Nevertheless, we will also discuss how to recognise and avoid them.

Section VI

We will make you like our products

Chapter 22

Who to believe?

A key problem for us all as consumers of healthcare products and services is how to tell if a promoted therapy or product is actually genuine, or a scam. As explored in the preceding chapters, healthcare deception is so abundant it is not easy differentiating marketing hype from genuinely helpful therapies, even when they are promoted by celebrities, famous doctors or even our friends and family. This section explores the techniques used in marketing deceptive healthcare, and practical ways in which you can assess the risk of deception involved in engaging with any promoted health practice.

Are we all gullible?

'People are gullible', is a common refrain heard about fraudsters, used-car salesmen and even politicians, who repeat the same unfulfilled promises every election. So why do we seem to be so trusting as to be naïve about the risks of deception involved in health products? In the eighteenth century, the Scottish philosopher Thomas Reid suggested that humans have a natural propensity to be trusting:

> *The wise and beneficent Author of nature, who intended that we should be social creatures, and that we should receive the greatest and most important part of our knowledge by the information of*

others, hath, for these purposes implanted in our natures two principles that tally with each other. The first of these principles is a propensity to speak truth… [the second] is a disposition to confide in the veracity of others, and to believe what they tell us.

Reid's ideas imply an assumption that people have a natural inclination to be honest and believe others are also truthful in their interactions. Many other philosophers and psychologists, such as Daniel Gilbert, have also made this claim, arguing that humans are fundamentally trustful, not to say gullible.[433] Clearly, the limits of human gullibility are well documented.

The case of the flesh-eating bananas

In 1999, a series of chain emails spread in North America warning of a spate of imported 'flesh-eating bananas'. The email reported that bananas were infecting people with necrotising fasciitis, a severe disease which results in the destruction of parts of the body's soft tissues with symptoms that include red or purple skin, severe pain, vomiting and fever occurring before one's flesh finally disintegrates and peels away. According to the email chain, the Food and Drug Administration (FDA) was trying to cover up the epidemic to avoid panic. The disease is real, but the banana threat was pure nonsense, of course; however, by the 28th of January the worry was sufficient for the US Centers for Disease Control and Prevention (CDC) to issue a statement denouncing the rumour. Unfortunately, this only added to its impact. Within weeks, the CDC was hearing from so many anxious callers it had to set up a banana hotline. So why do so many false beliefs persist in the face of hard evidence? And why do attempts to deny them only add flames to the fire? It's not a question of intelligence and, as explored previously, even Nobel Prize winners are not immune.

Trust versus gullibility

Some scientists who have explored gullibility have focused on the relationship between a negative trait of gullibility and positive trait of trust, as gullibility involves some form of trust. Stephen Greenspan, a psychology professor from the University of Rochester, writes that exploiters of the gullible are simply: '...people who understand the reluctance of others to appear untrusting and are willing to take advantage of that reluctance'.[434] Examples in folklore, literature and modern media abound, such as Pinocchio, the emperor in *The Emperor's New Clothes*, and even Eve in the Garden of Eden, in the *Bible*. There is even evolutionary support for our tendency towards trusting others. Human societies rely on effective communications between individuals to survive, to find sources of food and safe water, and to avoid dangers. So, there is good reason to trust other members of your community. However, humans do not always strive for the best interests of the social group and may be more interested in furthering their own objectives. This means there is the risk of gullibility, where trusting in others leaves us open to being accidentally or intentionally misinformed. Here, other factors have been proposed to come into play to maintain a general level of common trust in society (and reduce the risk of gullibility), which the psychologist Dan Sperber has termed 'epistemic vigilance'.[435]

Epistemic vigilance

Epistemic vigilance suggests that, despite the risk of being lied to, trusting in communications generally remains advantageous to us. In general, this proposes that rather than evolution leading us to being trusting, it has led us to refrain from lying too frequently or too blatantly because the chances are high that we will be found out or incur negative consequences. In other words, rather than the main rationale for gullibility being the positive factor of human trust (as Reid and Gilbert suggested), it is the inhibiting factors, such as social disapproval and the consequences of lying, that maintain our trust in others.

There are a number of mechanisms suggested to be at work here. Firstly, epistemic vigilance only comes into play when there is relevance or self-interest in the issue being communicated. For example, one is unlikely to care if a reported football score is true or false if one has no interest in football. Therefore, vigilance may be low with issues outside one's sphere of interest. Secondly, there is also a mutual vigilance at play. Our mutual trust is that generally, in day-to-day communications, we accept each other's tendency towards truthfulness to avoid unnecessary challenges, and therefore need to be vigilant only in rare and special circumstances. We could not be mutually trustful unless we were also mutually vigilant. Additionally, human reasoning is also argued to maintain vigilance. When new information is communicated, we first rationalise if the source is regarded as reliable. If not, the new information can simply be rejected as untrue. If the source is regarded as reliable, then the information is considered in the context of our pre-existing beliefs. If these beliefs are not held with much conviction, they can be corrected to take account of the new information. If we are confident about both the source and our own beliefs, then some conflict is unavoidable. We must revise either our background beliefs, or our belief that the source is reliable. Further evidence will be necessary to decide which. Overall, epistemic vigilance is not seen as the opposite of trust (unlike mistrust), but the mechanisms that prevent blind trust.[435]

Psychologists have also suggested that such vigilance mechanisms can easily be countered, and hence our gullibility be manipulated. For instance, if you distract people from thinking too deeply, for example by a direct appeal to emotion (see below), this may prevent vigilance and they may spontaneously accept what they are told. Alternatively, by making false information seem mundane and from trustworthy sources we can circumvent mutual vigilance. Interestingly, these were also the ideas behind early mind-control and brainwashing ideas in the 1950s. There is evidence such manipulations can work, and can result in people rejecting commonly accepted notions, joining cults, or even believing in outlandish ideas such as the world is run by lizard people. Unfortunately, we all have a tendency towards gullibility, and this is how health scammers make a living.

Who is the target?

Health scammers are very careful about selecting the best target populations to market their products and services to. For example, as explored in Chapter 4, research suggests the main users of alternative health products and services are well educated, employed women, and particularly those with chronic health concerns.[21] Exploring the main marketing of goop and other wellness businesses demonstrates a clear focus on this sector.

In our recent research into health scams, I and my colleagues found that the vast majority of Internet-based health scams targeted younger men and women with body-image products. For young women these are most frequently skin care or weight-loss products, and for young men, body-building merchandise. In older adults, the scam marketing switched to focus more on specific medicinal products for chronic conditions such as arthritis, cancer, diabetes and immunological diseases – all conditions that are difficult to treat with conventional medicine.

The most extreme example of this sort of targeted activity is probably those specialist clinics offering experimental therapies to cancer patients (see page 53). Another large group of scams focused upon lifestyle and wellness products, targeting middle-aged people, specifically tailored to appeal to adults with claims of more intangible benefits, such as anti-ageing or immune-boosting effects, or nutritional enhancements. A sub-group of these wellness scams targeted (mainly) men with products aimed at sexual enhancement.

The power of social media

As there are now more than three billion active social media users worldwide, the web and social media are being extensively used as a popular platform for businesses to extend their reach online. Over 70% of small companies now have one or more social media accounts. With such a large social media population, using publicly harvested data from major search engine providers, social media providers and businesses, health scammers now use targeted advertisements to find their ideal audience and extend their online reach. For example, if you search for content on treating acne online, you will not be surprised to see that your social media and web browsing activity becomes filled with advertisements for skin-care products. By profiling users' web-browsing and social media content use, advertisers use sophisticated algorithms to identify specific user groups and target products to them, even at an individual level. Even reading one news article on botox therapy can result in a deluge of pop-up advertisements proclaiming 'Hey, botox lover, wait until you see our latest offer…'

Unfortunately, you are just as likely to encounter bogus products or services from health scamming businesses as you are genuine medicines in such advertising, and probably more so as Internet-based advertising is very poorly regulated. Much of it arises internationally; for example, much of the Canadian targeted advertising comes from the USA.[21] Just as genuine healthcare businesses and pharmaceutical companies have become very skilled at marketing and designing attractive advertising campaigns, so too have the crooks selling deceptive healthcare products.

Mixing it up with half-truths

Another tactic designed to engage people with deceptive healthcare is to mix elements of truth with falsehoods, in order to make a product or service seem more appealing. This is a very old trick, and is even discussed in the *Quran*, which advises '… do not mix the truth with falsehood or conceal the truth while you know [it].' It is no secret that politicians often lie, but often they do so simply by telling the truth. That rather confusing statement becomes clearer when you consider that most of us have probably done this at some time or another. A common example might be if your daughter asks if she can go out with her friends and you respond by asking if she has finished her homework. She responds: 'I've written my essay on global warming for my science class.' Whilst this may well be true, and sounds affirmative, she has actually avoided answering the question.

Paltering

Misleading by telling the truth has become so pervasive today, psychologists even have a word to describe it: 'paltering'. By emphasising other facts, instead of answering questions, we can imply something is truthful when it is not. For example, when a used-car dealer describes a car as a 'peach', or when an estate agent describes a location as 'highly desirable', these may not be overt lies, but are vague and can mislead. A more classic example is when a financial advisor who knows a recession is likely says to a potential customer, 'As you know, over the last 10 years our portfolio has grown by 10% a year.' This answer is technically true, but it doesn't highlight their expectation that performance will most likely be flat or drop in the year ahead. Professor Todd Rogers, a behavioural scientist at the Harvard Kennedy School, notes that politicians do this all the time. In his work he found that paltering was an extremely common tactic used in negotiation. Over half the 184 business executives in one of his studies admitted to using the tactic. The research also found that the person doing the paltering believed it was more ethical than lying outright.[436, 437] For example, rather than stating that a skin product can definitely cure acne, an advertisement will provide testimonials from people who have used it along with a proposed scientific explanation of how it works.

Misleading statements

It is also difficult to spot a misleading 'fact' when we hear something that sounds like it is true. For instance, the *Washington Post* fact checker reported that Donald Trump had made 10,796 false or misleading claims over his first 869 days in office. For example, he stated that: 'They [Mexico] send in $500 billion worth of drugs, they kill 100,000 people, they ruin a million families every year. If you look at that, that's really an invasion without the guns.' The White House Council of Economic Advisers did in fact estimate in a 2017 report that 'the economic cost of the opioid crisis was $504.0 billion' in 2015. However, this was not all a result of drugs coming across the border from Mexico. It also included people who had abused prescription painkillers such as OxyContin and Vicodin (see page 93) and individuals who abused heroin and/or other illicit opioids. CDC has said that prescription drugs were involved in more than 35% of all opioid overdose deaths in 2017.[438]

The alkaline water scam

The 2017 often-seen health scam promoting the health benefits of alkaline mineral water offers an excellent example of where half-truths (see page 285) are used to promote the sale of a supposed health product. It was claimed that alkaline water could help neutralise acid in your bloodstream because we consume more acids than alkali, and alkaline water had a higher pH level (a measure of acidity, where lower numbers are more acidic) than plain tap water. This is even currently being proposed by a dietitian on the Mayo Clinic website at the time of writing! Other claims included that alkaline water could provide you with valuable antioxidants, detoxify you and lengthen your life. Some ionised versions also claimed to provide more oxygen to the body. This is, of course, mostly wrong and certainly misleading. Whilst tap water does have a pH of around 6.5-8.5 (more acidic than most alkaline water products), and it is correct to say we ingest more acids than alkali in our diet, the body has a number of physiological mechanisms that regulate the acidity of the blood to keep it within a very narrow pH range of 7.35-7.45. So, any extra alkali ingested in water is countered immediately by compensatory physiological mechanisms and by the kidneys rapidly excreting more alkali and less acid to maintain a balance. Therefore, an increased alkali state (metabolic alkalosis) cannot be induced by oral alkali administration by drinking alkali-water when kidney function is normal. You simply can't drink enough of it to do so, and even if you could it would be a severely dangerous thing to do. Body cells and tissues don't respond well to either acidic or alkaline environments outside this narrow normal blood range. As for the antioxidants, as discussed in Chapter 13, the benefits of these have not been demonstrated. Additionally, adding some oxygen, or shifting ions around to neutralise some of the acidic hydrogen ions in the water, does not create antioxidant water and cannot provide our cells with extra oxygen (that involves breathing, not drinking).

Not unsurprisingly, goop is still promoting alkaline water, currently marketing a product called Flow, that apparently '... has more healthy minerals than most bottled waters' and also offers crystal-infused water bottles retailing at $85 USD each. The website states 'According to crystal lore, smoky quartz anchors the root chakra, amplifying good intentions, cultivating serenity, and guarding against bad vibes'. Certainly, staying hydrated is important, but physiologists, physicians, nurses and dietitians alike will advise you to simply drink water when you are thirsty, and that treated tap water is perfectly fine. As far as balancing your energies go, no matter how many fanciful terms are used, a rock in a water bottle cannot crush your negative energies or prevent 'bad vibes'. Much of the hyped marketing that mixes facts and false information together in order to sell products also uses the appeal of science, and usually these products trade on pleasant aesthetics as well; after all, a water bottle with some quartz in it looks very cool.

Chapter 23

The appliance of science

As noted, a common characteristic of deceptive health practices is a tendency to claim that the products are based on science when in fact they are not. Science sells, and claims of being scientific add credibility. The problem is, as most people are not scientists or university professors, differentiating science from pseudoscience is frequently difficult, and sometimes even for health professionals. Surprisingly, most health professionals are actually not well versed in the philosophy of science, or even in the more technical aspects of scientific research methods. To understand these distinctions more clearly it is worth briefly exploring the nature of science, non-science, pseudoscience and quasi-science in relationship to scientific inquiry.

Science

Simply put, science is a way of understanding the world. The term comes from the Latin *Scientia*, meaning knowledge. Science was originally synonymous with philosophy in the ancient world and today the term is still commonly used to describe any field of organised study. However, technically it is a system of acquiring knowledge through the use of explanations and predictions that can be tested. The key element of scientific inquiry is that it involves evidence and explanation of occurrences by observation and experimentation. In reality, the definition of science itself has come under scrutiny many times, prompting the UK Science Council to publish this definition in 2009, which works well here:

> Science is the pursuit of knowledge and understanding of the natural and social world following a systematic methodology based on evidence.

Non-science

Non-science really refers to inquiry that does not involve the process of empirical verification or the scientific process to generate knowledge. Many of the greatest human achievements represent non-science, and such disciplines do not require a systematic methodology based on evidence. They are activities that don't purport to be scientific and are easily identified as non-scientific in their nature, including the arts, religion and even philosophy. They usually involve creative processes, the acceptance of subjective knowledge, belief, revelation or faith in establishing their epistemological basis. The rejection of the principles of scientific inquiry is also frequently acknowledged in much postmodern thinking, which can also be categorised as non-science. Although non-scientific approaches to knowledge are widespread and highly valued in peoples throughout the world, they are not as highly valued within evidence-based public healthcare policies. In effect, non-science represents an alternative to scientific thinking, and these approaches have gained ground in some societies, illustrated by the growth of complementary and alternative medicine in many countries.

Quasi- or proto-science

Quasi-science (or proto-science) is another term that may be encountered, and may be difficult to separate from pseudoscience (see below). Quasi-science resembles science, having some of its form, but not all of the features of scientific inquiry, and proto-science is really a form of this where there is the potential for the ideas to be expressed in scientific terms and further developed scientifically. Quasi-science involves an attempt to use a scientific approach but where development of a scientific theoretical basis or application of scientific methodologies is currently insufficient for the work to be determined as an established science. Differentiating quasi-science from pseudoscience or bad science is complex and there is certainly some overlap, and some quasi-science does fall into the realms of pseudoscience. Largely, quasi-science can be considered work involving commonly held beliefs in popular science but where they do not yet meet the rigorous criteria of scientific work. This is often seen with pop science that may blur the divide between science and pseudoscience among the general public and may also be seen in much science fiction. For example, ideas about time travel, immortality, aliens and sentient machines are frequently discussed in the media, although there is insufficient empirical basis for much of this to be seen as scientific knowledge at this time. Quasi-science does not normally reject, or purport to be an alternative or new, science and may be developed, with an application of rigorous scientific methods, into scientific work. Some alternative medicine, such as traditional Chinese medicine (TCM), is probably best regarded as quasi- or proto-science in that it does involve recognised associations between traditional remedies (e.g. herbal remedies) and their effectiveness in treating specific medical problems. However, this association has not been developed or tested in a scientific way, and therefore its use is not really based on scientific validation.

Pseudoscience

Pseudoscience is something that is often difficult to identify but can be thought of as disciplines, inquiry or work that claim to be scientific, but upon closer inspection are found not to be so. Interestingly, pseudoscience and non-science are frequently conflated, but they are actually quite different. The word 'pseudo' comes from the Greek for 'false', and in this case applies to things that are deceptively claimed to be scientific when they are not. Pseudoscientific practices employ non-scientific methods and cannot be reliably tested or verified, and lack supporting evidence. They also frequently adopt highly implausible theoretical positions (but to be fair, so do many scientific theories, so this may not help in differentiating them).

Pseudoscience is more easily characterised by vague, exaggerated or unfalsifiable claims (such as claims that the effects of prayer can be measured), and an over-reliance on confirmation rather than rigorous attempts at refutation. This is frequently seen with claims of scientific evidence in studies that put their conclusions before the hypotheses – for example, 'my new therapy works miracles, and I will now prove it to you'. Key features also include vague or impenetrable theories that are claimed to only be truly understood by an inner cabal of experts or gurus, a lack of openness to academic challenge and evaluation by external investigators, and the absence of established scientific processes in theory development and testing.[439] Pseudoscience is also often characterised by conspiracy arguments in that proponents argue their discipline is besieged by a narrow-minded positivistic scientific community, and that medicine or Big Pharma are hard at work to undermine them.

Overall, pseudoscience can be identified by the attribution of scientific claims or narrative to something that is clearly not evidence-based for the purposes of promoting or marketing and selling a product or service. Adding scientific-sounding language enhances the marketability of the item, and frequently pseudo-technical jargon is used to make products or services sound more scientific, such as: 'Our ozone-activated drinks enhance psychotropic brain waves.' Unfortunately, separating pseudoscience from science is far from easy, and the demarcation between the two has caused much debate in health disciplines. Pseudoscientific beliefs are also big business and support multi-million-dollar industries. They are widespread in the media, amongst university students, school science teachers, also occur in expert testimony, environmental policies, and even sometimes even in science education! A key example is the USA seeing the revival of efforts to ban the teaching of evolution or to insist that 'creation science' be given equal time in the high-school curriculum.[440] A number of US states currently offer 'creation science' content in public schools.[169, 441] Of course, the best way to be able to identify pseudoscience is to know as much as possible about science.

Bad science

Lastly, we have bad science, which is simply scientific work that is carried out poorly or with erroneous results due to fallacies in reasoning, hypothesis generation and testing or the methods involved. Science, like any human endeavour, can be carried out badly, and often with the most noble motives. Occasionally, scientists deliberately mislead for personal gain, but in most cases bad science results from errors in the scientific process. Sometimes these errors are the result of poor practices, or the researcher's unconscious imposition of their beliefs, looking for the answer they believe in. Science is an extraordinary process but has one notable flaw: 'It is carried out by people who are themselves unavoidably influenced by their own beliefs, and who are sometimes trained insufficiently and who make mistakes.'[198]

Naturally, it's good for you

Another common strategy to make health products more appealing is to claim they are natural, or are naturally produced, and therefore superior in some way. This too, is one of the oldest marketing techniques and relies on something known as the 'naturalistic fallacy'. This is a well-known logical fallacy and has several meanings in contemporary use. It is often used to refer to a claim that what is natural is inherently good and that what is unnatural is inherently bad (the appeal to nature). This was the basis for social Darwinism and also contemporary right-wing radical politics, in the belief that caring for the poor and sick gets in the way of evolution, which depends on the survival of the fittest. Interestingly, these ideas are currently being promoted by some anti-vaccination activists, although often citing God's natural order rather than evolution. In another example, in a recent TV broadcast of a COVID-19 restriction protest, I saw a protestor waving a 'Sacrifice the Weak' placard. Of course, those making these arguments always assume the health issue they are concerned with will somehow not affect them or their families.

More often the term 'naturalistic fallacy' is used as an expression of David Hume's (1711–1776) famous 'ought from is' problem. This describes the error of deriving what 'ought to be' from what 'is' without causal evidence (also known as 'Hume's guillotine'). Hume's point was that it is not obvious how we can get to make prescriptive statements from descriptive ones. For example, in the statement 'Murder rates have increased, so we ought to bring back capital punishment', there is not a logical causal connection between the two clauses. One does not logically imply the other, as there are other things that could reduce murder rates rather than capital punishment. The philosopher George Edward Moore (1873–1958) also argued that naturalistic fallacy is committed whenever someone attempts to prove a claim about ethics by applying the term 'good'. Moore refuted the possible identification of moral properties from natural ones. For example, it makes little sense to apply morals about how we ought to behave based on how other animals behave in the wild.

In deceptive healthcare we see both versions of the naturalistic fallacy frequently. A prime example is when some practitioners resort to the appeal to nature to justify their practices, using phrases such as 'all natural' to imply that products are environmentally friendly and safe. However, whether or not a product is 'natural' is irrelevant to determining its safety or effectiveness, and natural may not be environmentally friendly. For example, organic avocado production is very environmentally unfriendly as a monoculture consuming far more water than equivalent crops, creating significant loss of biodiversity and water stress.[442] We also know many natural substances are deadly, and many natural remedies available today are mass-produced by machines on production lines similar to other drugs (e.g. homeopathic remedies). Another example of the naturalistic fallacy is the claim that organic food is better for you. Organic food is not inherently better for you nor does it have any characteristic of 'goodness' simply because it has an 'organic' label on it. Food grown organically is produced without synthetic pesticides or fertilisers, but that doesn't mean no pesticides or fertilisers were used, and most is grown using modern intensive farming techniques. It may taste better, so this could be considered a half-truth from that respect, but its nutritional value will not be significantly different from non-organic foods, and it has no inherent virtue of being more natural than any other crops.[443, 444, 445] Finally, it is useful to remind ourselves that viruses and bacteria are just as natural as fruit and vegetables.

Clinical significance and importance

'Clinical significance' or 'clinical importance' are other terms frequently encountered in healthcare research that are often misunderstood. Practically, these represent the same thing, which is a way to consider if the difference between a new therapy and a pre-existing therapy is large enough to support changing practice. In other words, are the outcomes of a new study exploring a new drug or therapy clinically important enough to implement change? The usual practice in health research is to conduct trials comparing a new or altered therapy in a randomised group of patients, with some getting the new treatment and others the standard treatment (as the control). The results are then tested using inferential statistics to see if there is a meaningful statistical difference, and when so, reported as being 'statistically significant', which means in practice there was a measurable difference. If this difference is in favour of the new therapy, researchers will then generally argue it is advantageous.

However, as there is always some risk in extrapolating the results of a study on a small sample to the general population, health scientists usually consider a small improvement with a new therapy as insufficient evidence to justify altering clinical practice. We would certainly not alter an approach if study results were not statistically significant, but when they are, we also have to consider if the finding is actually important enough to change practice. Therefore, the question then arises, when is the difference between two therapies large enough to support changing practice?

The importance of clinical judgement

Statistics alone cannot really help answer this question. It becomes one of clinical judgement, considering the degree of benefit of the treatment, the respective side-effects of the two treatments, their relative costs, our professional comfort with delivering the new therapy and, of course, the patient's preferences. For example, in pain management a study might find a new analgesic might perform slightly better in terms of demonstrating a reduction in a self-reported numerical pain score of 0.5 more than another similar drug (on a 0-10 scale, with 0 being no pain and 10 being worst pain imaginable), but this is a very small change and the new drug might be more expensive, less easily available and have more side-effects, so clinically for the small benefits it might not be worth changing.

Risk calculation

Therefore, establishing the actual clinical value of any therapy, and particularly a new one is a complex process, and also frequently misunderstood. Often those opposing new therapeutic interventions and those promoting health scams will either ignore clinical significance or misuse it to confuse issues in support of their own agenda. Nonetheless, there are tried and tested practical statistical techniques to help scientists quantify the value of new treatments and compare risks, such as relative and absolute risk, commonly known as relative risk reduction (RRR), and absolute risk reduction (ARR).

In healthcare, risk refers to the probability of a bad outcome in people with a disease. When we need to consider the risk of treatment versus no treatment, ARR is used comparing the outcome rates of those who receive a therapy to those who do not. In the world of clinical practice, this rarely happens as people are normally receiving some kind of treatment, so RRR is more often used, where the risk of a new treatment is compared with an existing treatment. Other methods used include the odds ratio (OR – measure of association between exposure and an outcome), hazard ratio (HR – ratio of the hazard rates compared with exposure), and the number needed to treat (NNT – a relative measure of how many people we need to treat with the new drug to be of benefit to one patient). Further exploration of these tools is beyond the scope of this book, but health researchers will use these different measures to establish the actual clinical value of any therapy. However, their use is often unintuitive and therefore health scammers will often avoid discussing them and simplify their discussions of evidence in the support of the therapies they sell by using simpler arguments that people can more readily understand.

The public perception of risk

A good example here is public immunisation programmes. These have been highly successful in reducing the incidence of vaccine-preventable diseases, with new and improved vaccines being developed, such as the vaccine against the human papillomavirus (HPV) and now the various anti-COVID vaccines. However, because vaccine-targeted diseases (such as Tuberculosis) are now less common, they are a victim of their own success. As people don't encounter these diseases much any more, people find it more difficult to weigh up the risks of these diseases compared with the perceived risks of adverse events following immunisation, especially when new and altered forms of existing vaccines are introduced. This area of healthcare policy is particularly problematic as frequently there are minor symptoms that arise following immunisation due to the way in which the vaccines activate an immunological response (such as some localised pain and redness at the injection site, or a mild fever). Public and mass media attention has shifted away from these diseases to vaccine safety, and as discussed previously, there is now a strong anti-vaccination movement. As vaccines are given to healthy people (especially infants and children) there is now low public tolerance for any adverse events. Therefore, the actual clinical risk versus the public perceived risk may differ widely, and health scams make use of this fact by using the appeal of simple explanations to complex health problems.

Make it simple

A tactic often used to make health products more appealing is to grossly simplify either the health issue being addressed or the effects of the health product or service. This may be done either negatively or positively, depending what the desired goal is. For example, claims that diabetes can be cured simply by not eating some types of vegetable, weight loss is simple if you stop eating tomatoes or that measles is a harmless illness. In reality, diabetes mellitus involves problems with people metabolising blood sugar effectively, and simply reducing the intake of carbohydrates does not help everyone, and a diet too low in sugars can cause other problems such as muscle catabolism. Likewise, weight-loss requires multiple strategies, and measles has serious effects on some people and regularly sends some into hospital intensive care units or even kills. One famous example is the author Roald Dahl's daughter, Olivia, who died of measles encephalitis, aged seven, in 1962.

Another commonly seen example here is the claim that genetically modified organisms (GMOs) are bad for you. Whilst it sounds scary in that genetic engineering is being applied to the food we eat, in the anti-GMO mythology currently circulating, it is implied that nefarious scientists are working away in laboratories creating mutant 'Frankenfoods' that will wreak havoc on humans and the natural world. The reality is a bit more complex, in that scientists are researching, genetically modifying and testing plants to be cheaper, grow faster, be more resistant to disease and to include more nutrients so we can feed the growing world population. Agroscience has been doing this for decades and, without it, feeding the world's population would be all but impossible.

The primary simplification here is in simplifying the differences between genetic modification and genetic engineering. Most of the public are unaware of this difference. Genetic modification has been done for centuries, and may occur through traditional breeding methods like selective breeding or crossbreeding between plants or animals within the same species, or human manipulation of genes. Genetically engineered (GE) foods refer to foods for which DNA has been artificially altered by manipulation, often by inserting genes from unrelated species, to introduce desirable new traits to that organism. This is the key difference between GMOs and GE foods. GE foods are basically an extension of GMOs and have been around since the 1990s. Gene editing is a newer and more precise method of GE which hopes to avoid the bad associations with GMOs of the past. GE crops must meet the same safety standards as foods from non-engineered crops and must have been tested rigorously for toxicity, allergenicity and long-term safety before they are licensed for public use. Currently, there are no GMO or GE foods on the market that do not meet these standards. Much of the corn, canola and soybeans in the United States has engineered genes that protect them from insect or herbicide damage, and in Canada GE canola, soybean, corn, potatoes and sugar beet crops are currently grown. Again, applying the terms good or bad to these products is a gross oversimplification designed to derive an emotional response, rather than explore the risks and benefits.

Anecdotal evidence

Another way that health scams frequently simplify issues is by the use of anecdotal evidence rather than citing more complex statistical evidence from scientific studies. Research indicates that anecdotes can easily overwhelm a more scientific scrutiny, and so are frequently seen in health scam marketing (as discussed in the next chapter). In a well-known 2013 experiment where participants read eight science news articles arriving at dubious conclusions, the inclusion of anecdotal stories decreased the ability of the participants to use scientific reasoning.[446] Anecdotes are powerful tools, and marketers of health products know this.

Magical thinking

Promoting the acceptance of magical thinking is another way that deceptive healthcare providers simplify issues to promote a product. Magical thinking involves believing that one event happens as a result of another without any plausible link of causation, and many people hold magical beliefs of some sort. For example: 'I broke a mirror; therefore, I will get bad luck.' Results of many psychology studies confirm that such beliefs are common, and do affect behaviour.[447, 448, 449]

In a 2016 study, Dr Roger Cutting and I explored if final-year science-based professional students held magical beliefs and if this altered their behaviour in observable ways. We found that many students did hold magical beliefs but they generally discriminated between scientific and pseudoscientific ideas effectively. However, pre-existing paranormal beliefs in these students was quite common (37% believed that psychics could accurately predict the future and 33% that it was possible to communicate with the dead) and this was associated with an increased likelihood of students finding paranormal reports scientific, believable and credible.[169] Perhaps, a more refined definition of magical thinking would suggest that this involves believing in things more strongly than either evidence or experience justifies. This tendency for a large part of the population, to hold beliefs that require faith over scientific evidence, is an advantage for marketing purposes. By making simple claims of magical properties for health products and implying these are related to mystical events beyond current human understanding, this appeal to the unknown permits the avoidance of any complex rationales or questions about how the product actually works. These strategies are often observed in marketing, such as in claims that an age-reversing moisturising cream is based upon 'ancient Vedic knowledge' or some such hokum.

Chapter 24

Social influence

A key aspect in marketing is the power of social influence. Psychologists and advertisers have spent decades studying the power of social influence, and the way in which it controls people's opinions or behaviours. Specifically, social influence refers to the way in which we change our ideas and actions to conform with the behaviour of: a perceived authority, a particular social group, someone with a particular social role or a minority within a group that wields influence. For example, children in school soon learn the social expectations within a class of their peers, such as not appearing too clever by answering questions all the time, or not being a tell-tale on other classmates' misdeeds. Classic examples of where advertisers have used this for effect over the years have been in the sale of cigarettes and alcohol.

The appeal of the popular image

The Marlboro cowboy helped Marlboro's red-label cigarettes gain a reputation for being the smoke of choice for cool, rugged men everywhere in the 1950s (even though the brand was originally marketed as a woman's cigarette). New scientific evidence on the dangers of smoking had pressured the tobacco industry to develop filtered cigarettes, which were designed to appear as healthier alternatives; Philip Morris & Company needed a way to sell these filtered alternatives to men. The previous 'Mild as May!' slogan it used for its filtered product was hardly likely to appeal to men, and so in 1954, the company unveiled the Marlboro Man, the brainchild of the advertising agency Leo Burnett Worldwide. Whilst other brands used actors and athletes to routinely endorse their products (some, like Camel cigarettes, even used doctors), Marlboro used their rugged cowboy, as westerns were a popular medium at the time (much like superhero comics and movies are today). Now men could feel like tough hombres smoking a Marlboro, because it was apparently the choice for the wind-swept hunky cowboy. Marlboro sales grew from $5 billion in 1955 to $20 billion in 1957, and by the '90s, Marlboro's advertisements were so pervasive that one study showed that nearly 90% of schoolchildren recognised the cigarette-brandishing cowboy. The Marlboro Man campaign was eventually retired following the 1998 Tobacco Master Settlement that became American federal law, where tobacco companies agreed to stop using cartoons and human advertising to sell their products.[450]

Endorsement and group behaviours

Social influence involves stimulus from friends, family, peers and other respected social groups and relies on emotional pressure to conform to social norms. Common techniques include the use of endorsement by trusted figures (including celebrities) or language that promotes trust such as 'mom's remedy'. Patti LaBelle-branded sweet potato pie case is a good example of this in the USA. Thanks to a viral video, posted on Facebook in November 2015 when comedian James Wright Chanel simulated transforming into the singer and started belting out some of her signature songs in between bites of her signature pie, a national frenzy has ensued in the US, and two days later, outlets were reporting that the pies were completely sold out. Additionally, social influence can also be enacted by negative endorsement, encouraging people to feel a part of one social group through the distrust of another. For example, phrases such as 'Dentists don't want you to know this' capitalises on the fact most people dislike visits to the dentist, and the social meme that dental health professionals are conspiring against people to maximise profits.

Social conformity

One reason that social influence is so powerful, and people readily accept it, is that we often conform to the norms of a group to gain acceptance by its members. Supporters of sports teams voluntarily wear their teams' shirts to identify with other fans. Teenage friends also tend to wear similar clothing to their peers to experience a sense of belonging. Conformity can also encourage cooperation to achieve a shared goal, such as by joining a mental health charity group to help fight the stigma associated with mental illness. This may make advocacy more powerful than through separate people acting on their own. However, this can also lead to a conformity of views, resulting in what is known as 'groupthink'. This occurs when group members adopt agreed views and actions in the pursuit of their goal, but reject criticism from any individuals who question aspects of them. A recent illustration of this was when some fundamentalist Christian anti-vaccination campaigners posted pictures on social media of themselves wearing T-shirts proclaiming: 'Spoiler Alert: Jesus wasn't vaccinated!' Their goal was to influence Christian parents (and others) to stop immunising their kids, proudly rejecting any critique of the irrationality of this by others outside of their group. However, this lack of critical thinking can have a negative impact on the group's performance as its ability to adapt to changing conditions becomes hampered, and it becomes tunnel-vision-like in its outlook. Conformity to a narrow set of behaviours and views can discourage the development of new ideas that could improve the likelihood of the group reaching their goals, or cause them to be ostracised by wider society.

Famous and infamous experiments on social conformity

Whilst social influence can have a positive effect on behaviour, its disadvantages have been widely researched, most famously by psychologists such as Stanley Milgram and Phillip Zimbardo. In the 1960s, Yale psychologist Dr Stanley Milgram undertook a series of experiments to explore the willingness of subjects to obey an authority who instructed them to perform acts that clashed with their personal morality. The experiment involved the subjects being ordered by a researcher to administer electric shocks to other people who answered a question incorrectly. No actual shocks were administered as it was a set-up (and the people receiving the fake shocks were actors), but the subjects pressing the button to administer them were unaware of this and thought they were administering painful stimuli. Over half of them continued to administer shocks up to 450 volts (labelled clearly as dangerous) when ordered to do so by the researchers. Milgram received a lot of criticism from the scientific community for these experiments as they were clearly psychologically abusive to the subjects.

In 1971, researcher Phillip Zimbardo performed another infamous psychology experiment, this time to explore the relationships of authority and subservience between guards and prisoners. Twelve male Stanford University students were selected to play prisoners and live in a mock prison. Another 12 were given the role of guards. Roles were assigned randomly to the subjects at the start, but after a couple of days the guard actors started becoming actually physically abusive, whilst some of the prisoners became passive and, at the guards' request, inflicted punishment on other prisoners. Five of the subjects were upset enough by the process to walk out of the experiment early, and the entire experiment was stopped after six days as Zimbardo himself finally realised he had permitted the abuse to continue. Again, this study was widely criticised because of its potential harm to its subjects for questionable scientific benefits.[451]

Largely, psychologists suggest people conform for one of two reasons: either to become more informed so they can act more effectively (informative social influence) or to match the views and behaviour of a social group (normative social influence). In informative social influence, people turn to others in the hope that they will provide them with useful information. By accepting this information (regardless of its accuracy), the person has become subject to social influence. An example of this would be deferring to others in the group to answer a question about which city is the capital of a country when unsure, and accepting their view. In the latter form, people want to fit in with friends and colleagues, and to be liked and respected by other members of their social group. They value the opinions of other members, and seek to maintain their standing within the group. Therefore, individuals will adjust their own attitudes and behaviour to match the accepted norms of the group. For example, kids joining street gangs may be persuaded to steal or harm someone as an initiation, and do so to become accepted.

Probably, the best-known experiment testing this was undertaken by the psychologist Solomon Asch in the late 1950s. Asch got groups of students to participate in a vision test. In reality, all but one of the experiment volunteers were accomplices of the researcher, and the study was really about how the single subject would react to the other participants' behaviours. The subject was unaware that the other participants were accomplices, thinking they were all simply other volunteers. They were all shown a series of visual tests with two cards. The first one had a line on it and then the second card had three lines on it marked A, B and C (Figure 1).

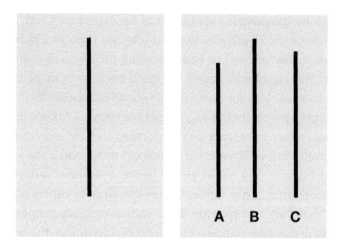

Figure1: The Solomon Asch test example

The participants were then asked to say which line on the second card matched the line on the first in length. The experiment was managed so the researcher's confederates answered first and in the first two tests they all gave the correct answer. Following that they all stated the same wrong answer. There was also a control group, with no pressure to conform to an erroneous view. In the control only one participant out of 35 ever gave an incorrect answer. In the experimental group, when surrounded by individuals all voicing the same incorrect answer, 32% of the participants provided incorrect responses on a high proportion of the questions, and 75% of the participants gave an incorrect answer to at least one question.

Since then, numerous studies have repeated Asch's conformity experiment with varying results. The 'Asch conformity effect' appears to be an unpredictable phenomenon rather than a stable tendency of human behaviour. Many other studies have found similar conformity, but some have not, suggesting conformity may have social context in itself. Nevertheless, the peer reinforcement suggested here would help explain how some belief structures (such as specific religious beliefs) are passed on from one generation to the next.[102]

Minority influence

Whilst conformity to a social norm usually occurs in response to a majority, sometimes individuals or minorities within a group can also exhibit social influence. This is known as minority influence, as the views are contrary to group norms. If the view is consistently stated by a respected member of the group, the attention of the other members is drawn to it and they may be led to consider the merits of the minority opinion. A minority view exerts an informative influence by presenting new information that may be unknown by the majority. In this way, celebrity social influencers such as Oprah Winfrey or Gwyneth Paltrow, can hold a significant effect upon their followers by the process known as conversion. This is where an influential minority is able to convert a sufficient number of members, so their view becomes the opinion held by a majority of individuals within the group. Minority influence is more effective when the person expressing the view is an established member of the group and displays consistency in their view.

Free will and subconscious influence

Promoting products via social influence is really a form of subconscious marketing. For at least a century, brands and advertisers have been seeking to shape consumers' thoughts, attitudes and behaviour, without us even being aware of it. Neuroscientists suggest that many decisions are made in the subconscious mind long before we are even consciously aware of it. Experiments by Benjamin Libert in the 1980s and, more recently, Gabriel Kreiman of Harvard University have demonstrated that electrical activity in a motor area of the

The New Alchemists

brain involved in initiating movement can be detected in the brain up to several seconds before someone is aware they have made the decision to move! As for what this means for one of the longest-running debates in science – the question of whether we do or do not have free will – is another matter. Though the philosophical implications of these results are open for debate, neural determinism (as defined as the mediation of all mental states by processes in the brain) remains evident, even if we assume the centrality of conscious awareness in action control. Neurophysiologist Karim Fifel suggests that 'Neuroscience may in no way interfere with our first-person experience of the will, it can in the end only describe it … it leaves everything as it is'. In other words, these findings do not necessarily counter the notion of free will but suggest the neurological mechanisms involved in decision-making are far more complex than simply unconscious versus conscious divisions of sentience.[452]

Regardless of philosophical debates about free will, contemporary neuroscience has demonstrated that decisions are made in our subconscious mind long before we are consciously aware of them, and there are numerous examples. Perhaps some of the most entertaining are those performed by illusionists such as Penn & Teller, James Randi, David Blaine or Derren Brown. In one fascinating example (which can be seen on his YouTube video site), Brown exposes two members of an advertising agency to numerous subconscious visual cues during their taxi ride to a location where they have been asked to design an ad campaign. They are then asked to design some preliminary advertising ideas and sketches for a novel campaign. The ideas they came up with after an hour or so are then compared with sketches that Brown had prepared beforehand and sealed in an envelope. The ideas of the two advertisers are almost completely identical to Brown's sketches. At the end, Brown demonstrates all of the numerous visual cues the two men were exposed to beforehand, that subconsciously

310

influenced their design, demonstrating how much information our subconscious mind is absorbing all of the time.[453]

The rise of social media

The advent of social media has created a new and powerful medium for the enactment of social influence. If a social media user selects an advertisement and endorses the product or company, they reveal an affinity for the brand that can be a powerful source of promotion. For example, in one recent study alcohol advertising on social media was found to be particularly successful in encouraging people to drink.[454] Research has long indicated a positive effect of social influence on brand choice.[455, 456] By advertising in social media streams, advertisers can help create advantageous associations between their brand and the user's social group. This has been a huge growth area in the advertising industry. The term 'influencer marketing' increased by 325% in Google searches over 2017-18, and new platforms targeted for influencer marketing change almost daily, although Instagram, Facebook, YouTube, SnapChat, Vine, Twitter and Pinterest all remain popular at the time of writing. Numerous new web-businesses have now appeared providing services that match brands, and with the best influencers using databases. The influencers sign sponsorship contracts to endorse specific products or brands in their feeds. Even influencers with smaller followings (known as nano-influencers) can make between $30,000 and $60,000 a year doing this, whilst celebrity influencers with millions of followers make hundreds of thousands of dollars per post. For example, singer Ariana Grande reportedly made $996,000 per Instagram product post in 2019.[457]

Following this growth, influencer marketing agencies have now appeared, where teams of people provide consultancy to help a brand identify the right influencers for it, regardless of platform. Simply searching for the term 'influencer marketing platform' reveals numerous examples of such businesses. Researchers have also explored the characteristics of the influencers in attempts to identify who are the most persuasive users in a social network. Data scientist Eytan Bakshy and colleagues established in a 2010 study that, as might be expected, the most influential users on Twitter were the ones with the largest number of connections. However, they also found that individuals with an average number of connections were likely to be the most cost-effective method of spreading influence.[458] Social influence is, then, a tried and tested phenomenon, and as well as its use for advertising genuine products, it also appears to be one of the strongest factors that stimulate people to engage with internet health scams.[261]

Chapter 25

Health scams and detecting deception

Internet health scams

The era of the Internet has brought with it both positive and negative effects. Internet fraud is one of them. It is a type of deception that makes use of the Internet as the communications medium and involves anything from the hiding of information or providing false information, but where the purpose is tricking victims out of money or property. Largely, it is not considered a single, distinctive crime but a range of illegal and illicit activities that are committed in cyberspace. Legally, however, it is differentiated from simple theft since, in this case, the victim voluntarily and knowingly provides the information, money or property to the perpetrator. It is also distinguished by the way it involves offenders separated from the victim in location and sometimes in time (where the fraud may happen a long time after communication has occurred).

Cybercrime

According to the UK's National Crime Agency, criminal offences involving a computer to either commit or target crime (cybercrime, as it is more commonly referred to) continues to rise in scale and complexity, affecting essential services, businesses and private individuals alike. Cybercrime costs the UK billions of pounds, causes untold damage and even poses a threat to national security.[459] The FBI's internet Crime Complaint Center (IC3) received about 350,000 complaints in 2018. Victims lost over $2.7 billion in online fraud, an increase of 70% in losses compared with the previous year.[460] The Canadian Anti-Fraud Centre (CAFC) has also documented a similar rise in cybercrime over the last five years, particularly where the Internet is used as the medium.[21] One study, conducted by the Centre for Strategic and International Studies (CSIS) and McAfee, suggested cybercrime costs the global economy $600 billion a year, which translates into around 0.8% of total global GDP.[461] Online fraud appears in many forms. It ranges from fake emails soliciting money to online scams selling fake products.

Types of health scam

A growing sector of this type of cybercrime is internet health scams (IHS), which focus on opportunistic commercial gain involving the sale of health products that are either entirely fake, or have claimed effects with little to no substantive evidence of efficacy for the purpose advertised.[21, 261, 462] Many IHS practices exist in a grey area of legislation and remain unchallenged in case law, an example being the promotion of products by celebrities or qualified health practitioners.[21, 335] Others are technically legal, such as click-fraud, which involves hidden computer code that automatically generates fake mouse clicks on an advert when a website is visited that contains web advertisements that pay the website owner(s) per click on the advert, or other similar mechanisms. These drain revenue from the advertiser to the website owner when the adverts have not really been viewed. Perpetrators of IHS have become adept at disguising the commercial sales of unproven or ineffective remedies and cures with those of genuine health products and services. These scams range from the overt sale of completely bogus health items (e.g.

radionics machines) to the mass-marketing of ineffective therapies (e.g. green coffee for weight loss). More sophisticated frauds avoid legal issues by offering costly seminars that teach esoteric techniques for healing (or other intangible health benefits) rather than actually selling products directly. Additionally, as the web is an international medium, sites hosted outside of the country they target can also avoid regulatory challenges, and legal action. For example, sites advertising outside of Canada can effectively circumvent the Canada Food and Drug Act regulations that ban the advertising of misleading and direct-to-consumer drugs and medical products.

As noted previously, research indicates that few people (about 1%) exposed to IHS actually lose money to them. However, even with this low rate of return, the ability to mass-market these activities cheaply on the Internet with virtual impunity makes this sufficient to support a highly lucrative business. The non-financial impact of these activities is more difficult to establish but includes the negative experience of feeling humiliated over being scammed or perceived as naïve. However, a more serious concern is that engaging with many of these dubious health practices may actually prove hazardous to health.

The psychology of scamming and susceptibility to persuasion

As we have seen, the healthcare industry is rife with advertisements for health products and services from miracle weight-loss supplements to cancer cures, but whether they actually work or are simply scams can often be difficult to determine. Over the years, social psychologists have established several mechanisms that influence why people engage with scams, and people's perception of risk and their susceptibility to scams and Internet fraud.[1,463] Three distinct characteristics associated with increased risk-taking behaviours in consumers have been identified:

1. the use of alternative routes of persuasion
2. the exploitation of attitudes and beliefs affecting social interaction
3. the use of persuasion and influence techniques.[261, 462, 464]

Alternative routes of persuasion

Alternative routes of persuasion use emotional shortcuts that bypass logical arguments or evidence about benefits. An example would be making a prominent statement in an advertisement that triggers excitement or fear, such as those used by some alternative practitioners suggesting modern drugs are poisons promoted by Big Pharma. This appeal to emotion sidesteps logical analysis and often triggers consumer interest without deeper thought about a product.

Attitudes and beliefs about social interaction

Exploiting attitudes and beliefs involves differences between the consumer's attitudes and those of the fraud perpetrator. Normally, a customer is habituated to trading practices where they expect both they and the vendor are engaged in an honest transaction of genuine value. In the case of a scam, the consumer still retains this belief until they become aware of the fraudulent nature of the transaction. The fraudster, however, has a completely different view of the social interaction, and is aware from the very start that this is a deceptive transaction with a goal of extracting money from it without any regard for the ethical obligations of fair trade.

Persuasion and influence techniques

Finally, fraudsters use persuasion and influence techniques that are associated with increased consumer risk-taking and concentrate on exploiting personality traits that correlate with an increased likelihood of engagement with risky products or services. These include: a dislike of premeditation, a dislike of changing one's mind (consistency), sensation seeking, needing self-control, valuing social influence, openness to taking risks, positive attitudes towards advertising, a need for meaning and purpose (cognition), and a preference for uniqueness.[462, 465, 466] As previously discussed, its seems in health scams social influence is a key factor; however, all are used by scammers.

Memes

One scam marketing technique that is frequently seen is the use of memes. Memes are a means of carrying cultural ideas, symbols or practices, via media such as the Internet, which promote social engagement. Health scammers often appropriate memes to promote their product. For example, the use of phrases such as 'one weird trick' or 'mom's odd tip' are frequently seen in web-based health scams. Presenting the product as unconventional allows it to appear novel, encouraging people not to disengage right away. If a product is marketed as 'mom's home remedy', it has the cultural significance of being considered safe and socially trusted. If marketed as 'weird', consumers tend to view it as something that is not widely known. Another common meme is to present a product as something mysterious, as in 'Doctors don't want you to know this!' This taps into the meme of mistrust of medicine, government, or the notion of Big Pharma. These techniques are often effective with people who desire rapid solutions for complex health problems. It is also worth noting that advertisements may use these factors to serve another purpose besides selling something directly, such as to identify which consumers might be susceptible to buying other products or providing remuneration from click fraud (such as pay per click advertising – see page 314).

Risk of deception

The good news is, as we become aware of the techniques fraudsters use and the personality traits that might make us more susceptible to their approaches, we can take action to avoid being taken in by them. To this end, in research into the nature of Internet health scams in 2018, my colleagues and I devised a simple screening tool to evaluate if health products and services being advertised are likely to be scams or not.[21] This is not as easy as it might first appear, as there is no way to completely screen out if a product is deceptive or not, but by looking for certain traits we can establish a 'risk of deception' for any product or service.

The Risk of Deception tool was devised by a team of nurses, doctors, physiotherapists, pharmacists and a social worker, and assigns points based on the characteristics of the advertisement and the type and number of persuasion characteristics found in it. For example, if the ad includes a celebrity endorsement, it gets one point; if it uses pseudo-technical language, it gets another point, and so on. More points are added if the ad uses 'mystical' language or claims that the product is very rare or in short supply. The higher the overall score, the greater the probability that the ad is a scam and any high-risk advertisements are almost certainly health scams.

The tool was originally developed based on research carried out by researchers at the University of British Columbia School of Nursing in 2018.[21] Following a review by the British Columbia Centre for Collaboration Motivation and Innovation, to make the original framework developed for health professionals more accessible to the public, the following tool was developed as a means to test the risk of deception of any healthcare advertisement (Table 2).[467]

Table 2: Are health and wellness advertising claims truthful?

There are a lot of health and wellness adverts on the Internet, TV, magazines, and newspapers. Most say they can help you to improve your health or quality of life. Some are helpful but many are scams. **So, is it truthful?**
Instructions: Use the information below to check a health or wellness advert and give it a 'risk of deception' score. The higher the score, the more likely it's a scam: • Each box has a claim worth points. • If you think the advert includes this item, add points as indicated in the blank box on the right-hand side of the page. Use your judgement to choose which ones you think apply, even if not exactly as stated. • Then add up all your circled points to see if it may be a scam.

Characteristic	Points
1. Does it offer a **'Free gift or sample'** if you: • participate in a phone call, or email them, • sign up for a newsletter, take out a subscription, or • go to a meeting?　　　　　　　　　　　　1 point	
2. Does it include comments about people who recommend, like, or hide it, such as: • '…millions of satisfied customers' or, • 'Mom's tips/tricks', or, • 'Doctors don't want you to know this'　　2 points	
3. Does it make **amazing claims**, including before and after photos, or real-life stories?　　2 points	
4. Does it suggest the product is **hard to find**, rare or in short supply?　　　　　　　　　1 point	
5. Does it suggest a **famous, well-known or respected person likes or uses it**?　　　　　2 points	
6. Does it include many **hard to understand words, with repetition or jargon**?　　　　　1 point	
7. Does it claim to be **based on science**, but seems to lack a scientific approach and seems more like **dubious/fake science** to you?　　　2 points	

8. Is there any real proof it actually works? (choose one category only) **Very low:** No proof 4 points **Low:** Some proof, but unclear sources such as stories from users 3 points **Moderate:** Some proof, but no agreement by medical professionals it works 2 points **Good:** Solid proof from scientists but it has not been in use for long by medical professionals 1 point **Excellent:** Lots of solid proof from scientists and it has been used in hospitals or clinics by medical professionals for a long time 0 points	

Beliefs as inclinations

Unfortunately, no system is a guarantee that a product or service is not fraudulent or safe, but by using clear and critical thinking skills we can remain consistently wary of the influences that put us at risk for deception and also attempt to avoid our own biases, or any tendency towards magical thinking. Does your rationale for believing in something stand up to scientific justification, or is it really based more on faith over evidence? A good place to start here is to explore the Oxford University Centre for Evidence-based Medicine's *'Catalog of Bias'* (www.catalogofbias.org) and ask oneself: 'Do any of these biases apply to me, or the arguments I am using to support my beliefs here?' Another simple question is to ask is 'Does this one piece of evidence I have found that confirms my beliefs outweigh the others that run contrary to it?' Being cognisant of why we believe what we do is an important aspect here, and is influenced by many things besides reasoning. This includes considering the weight of any scientific evidence for a claim but also what our parents and families taught us, what we want to believe is true, and what our experience suggests should be true. By consciously identifying our desires and biases, and their causes, it is possible to work free from their negative influence on our thinking and become more objective in analysing health claims. Demanding proof when proof seems demonstrable (especially quality scientific proof) is one way to do so, and attempting to remain intellectually neutral towards what hasn't been proven or isn't provable, even when you find yourself emotionally drawn to believe it. Trying to regard our belief as an inclination, rather than absolute, is another useful approach, so that we are not tempted to act with more confidence in the belief than is justified.

Trust and maintaining authority

Another important consideration here is the tendency to let others think for us. Most of us are busy people and, unfortunately, do not have the time or resources to investigate every health claim. Often a journalist presents a position about a topic and has their view accepted unquestioningly, or a friend makes a statement about a health practice and everyone accepts it as true without bothering to investigate further. Many of us do subjugate our judgement on health matters to faith in others and we all tend to cling not only to the things we believe in, but also to the reasoning that leads us to believe them. No one can be an expert in all aspects of health, and even expert health professionals tend to specialise in one aspect or another, and refer to others when problems relate to areas outside of their expertise. However, trust in health professionals should not be unqualified, and it is important that when trust is given it is earned through genuine expertise and qualifications, rational explanations of treatments that make sense and are given unreservedly. This means being vigilant about the faith-based health decisions, as they often end badly if trust is not carefully considered. In the final section we explore how to establish more positive behaviours relating to our own health, meaningful and productive relationships with health professionals and avoid some of the pitfalls of misplaced trust.

Section VII

Conclusions – who do you trust?

Chapter 26

Don't believe everything you think

By this point, any reader who has persevered this far would be forgiven for thinking that every aspect of modern healthcare is fraught with potential disaster and all so-called health professionals are completely untrustworthy charlatans. Nevertheless, despite the problems with contemporary healthcare we have discussed here, there is good reason to be optimistic. There have been huge developments in health science with a corresponding positive impact on human health. Infant and maternal death rates are at an all-time low in the UK and Canada, and new treatments have meant many previously fatal conditions have now become treatable. Progress in scientific healthcare has been quite remarkable, and despite all the flaws in the current system, for most people with access to it, it has proved hugely beneficial. We have seen massive advances in vaccines for infectious diseases, antibiotics, solid organ transplant, orthopaedic surgery, cancer treatment, reproductive technologies, medical imaging, genetic screening and much more. Modern immunisations mean many serious infectious diseases are now a thing of the past, and people are generally adopting more healthy lifestyles and living longer. Health promotion has become an important part of modern healthcare and just considering the improvements in health today compared with our parents' generation should provide ample evidence of the progress we have made with our improved knowledge about healthy behaviours, treatments and the eradication of many significant health problems. Overall, although the pace of innovation may have slowed from the implementation of new pharmaceuticals, antibiotics and surgical advances that occurred between the 1950s and 1980s, scientific healthcare and biomedicine continue to provide remarkable new therapeutics and preventative measures, such as the COVID-19 vaccine. Overall, scientific healthcare has proved to be, and continues to be, a massive benefit to overall human wellbeing. Unfortunately, however, access to it remains out of reach for much of the global population.

Health universally remains a major public concern, and many conditions remain untreatable or are poorly managed in our existing public health systems (especially chronic illnesses). We also have a long way to go to eradicate disease, and it's likely we may never completely do so, as new infectious viruses (such as SARS-CoV-2) do arise. There also remain numerous acute and chronic health issues that we still do not really understand well, or have no effective treatments for or ways to prevent. Nevertheless, research is ongoing for solutions and ways to improve the lives of those who suffer, so, there is certainly no reason to become pessimistic. Things can undoubtedly be improved, but threats to the progress made in public healthcare, such as arguments to privatise public health systems like the NHS, or the growth of anti-science, anti-vaccination, and regressive movements rejecting biomedicine, continue to arise and should be firmly resisted.

The myth of perfect health

A quick online search for the term 'perfect health' will reveal literally thousands of books, videos and websites which all profess to have the answers to living a perfectly healthy life. Some provide an ingenious seven-step process to maintaining health, or similar advice that promises a simple solution to all our health issues. As we have seen, many celebrities also make a good profit out of professing as much. We have most likely also all heard stories about people who smoked like chimneys and lived into their 90s, or folks who were never sick a day in their entire life. More often than not, those stories are about someone indirectly related to the raconteur, and also frequently end up with the subject coming to an untimely end despite their 'perfect health'.

The hypochondriac mind and the blame game

As a nurse, I learned a long time ago that perfect health is a myth. In most cases where we find someone having a health issue resulting in aches, pains, fevers, bruises, rashes or a runny nose, what we are seeing is their body responding with symptoms because it is doing its job in protecting the body and healing. The immune system and mechanisms kick in to tackle foreign invaders such as a viral, bacterial or fungal infection that is challenging the body, and inflammatory processes occur to help heal physical damage to the skin or muscles. These are signals that the biological machine that makes up our body is actually working fine. However, that doesn't stop us worrying excessively every time we get a headache ('must be a brain tumour...') or a chest pain ('must be a heart condition...'). This is unfortunately a very common human response, and often it seems the worst culprits for such hypochondria are doctors and nurses.

Many chronic conditions are hard to diagnose, and some are frequently misdiagnosed, such as hypothyroidism, which is why it is always wise to persist and seek a second opinion with ongoing health issues. Nevertheless, most of us are lucky enough to be unafflicted by these significant medical problems and it is important to recognise that health and wellness are not about feeling good all of the time. Instead, being unwell at times is a perfectly natural state of affairs and to be expected. It is cyclical and characterised by periods of optimal performance and the unfortunate periods when we are not at our best and have succumbed to some minor ailment or other. In the majority of those cases, we will recover perfectly well, and there is no need for drugs, surgical interventions, special diets or supplements, or costly alternative medical interventions.

However, there will always be practitioners who take advantage of this and will be keen to make a quick (and fake) diagnosis of a non-existent chronic condition that all the other doctors have somehow missed, such as 'adrenal fatigue' or 'candida overgrowth', inevitably with the need for extensive follow up and/or purchase of treatments. These take advantage of this tendency to look for simple answers to complex problems and unrealistic expectations of perfect health. Often, due to the placebo effect, this seems to work for a period, especially as people cycle into a period of feeling well. We also know that as biological beings the body and mind function together as one and our mental health can directly influence our physical health. However, it is also fruitful to recognise this and discard the wellness myth and associated notions that healthy people never get ill, that you don't have time to feel unwell, or you likely have some mystery chronic illness, and also the perception that you are somehow to blame for your poor health. It is much more helpful to replace these negative thoughts of self-blame with an awareness that it is physically impossible to be perfectly well all of the time whilst actually living a normal, active life. We can certainly take steps to maintain our fitness and promote health; it is also important to recognise that much of our health status is beyond our direct control and depends upon genetic heritage and environmental factors and, at the end of the day, unhappily, dumb luck.

Being proactive about health

There are many things we can do to help maintain and improve our health, and rather than becoming obsessed about the possible micro-toxins in our foods or products, excessive cleanliness, or New-Age notions of spiritual purity, it is probably more helpful to focus on the simple and well-known strategies. For those of us unsure where to start, usually a discussion with a general practitioner, nurse, or registered dietitian (not a nutritionist) can be a good start. Simple pro-active health measures we can undertake include eating a balanced diet you enjoy (including plenty of fruit and vegetables), being physically active daily with regular exercise, getting enough sleep, adopting positive mental health and stress-coping strategies, spending time with friends, avoiding smoking and minimising or abstaining from the use of potentially harmful recreational substances (including alcohol). Although most of us living and working in contemporary society will struggle to do all this assiduously, and economic factors certainly come into play, eating well, being active and moderating excesses are likely still to result in improved health, so should be something we strive to achieve.

It is a waste of time and energy to strive for an unattainable state of risk-free perfect health. Doing so may well result in obsessing over our health and missing out on many of the things that make life worth living. The human body and mind are designed to be adaptable to new situations, and changes in our health over time are a normal part of life. However, this is often not the message sold by wellness gurus and health scammers, who promote a kind of mythical wellness that only exists in media fantasies. Fascinatingly, those promoting these ideals often cite wholesome natural living but (very obviously) indulge in many unnatural practices to promote and maintain their 'healthy' image. The use of cosmetic dentistry, restrictive diets, expensive personal trainers, tanning salons, hair implants, cosmetic surgical procedures and even airbrushed promotional photos are a huge part of the deception. In reality, these folks fare no better than the rest of us in terms of their health. These are really lifestyle choices, not heathy behaviours, and we are being sold a lie.

Avoiding ineffective interventions

Part of the modern drive towards evidence-based practice has been to establish therapies that are based on sound demonstrable science rather than the claims or preferences of experts. Even this has proved contentious amongst many physicians, nurses and other practitioners, particularly where a favoured and well-established therapy has come into question. It is important to reflect that our knowledge of health-science constantly changes and it is important to keep up to date with new information. The truth (as some of the examples in this book attest) is there are undoubtedly some current medical practices that are ineffective but are still practised, just as blood-letting was once argued as an indispensable medical therapy. Health professionals are often reluctant to discard therapies validated by both tradition and their own experiences based upon someone else's research. A good example here is to consider the case for the arthroscopic surgical treatment of knee joint injuries.

Arthroscopic and spinal fixation surgical procedures

Arthroscopy involves the surgical treatment of a knee joint using a narrow tube attached to a fibre-optic video camera through a small incision, about the size of a buttonhole. The view inside the joint is transmitted to the surgeon via a high-definition video monitor. Arthroscopy has been the treatment of choice for knee injuries for many years. Following the development of fibre-optic tubes in the 1970s, this treatment for knee injuries became commonplace, especially for meniscal tears, rupture of the anterior cruciate ligament (ACL) and even osteoarthritis of the knee. Arthroscopy of the knee remains one of the most common orthopaedic procedures and is performed millions of times worldwide each year. I have even had it done myself, for a knee injury following a skiing misadventure back in 2006. However, a significant problem with it is that the evidence for its effectiveness remains uncertain at the very least.

For osteoarthritis (wear and tear damage) and meniscal tears (traumatic damage) the idea is basically to file down or cut rough knee cartilage away. It sounds like a good idea, but in most cases, it doesn't seem to work. Back in 2002, pioneering orthopaedic surgeon Dr J Bruce Moseley and colleagues published a fascinating and controversial study that showed that people who received fake arthroscopic knee surgery for osteoarthritis had results that were just as good as people who received the real surgery.[468] This caused some to raise concerns over the ethics of this work. However, all of the participants were fully informed of the details of the study. Since then, numerous other researchers have generally been finding the same thing about arthroscopic surgery for knee pain. In 2008, in what should have been the death knell for the procedure for osteoarthritis, a large-scale Cochrane Collaboration scientific review concluded that 'there is "gold" standard evidence that arthroscopic debridement has no benefit'.[469] In 2013 the American Academy of Orthopaedic Surgeons reiterated this in their guidelines on treatments for knee arthritis.[470]

Unfortunately, the evidence for the effectiveness of arthroscopy knee surgery for damage to the meniscus has suffered a similar fate. There is now a general consensus that arthroscopic surgical meniscectomy or meniscal tear repairs are ineffective, resulting in no better outcomes than sham surgery (where a surgical incision is made, but no repair undertaken in a study) or physiotherapy.[471, 472, 473, 474] Even its value for cruciate ligament injury repair has now become questionable.[475] The evidence is now overwhelming that arthroscopic knee surgery just doesn't do what it is supposed to for many conditions, something well-intentioned and highly-educated doctors had assumed for many years. However, unfortunately it often takes some years for these research findings to translate into changed healthcare practice as happened with spinal fusion surgery.

Spinal fusion surgery offers another example, and is an operation that welds together adjacent vertebrae to relieve back pain from worn-out intervertebral discs. Unlike many surgical procedures, it was actually tested in clinical trials, but unfortunately, these reported that the results of the surgery were no better than alternative treatments, like physiotherapy and exercise. These studies were completed in the early 2000s and should have been enough to greatly limit or stop the surgery, but by 2012 spinal fusion surgical rates in the USA had actually increased, and the results of the clinical trials seemed to have had little effect on practice.[476, 477] Eventually, Blue Cross indicated it would no longer pay for the procedure, and other insurers followed suit, and it has now fallen out of favour.

Dr David Kallmes of the Mayo Clinic, an author of another study that failed to demonstrate any benefits of a similar spinal-fusing procedure (vertebroplasty), suggested doctors continued to do these operations because insurers pay and because doctors remember their own patients who seemed to do better afterwards. When they read a negative study on their procedure, they tended to conclude that the other surgeons must have done it differently.[477, 478] This sort of expert-based (rather than evidence-based) practice creates a sort of inertia in clinical healthcare, even when research finds a practice or therapy is unhelpful, or a new therapeutic is developed; it can take years for it to take hold and practices to change.

So, if doctors are still not in agreement over many treatments, how does a typical member of the public with no healthcare expertise figure out if a recommended drug or treatment is likely to be useful to them? Luckily, there are strategies that can help, and keeping informed on the effectiveness of medical therapies is easier than ever today; the days when a single physician's advice was trusted as the word of God have thankfully long since gone. Firstly, for any health problem it is worth considering if the issue is likely to get better or not on its own.

Regression to the mean and the trajectory of illnesses

The nature of any health measurement in a population involves a phenomenon known as 'regression to the mean' (also known as 'reversion to mediocrity'), which is a fascinating and totally unintuitive concept. It originally comes from genetics and was popularised by Sir Francis Galton (1822–1911) over a century ago. It is the observation that, if a measurement of some variable is extreme (high or low) on its first measurement, it will tend to be closer to the average (or mean) on its second measurement, and if it is extreme on a second measurement, will tend to have been closer to the average on the first measurement. This is all rather puzzling, but actually a well-documented statistical fact, that on the whole things tend to move towards an average baseline over time. In finance it is used to note that, with investments over time, returns can be very unstable over short periods but overall, very stable (and more predictable) in the long run.

Let us take a simple example to see how it works. Say we take a group of students who take a test asking them to randomly answer yes or no to a set of 100 yes/no questions. Statistically, some will score above 50% and some below, purely by chance. The mean should fall around 50%. Following this, if we then take 10% of the top-scoring students and give them a second test on which they again choose randomly, their mean score would again likely be close to 50% (as the reason they scored high initially was purely by chance). Therefore, the mean of these students would 'regress' back towards the mean of all students who took the original test (even though they were in the top 10% as the selection was random in both cases). It is important to note that without random chance the scores will not regress to the mean, but most real world situations are a combination of an actual effect (such as knowledge or skill), and an element of chance.[31] Regression to the mean is also an observation of performance of a population over time, and not an individual causal predictive phenomenon. So, it can't be used to predict how a particular person will score or respond to a drug over time.

Nevertheless, regression to the mean is an important concept in healthcare as it suggests that illnesses have a cycle and follow patterns in a population and, in some cases, symptoms will resolve on their own. For example, when a person has a cold, the disease normally progresses through a process of active viral infection, with all the symptoms, to a resolution as the immune system overwhelms the infection. The majority of cases will follow this trajectory and require no medical intervention, other than possibly measures to make the symptoms less unpleasant. However, in terms of health psychology, we also know that people tend to seek professional healthcare when their symptoms are at their worst and then tend to assume that whatever they did at that stage probably helped resolve their illness. So, we might think a specific herbal tea we drank when we were feeling most terrible was what helped cure our cold. We also see this a lot with claims of miracle cures, where it is not unusual to hear someone assert that a veggie-smoothie diet cured their cancer, despite the fact they only started the diet after several rounds of chemo and radiotherapy.

In health research, this concept means it is necessary to consider that what we are observing as patients respond to a specific therapy might simply be regression to the mean. It is not always clear why, but statistically it is to be expected that some illnesses (even cancer) will resolve spontaneously for some people over time. If one medical trial of a new drug suggests that it is has outstanding results, outperforming all other treatments for a condition, then we know that it is more likely that the outperforming drug or treatment will perform closer to the mean in a second trial. So, even when a therapy is effective, the real results will be a mix of some positive results due to the intervention and some that would have improved on their own.

Cause and effect

As humans we are naturally prone to look for causal relationships to explain things, and so tend to see causal relationships even when there are none, such as the erroneous claims of autism or sudden infant death syndrome (SIDS) being attributed to vaccines. As noted above, people intuitively tend to consider whatever they did at the peak of their illness or immediately before they started to feel better is most likely what resulted in the improvement, be it taking antibiotics or smoothies. Unfortunately, this kind of intuitive thinking and justification for a health intervention does not reflect the real world where there are always outliers, and so such thinking provides a poor basis for developing meaningful health knowledge.[479] Regression to the mean is another good reason why we need repeat studies to reinforce findings, and should never accept the findings of one study or incident as good evidence. A useful tactic modern health scientists use is to examine multiple studies in a meta-analysis (a statistical analysis of data combined from multiple similar studies) or a systematic review (comparing the results of multiple studies of the same issue).

In terms of practical applications, regression to the mean suggests we should be cautious of making unnecessary intuitive leaps as to the value of any specific therapeutic interventions we observe and consider the known illness trajectory for the specific problem. There will always be serious conditions that require immediate and highly invasive interventions (such as emergency drugs or surgery). However, for the less serious illnesses that most people experience, a less interventionist approach, letting the body heal with a few simple, symptom-management measures may be more productive than diving into seeking novel medical, or alternative, treatments. Sometimes a health issue may take many months to fully resolve, and the trend in modern medical care is now moving away from more invasive interventions unless absolutely necessary.

Given our knowledge of regression to the mean, being cautious about any suggested miracle-cures or invasive interventions for health issues is probably a reasonable approach. For example, for lower back pain, various health professions over the years have recommended opioids, surgery, physical manipulation, acupuncture, chiropractic and even IV vitamin boosters and coffee-enemas. The quality of evidence on the effectiveness of these for the condition runs from mediocre to non-existent. However, for most people, providing the body with plenty of time to heal with a nutritious diet, rest, stress reduction practices, gentle therapies such as physiotherapy, building up exercise as tolerated and using non-opioid analgesics as much as possible, is probably a wiser strategy in terms of both promoting healing and avoiding the risks of adverse effects from the actual treatments. Unfortunately, at this time we still do not have a simple fix for chronic back pain (despite what chiropractors may tell us).

The power of placebo and nocebo

Understanding the nature of the placebo effect is also worth spending time considering here, as this is actually quite a complex phenomenon. There is now considerable evidence that our expectations to get better have significant effects on how we actually feel, and we certainly hear a lot about the placebo effect in the media. A placebo (Latin for 'to please') is the measurable, observable, or experienced improvement in health or behaviour not attributable to any medication or treatment that has been administered. It is frequently argued that the placebo effect is really mind over matter, and it has become a catch-all term for a positive change in health not attributable to a therapeutic intervention. However, it isn't quite that simple, and the changes seen with placebos are most likely due to a number of factors. These include:

1. Regression to the mean: The fascinating statistical phenomenon (discussed above) that, if a variable is extreme on its first measurement, it will tend to be closer to the average on a second measurement;

2. Spontaneous resolution: Leave people alone and they often get better without any therapeutic interventions (much to the chagrin of many surgeons!). A proportion of the population will naturally resolve an illness without treatment. This is a good argument for minimising interventions, versus a 'let's throw the kitchen sink at this health problem' approach;

3. Reduction of psychological stress: Mental stress has a direct physiological effect on the body through what is known as the neuro-endocrine response, and a reduction in stress can have positive physiological benefits;

4. Misdiagnosis: Frequently health conditions are misdiagnosed (especially in early phases), and even today many physicians will attest differential diagnosis remains as much an art as a science; and lastly,

5. Subject expectancy or classical conditioning: Remember Pavlov and his dogs? If we associate one specific thing (such as a tablet) with another (such as good sleep), we learn they go together, and one can trigger an expectation of the other.

The placebo effect is nicely characterised by this quote:

The physician's belief in the treatment and the patient's faith in the physician exert a mutually reinforcing effect; the result is a powerful remedy that is almost guaranteed to produce an improvement and sometimes a cure.

Petr Skrabanek and James McCormick. [480]

In this way we can see that the placebo effect can influence our health experiences, and can also be used to support many useless health practices such as nutritional supplements (of the 'super-food' variety), drinking sharks-fin soup or eating rhino horn for increased potency.

In scientific drug testing, researchers frequently use controls of inactive substances (e.g. sugar pills) but have to consider that in some cases these will actually produce an effect similar to what would be expected with the active drug. It is also possible to counter the placebo effect with large samples and, more particularly, double-blinded (where neither the researcher nor the subject knows if they are taking the active drug or control substance) and repeated studies. Indeed, in scientific clinical trials, researchers are now required to take the placebo effect into account in their studies (a requirement for this was introduced in a revision of the Declaration of Helsinki (The World Medical Association's policy statement on the ethical treatment of research subjects, first adopted in 1964).

Overall, the placebo effect can be very powerful, and amazingly some researchers have suggested it could even account for 25-50% of the effects observed in a clinical drug study![481] Strangely, there is also some growing evidence that the placebo effect is getting stronger, and currently we are not really sure why. Clinical trials on a range of medications used for treating different psychological and physical health problems suggest that differences in the size of positive effects relative to placebo effects are decreasing.[482]

A related phenomenon to placebo is the 'nocebo' (Latin for 'to harm') effect, which is basically the same as the placebo effect but this time the subject experiences negative, harmful, unpleasant or undesirable effects after receiving an inactive substance. Nocebo responses are thought to be due to a subject's pessimistic belief and expectation that the drug or treatment will produce negative consequences. One well-known example of this is, the physician researcher C K Meador once suggested, the fact that people who believe in voodoo can actually die because of their belief.[483] Other studies have also demonstrated this effect. In a well-known cardiac study, women who believed they were prone to heart disease were nearly four times as likely to die as women with similar risk factors who didn't believe this.[484, 485]

These effects appear to be mediated by higher brain centres but, as discussed earlier, the subconscious mind is easily manipulated, so the human brain appears very susceptible to placebo and nocebo effects. Since people's beliefs and fears are so highly varied, it may well be that many things that are unnoticed by health professionals, such as the colour of the pills prescribed, the words used to provide information, and even the environment in which treatment is provided, may all be infused with unintentional meanings for the patient and have profound effects (positive or negative) on their response to a therapy.

There are also ethical issues to be considered when using nocebos in research. I sit on a university behavioural research ethics committee, and clearly research using nocebos is problematic here. Even with placebos the question frequently arises whether it is ethical to deceive patients in this way for the sake of science (even if they know they 'might' receive a placebo in the study). In general practice it is also questionable whether it is ethical for physicians to give antibiotics for viral infections, and vitamins for fatigue. These are still relatively common practices, despite the fact that research tells us they don't work for these issues and this is not for the overall good of the population. So, it seems there is lots of room for more research into this interesting phenomenon, and its implications for healthcare practice. This only serves to illustrate the powerful effects of psychosocial factors that influence our health.

Chapter 27

Conclusion

Taking back charge of your health

Despite all of the numerous problems with current healthcare systems, regulation, health research, Big Pharma, alternative medicine and health scammers, there is still much we can do to positively influence our health and wellbeing. Some health problems are always going to be a matter of genetics, environmental factors, bad health behaviours and/or bad luck, but attempts to put the blame on the individual for their illnesses by such things as fat-shaming, addiction guilt, lack of spiritual purity, or suggesting that people can simply will themselves well, are disingenuous. Although lifestyle factors influence our health profoundly, people do not usually get serious diseases simply because of the way they think or behave, but as a result of multiple factors. Modern healthcare needs to be multi-modal and holistic in its approach, but looking for quick magical solutions just doesn't work, and plays into the hands of deceptive health practitioners. Simply being aware of this and looking at what those marketing health services are actually saying with a sceptical eye can help considerably.

There are no absolutes

Most genuine health professionals and scientists will never

claim they have an absolute cure and will also openly admit they could be wrong, but give you reasons why they believe they are not. It is perfectly reasonable to ask questions about vaccines, drugs, surgeries or other medical therapies, and we should all actively do so. Good health professionals encourage questions and voicing concerns. However, it is also important to consider if the answers provided appear reasonable and not to dismiss them because they clash with our own prior beliefs, or those of our social group. It is also important to consider how members of that group respond to new information. For example, if a mother has heard the claim that there are aborted foetal cells in vaccines from her friends, and asks a nurse or physician about this, then that is perfectly reasonable and responsible. However, when it is explained how this is untrue and based upon misinformation and can be easily demonstrated as false, then a logical response is to report this back to those friends making that claim. If they then continue making these claims irrespective of the contrary evidence, or simply change tack to make another negative claim about vaccines, the chances are they are not being open to the possibility they are wrong, and simply want to maintain their position irrespective of its validity. A simple test is to ask someone making such health claims: what would make them change their mind? The answer may often be very revealing, and if nothing will change their mind, then their health advice is best treated with considerable scepticism.

Recognise deceptive tactics

Apart from being proactive in looking after ourselves and adopting healthy behaviours as discussed above, we can also become more aware of the nature of the problems and deceptions in the healthcare industry and thereby avoid scams and dubious practices. To recap, it is important to consider the following issues in any health professional interaction.

Qualifications

A useful protective behaviour is to look at the qualifications and behaviours of those making health claims. As we have explored, there are so many different dubious and diploma-mill health qualifications it is sometimes difficult to know if someone's credentials are meaningful or not. If the qualifications are conventional (e.g. a medical doctor, registered nurse or physiotherapist) and from a well-known publicly funded university, then you can be fairly sure they are genuine and their credentials reflect the quality expected of undergraduate, graduate and professional qualifications. If someone's professional qualifications appear to be from private, alternative medical colleges or the growing number of private New-Age universities and represent such vague things as interdisciplinary spiritual studies, transformative change, integrative healing, transdisciplinary energetics, somatic consciousness, nutrionics, or other vague neologisms, they should be prudently regarded with a high degree of suspicion. Unfortunately, the academic credibility of many such institutions is highly suspect. Being accredited as an educational institution in most of these cases simply means that someone has checked there are teachers, classrooms, rudimentary student services and programmes of study leading to awards on offer. Entry requirements for such programmes usually reflect the size of the student's wallet rather than their academic abilities. The high number of for-profit law schools in the USA that churn out graduates who cannot pass the bar exam is a good example of the sort of problems encountered here.[486]

Another significant issue here is that the people who graduate or purchase these qualifications often have an unrealistic view of their own expertise. I recently witnessed a self-professed expert researcher in vaccines making anti-vaccination claims about kids being turned into zombies by them on social media. She claimed a long list of qualifications to support her expertise, but in reality, was an estate agent with a range of online certificates, a dodgy law degree from a US School that was shut down for fraud years ago, and a Reiki Master certificate. Strangely, she also claimed she was once married to a doctor as evidence of her extensive medical knowledge. Although it may be difficult to ascertain the real value of health qualifications, a cursory inspection should be enough to give some sense of whether they have any genuine value or are illusory fabrications. Unfortunately, though, there are also many genuinely qualified people who do act unscrupulously, and as we have explored here, there are also a lot of 'highly qualified idiots' quite happy to champion irrational ideas in public forums. So, in addition to health qualifications, it is worth examining other aspects of the behaviour of someone selling a health product or service, particularly if they are claiming some exclusive knowledge or skill set, and of course, carefully explore the nature of the therapy being advocated.

Novel therapies

Being rigorous in exploring novel treatments is important, no matter how emotionally appealing they seem. For any suggested therapeutic intervention, be it drugs, surgery or diets, a practical first step is to check its historical use, and a good rule of thumb is to treat any new health intervention or social trend with a degree of scepticism until it has been established as an effective and safe practice. This does not mean that just because a health practice has had thousands of years of practice it actually works (as many ancient therapies don't really work), but it does prevent you becoming a guinea pig. For example, the use of e-cigarettes and vaping is currently a growing trend, and many users (including some doctors) are extoling the health benefits, especially as an alternative to cigarettes. However, at the moment long-term data showing that vaping is a healthier alternative than cigarette smoking does not exist. There may well be a high cost for ignoring potential risks, and the toxic effects of wood dust, asbestos and second-hand smoke are cases in point. At the time of writing, some significant health issues with vaping and respiratory illness are being reported, and the nature of the problem is unclear. The same is true of many novel therapeutics being sold. Certainly, it is possible new therapies may be highly effective, and for some there may be no choice as a novel or experimental therapy might be their last resort. Nevertheless, it is important to recognise that the use of any new drug or therapy is a significantly riskier proposition than the use of those with established safety.

The risk of deception
Finally, a simple way to explore the likelihood that a health product or service is a scam is to check it with the risk of deception tool described previously (see page 318). Anything that scores in the 'high risk of deception' category is in all likelihood a health scam. Also, we can forearm ourselves against health scammers and deceptive health arguments by looking at the sources of information that are being used to promote a product. If it is a therapy that is widely cited as helpful in numerous medical, nursing and other established health professional journals/ websites and is also supported by government sources (such as Health Canada, the US Centers for Disease Control and Prevention, the UK National Institute for Health and Care Excellence, or the global Cochrane Centres) it is likely to be genuine. Additionally, in exploring the value of therapeutics, bear in mind that there are self-interest journals that only publish studies about a specific type of therapy or approach and are therefore far less trustworthy as sources of information than journals or sources that explore a wide range of interventions. For example, alternative medicine journals rarely publish negative results, whereas quality medical, nursing and science journals will frequently publish studies that both succeeded and failed to demonstrate a useful intervention. If the sources promoting a practice are primarily web or social-media based,

The New Alchemists

members of the general public (e.g. anecdotes from concerned parents), alternative practitioners, conspiracy theorists and/ or New-Age wellness gurus, there is a much higher likelihood that the information is incorrect or simply a scam. Healthcare science is complex, and very often these sources have anti-science or other agendas and suggest ideas that are completely incorrect. Often, we can easily check these facts as being true or not, but sometimes the volume of information on the Internet far outweighs the accuracy. Reminding ourselves that the mass of information published on the web is not a good indicator of its truthfulness is sometimes useful. Another useful thing to ask is if those promoting the product or service are directly profiting from its sale in some way. If so, seek sources that do not do so, as these are likely to be less biased.

Navigating the deceptive landscape

In conclusion, there are plenty of reasons why we should continue to place our trust in science-based healthcare, and to be positive about the future of human health and our abilities to successfully navigate the minefield of health deception and fraud in modern society. It is equally important to value and protect the systems we have that are working. Public healthcare provision was a huge step forward for society. The implementation of the NHS was the first time anywhere in the world that completely free healthcare was made available on the basis of citizenship rather than the payment of fees or insurance. One only has to look at countries that do not have universal healthcare systems to see the huge benefits we have in countries that do (like the UK and Canada) and we should strive to protect such systems and ensure they operate efficiently using practices we know work.

There are, of course, many other forms of health scam and deception and we have not exhausted the subject here by any means. The world of academic plagiarism is another area, for

346

example, and is perhaps the most common ethical issue plaguing medical research publishing. Sometimes, strict disciplinary action is taken against the plagiarist, but often they only receive a warning.[487] Similarly, a huge number of predatory health journals and conferences have sprung up over the last decade that make money publishing junk health-science with practically (or actually) no scientific review on a pay-per-paper basis.[458] For example, some of my students sent in a spoof conference paper submission to one of these a few years back suggesting a novel method of reviving zombies with tissue transplants and had their paper accepted within 48 hours. I literally get about 10 of these requests by email every single day.

Notwithstanding, most health deception and health scams occur outside of public healthcare settings, so next time you encounter a health advertisement or practitioner that makes promises that seem too good to be true, it might help to try imagining your response to them if they were pitching some other commercial product or service, as when it comes to health it seems we are more susceptible to their approach. Imagine if they were a used-car salesman; would you be swayed by their sales pitch for the car with one previous careful owner, the vicar's wife who only used it on Sundays? Healthcare product advertisements often also make such surprisingly outrageous claims. As with our friend Jeff, back at the start of this book, we may even get some vague sense something is not quite right or above board, but we really want to believe so oddly tend to ignore our own intuition (especially when it comes to health).

At the end of the day, we will pay the price for our complacency here. The sad truth is, many health fraudsters are highly skilled manipulators, and do not always end up being held to account for their crimes, and many continue to profit from them. Health products and services remain a highly profitable enterprise as everyone is a potential customer, and so they are likely to remain a key area for marketing scams. But what's that I hear you say?

Never mind all that, there is a new Facebook post by a doctor recommending the health benefits of rutabaga extract, as used by the ancient Mesopotamians for centuries to prolong life, reduce stress, boost the immune system, cure hair loss and even raise the dead. Amazingly, he has a concentrated supplement in easy-to-swallow form, and it's on special offer this week, but only whilst stocks last. Great Scott, where did I leave my credit card...?

References

1. Modic D, Lea SEG. Scam Compliance and the Psychology of Persuasion. *SSRN* 21 June 2013. https://ssrn.com/abstract=2364464 or http://dx.doi.org/10.2139/ssrn.2364464

2. Fischer WC. German hyperinflation 1922/23 : a law and economics approach. Eul Verlag; 2010. 204

3. Bennett DJ, Jennings RC. *Successful science communication : telling it like it is.* Cambridge UK: Cambridge University Press; 2011: 462 pp.

4. Brown PG, Timmerman P. *Ecological Economics for the Anthropocene: An Emerging Paradigm.* New York, NY: Columbia University Press; 2015: 196-197 pp. (cited 3 May 2019)

5. WHO. Health Promotion: A discussion document on the concept and principles: summary report of the Working Group on Concept and Principles of Health Promotion. Copenhagen; 1984.

6. US Bureau of Labor Statistics. Healthcare Occupations : Occupational Outlook Handbook: U.S. Bureau of Labor Statistics. *Occupational Outlook Handbook* 2017. www.bls.gov/ooh/healthcare/home.htm (cited 23 January 2019)

7. Thorne S, Paterson B, Russell C, Schultz A. Complementary/alternative medicine in chronic illness as informed self-care decision making. *Int J Nurs Stud* 2002; 39(7): 671–683. www.ncbi.nlm.nih.gov/pubmed/12231024

8. Furnham A HY. Examining Health Beliefs, Attitudes and Behaviours Relate to Complementary and Orthodox Medicine Use in Chinese Population. *Altern Integr Med* 2013; 02(07).

9. Sirois FM, Salamonsen A, Kristoffersen AE. Reasons for continuing use of Complementary and Alternative Medicine (CAM) in

students: a consumer commitment model. *BMC Complement Altern Med* 2016; 16(1): 75. www.biomedcentral.com/1472-6882/16/75

10. Thomsen J. Ex-doctor says Trump dictated letter claiming he would be 'healthiest' president ever. *The Hill.* https://thehill.com/homenews/administration/385765-trumps-ex-doctor-says-trump-dictated-letter-claiming-he-would-be. Published 2018. (cited 12 February 2021)

11. Thomas K, Kolata G. President Trump Received Regeneron Experimental Antibody Treatment. *The New York Times* 2 October 2021. www.nytimes.com/2020/10/02/health/trump-antibody-treatment.html. (cited 12 February 2021)

12. Gillis C, Belluz J, Dehaas J. Do you trust your doctor? *Macleans Magazine* 16 August 2010 . www.macleans.ca/news/canada/do-you-trust-your-doctor/

13. Blendon RJ, Benson JM, Hero JO. Public Trust in Physicians — U.S. Medicine in International Perspective. *N Engl J Med* 2014; 371(17): 1570–1572. www.ncbi.nlm.nih.gov/pubmed/25337746

14. Steel-Fisher GK, Blendon RJ, Lasala-Blanco N. Ebola in the United States — Public Reactions and Implications. *N Engl J Med* 2015; 373(9): 789–791. www.nejm.org/doi/10.1056/NEJMp1506290

15. Brenan M. Nurses Again Outpace Other Professions for Honesty. *Ethics* Washington, DC; 2018 (cited 2019 Jan 29). https://news.gallup.com/poll/245597/nurses-again-outpace-professions-honesty-ethics.aspx

16. Gavidia M. Cancer death rates. *AJMC* 8 January 2020. Available at www.ajmc.com/view/overall-us-cancer-mortality-rate-reaches-26year-decline-but-obesityrelated-cancer-deaths-rise (cited 13 March 2021).

17. World Health Organization. Ten Threats to Global Health in 2019. *Emergencies* 2019 (cited 28 Jan 2019). www.who.int/emergencies/ten-threats-to-global-health-in-2019

18. Offit PA. Do You Believe in Magic? . Philadelphia, PA: Harper Collins; 2013 (cited 4 Dec 2015). www.harpercollins.ca/9780062222961/do-you-believe-in-magic

19. Johnson SB, Park HS, Gross CP, Yu JB. Use of alternative medicine for cancer and its impact on survival. *J Natl Cancer Inst* 2018; 110(1): 121–124.

20. Werneke U, Earl J, Seydel C, Horn O, Crichton P, Fannon D.

Potential health risks of complementary alternative medicines in cancer patients. *Br J Cancer* 2004 ; 90(2): 408–413. www.ncbi.nlm.nih.gov/pubmed/14735185

21. Garrett B, Murphy S, Jamal S, Macphee M, Reardon J, Cheung W, et al. Internet health scams — Developing a taxonomy and risk-of-deception assessment tool. *Heal Soc Care Community* 2019; 27(1): 226–240.

22. Kaboli PJ, Doebbeling BN, Saag KG, Rosenthal GE. Use of complementary and alternative medicine by older patients with arthritis: a population-based study. *Arthritis Rheum* 2001; 45(4): 398–403. http://doi.wiley.com/10.1002/1529-0131%28200108%2945%3A4%3C398%3A%3AAID-ART354%3E3.0.CO%3B2-I (cited 19 July 2017)

23. Patel DN, Low W-L, Tan LL, Tan M-MB, Zhang Q, Low M-Y, et al. Adverse events associated with the use of complementary medicine and health supplements: An analysis of reports in the Singapore Pharmacovigilance database from 1998 to 2009. *Clin Toxicol* 2012; 50(6): 481–489. www.tandfonline.com/doi/full/10.3109/15563650.2012.700402

24. Stevinson C, Honan W, Cooke B, Ernst E. Neurological complications of cervical spine manipulation. *J R Soc Med* 2001; 94(3): 107–110. www.ncbi.nlm.nih.gov/pubmed/11285788 (cited 20 July 2017)

25. Nielsen SM, Tarp S, Christensen R, Bliddal H, Klokker L, Henriksen M. The risk associated with spinal manipulation: an overview of reviews. *Syst Rev* 2017; 6(64). doi: 10.1186/s13643-017-0458-y.

26. Ernst E. Adverse effects of unconventional therapies in the elderly: A systematic review of the recent literature. *J Am Aging Assoc* 2002; 25(1): 11–20. www.ncbi.nlm.nih.gov/pubmed/23604886 (cited 20 July 2017)

27. Luke S, Fleming O, Stickney R. Woman Dies After Turmeric IV: *County Medical Examiner* - NBC 7 San Diego. San Diego 7 News. 2017 www.nbcsandiego.com/news/local/Woman-Dies-After-Turmeric-IV-416896783.html (cited 28 January 2019)

28. Aldach K. Alberta parents whose toddler died of meningitis were told to visit doctor, trial hears - Calgary - CBC News. *CBC News Calgary* 2016 www.cbc.ca/news/canada/calgary/raymond-toddler-death-trial-stephan-1.3481958 (cited 19 July 2017)

29. Lindsay B. BC health official voices 'grave concerns' after child

given homeopathic remedy using rabid-dog saliva. *CBC News* 2018. www.cbc.ca/news/canada/british-columbia/b-c-health-official-voices-grave-concerns-after-child-given-homeopathic-remedy-using-rabid-dog-saliva-1.4622494 (cited 28 January 2019)

30. Donelly B, Toscano N. *The woman who fooled the world : Belle Gibson's cancer con, and the darkness at the heart of the wellness industry.* Victoria: Scribe; 2017.

31. Goldacre B. *Bad Science.* London: Fourth Estate; 2008.

32. Goldacre B. A dose of reality. *The Guardian* 1 September 2008 www.theguardian.com/business/2008/sep/01/pharmaceuticals.drugs (cited 14 February 2019)

33. Davis BK. *Phlebotomy: From Student to Professional.* 3rd ed. New York: Delmar; 2011.

34. Kerridge IH, Lowe M. Bloodletting: the story of a therapeutic technique. *Med J Aust* 1995; 163(11–12): 631–633. www.ncbi.nlm.nih.gov/pubmed/8538564

35. Hays JN. *The burdens of disease: epidemics and human response in western history.* 2009; 374 pp. www.worldcat.org/title/burdens-of-disease-epidemics-and-human-response-in-western-history/oclc/961550627&referer=brief_results (cited 20 February 2019)

36. Bynum WF. The Weapon Salve in Seventeenth Century English Drama. *Journal of the History of Medicine and Allied Sciences* 1966; 21: 8–23. www.jstor.org/stable/24621560 (cited 20 February 2020)

37. Freud S, Strachey J, Freud A. *The Standard edition of the complete psychological works of Sigmund Freud.* Hogarth Press; 1962.

38. Kapsalis T, Litherland G. The hysterical alphabet : wherein we chart the course of that curious malady of the womb or hysterus known as hysteria, beginning with the letter A in ancient Egypt, with the actual kinds, causes, symptoms, prognostics, and several cures thereof. WhiteWalls; 2008.

39. Tasca C, Rapetti M, Carta MG, Fadda B. Women and hysteria in the history of mental health. *Clin Pract Epidemiol Ment Health.* 2012; 8: 110–119. www.ncbi.nlm.nih.gov/pubmed/23115576 (cited 20 February 2019)

40. National Research Council. Health Risks from Exposure to Low Levels of Ionizing Radiation. Washington, DC: National Academies Press; March 2006.www.nap.edu/catalog/11340 (cited 21 February 2019)

41. Macklis RM. The Great Radium Scandal. *Sci Am* 1993; 269(2): 94–99. www.nature.com/doifinder/10.1038/scientificamerican0893-94 (cited 21 February 2019)

42. Boenig H. *Method of Reducing Irritants in Tobacco by Gamma irradiation.* 3,358,694, 1967.

43. Gadbow D. State of mine: Many swear to benefits of inhaling radon. *The Missoulian* 2004; (cited 21 February 2019) https://missoulian.com/news/state-and-regional/state-of-mine-many-swear-to-benefits-of-inhaling-radon/article_de78e871-ad4a-5142-bdcc-6ed8c6883417.html

44. Volpini M, Giacobbe P, Cosgrove GR, Levitt A, Lozano AM, Lipsman N. The History and Future of Ablative Neurosurgery for Major Depressive Disorder. *Stereotact Funct Neurosurg* 2017; 95(4): 216–228. www.ncbi.nlm.nih.gov/pubmed/28723697

45. Heller AC, Amar AP, Liu CY, Apuzzo MLJ. Surgery of the Mind and Mood: A Mosaic of Issues in Time and Evolution. *Neurosurgery* 2006; 59(4): 720–739. https://academic.oup.com/neurosurgery/article/59/4/720/2559224 (cited 15 February 2019)

46. Bovbjerg ML. Rethinking Dr. Spock. *Am J Public Health* 2011;101(10): 1812; author reply 1812-3. www.ncbi.nlm.nih.gov/pubmed/21852654 (cited 15 February 2019)

47. Perkins A. Back to sleep: the doctor who helped stem a cot death epidemic. *The Guardian* 26 August 2016 www.theguardian.com/society/2016/aug/26/back-to-sleep-sudden-infant-death-syndrome-cot-death-peter-fleming (cited 15 February 2019)

48. Hattenstone S. Britain's contaminated blood scandal: 'I need them to admit they killed our son'. *The Guardian* 3 March 2018 www.theguardian.com/society/2018/mar/03/contaminated-blood-scandal-thousands-haemophiliacs-died-simon-hattenstone (cited 15 February 2019)

49. Government of Scotland PHD. Preliminary Report of The Penrose Inquiry, an independent Scottish public inquiry under the Inquiries Act 2005, chaired by the Right Honourable Lord Penrose. *The Penrose Report.* Edinburgh: APS Group Scotland. 2010; 2008. www.penroseinquiry.org.uk/preliminary-report/

50. Public I, Report I. *The Archer Inquiry - An Independent Public Inquiry Report on NHS Supplied Contaminated Blood and Blood Products.* London; 2009. www.archercbbp.com

51. Johnson M, Stokes RG, Arndt T. *The Thalidomide catastrophe : how it happened, who was responsible and why the search for justice continues after more than six decades*. Exeter: Onwards & Upwards Publishers; 2018. 263 pp.
52. Walsh F. PIP breast implants: 'serious lessons must be learned'. BBC News . 14 April 2012. www.bbc.com/news/health-18057761 (cited 19 February 2019)
53. Biomedtracker, Biotechnology Innovation Organization, Amplion. *Clinical Development Success Rates Pharma intelligence*. San Diego, CA.; 2016: 27 pp. www.bio.org/sites/default/files/Clinical Development Success Rates 2006-2015 - BIO, Biomedtracker, Amplion 2016.pdf (cited 27 February 2019)
54. Goldacre B. *Bad Pharma : how drug companies mislead doctors and harm patients*. London: Fourth Estate; 2012.
55. Lavoie D. Bristol-Myers Squibb to pay $515M settlement. ABC News. 30 Sept. 2007 https://abcnews.go.com/Business/story?id=3670595&page=1 (cited 1 March 2019)
56. Meier B. In Guilty Plea, OxyContin Maker to Pay $600 Million. *The New York Times* 10 May 2007 www.nytimes.com/2007/05/10/business/11drug-web.html (cited 1 March 2019)
57. Canadian Institute for Health Information. *Pan-Canadian Trends in the Prescribing of Opioids, 2012 to 2016*. Ottawa, ON: CIHI; 2017. www.cihi.ca/sites/default/files/document/pan-canadian-trends-opioid-prescribing-2017-en-web.pdf
58. Thomson Reuters. OxyContin drug maker mulls bankruptcy due to myriad lawsuits. CBC News 4 March 2019 www.cbc.ca/news/business/oxycontin-bankruptcy-1.5042149 (cited 5 March 2019)
59. Thomas K. J&J to Pay $2.2 Billion in Risperdal Settlement. *The New York Times* 4 November 2013. www.nytimes.com/2013/11/05/business/johnson-johnson-to-settle-risperdal-improper-marketing-case.html (cited 1 March 2019)
60. Wilson D. AstraZeneca Settles Case for $520 Million. *The New York Times* 27 April 2010 www.nytimes.com/2010/04/28/business/28drug.html (cited 1 March 2019)
61. Wadman M. Merck settles Vioxx lawsuits for $4.85 billion. *Nature* 13 November 2007 www.nature.com/doifinder/10.1038/450324b (cited 1 March 2019)
62. Pollack A, Secret M. Amgen Agrees to Pay $762 Million for

Marketing Anemia Drug for Off-Label Use. *The New York Times* 2012;12. www.nytimes.com/2012/12/19/business/amgen-agrees-to-pay-762-million-in-drug-case.html

63. Sifferlin A. Breaking Down GlaxoSmithKline's Billion-Dollar Wrongdoing. *Time* July 2012. http://healthland.time.com/2012/07/05/breaking-down-glaxosmithklines-billion-dollar-wrongdoing/ (cited 1 March 2019)

64. Manning S. NHS hit for millions by overcharging 'scam.' *The Independent* 15 July 2013. www.independent.co.uk/news/uk/politics/nhs-hit-for-millions-by-overcharging-scam-8708292.html (cited 11 September 2020)

65. Espiner T. Pfizer fined record £84.2m for overcharging NHS. BBC News. 7 December 2016 www.bbc.com/news/business-38233852 (cited 11 September 2020)

66. Reuters. Pfizer wins appeal against UK fine for epilepsy drug price hike. *Reuters News* 07 June 2018. www.reuters.com/article/pfizer-britain-fine/pfizer-wins-appeal-against-uk-fine-for-epilepsy-drug-price-hike-idUSL5N1T95EA (cited 11 September 2020)

67. Taylor Wessing. Court of Appeal Judgment confirms that Pfizer and Flynn should not yet be fined for excessive pricing of anti-epilepsy drug. *Insights* 12 March 2020. www.taylorwessing.com/en/insights-and-events/insights/2020/03/pfizer-and-flynn-should-not-yet-be-fined-for-excessive-pricing-of-anti-epilepsy-drug (cited 1 September 2020)

68. Elvidge S. Concordia faces fine for bad pricing behavior. *BioPharma Dive* 22 November 2017. www.biopharmadive.com/news/concordia-uk-cma-price-gouging-thyroid-drug/511560/ (cited 11 September 2020)

69. Almashat S, Wolfe SM, Carome M. *Twenty-Five Years of Pharmaceutical Industry Criminal and Civil Penalties: 1991 Through 2015*. New York, NY; Public Citizen 2018. www.citizen.org/documents/2311.pdf

70. Loftus P. Merck to Pay $830 Million to Settle Vioxx Shareholder Suit. *The Wall Street Journal* 15 January 2016. www.wsj.com/articles/merck-to-pay-830-million-to-settle-vioxx-shareholder-suit-1452866882 (cited 1 March 2019)

71. Celgene to Pay $280 Million to Settle Fraud Suit Over Cancer Drugs. *The New York Times* 25 July 2017. www.nytimes.

com/2017/07/25/health/celgene-to-pay-280-million-to-settle-fraud-suit-over-cancer-drugs.html (1 March 2019)

72. Reuters. Mylan finalizes $465 million EpiPen settlement with Justice Department. *CNBC News* 17 Aug 2017 www.cnbc.com/2017/08/17/mylan-finalizes-465-million-epipen-settlement-with-justice-department.html (cited 1 March 2019)

73. Cronin Fisk Ma, Feeley J. AstraZeneca to Pay $110 Million to Settle Texas Drug Suits. *Bloomberg News* 17 Aug. 2018 www.bloomberg.com/news/articles/2018-08-07/astrazeneca-to-pay-110-million-to-settle-texas-drug-suits-jkk6v647 (cited 26 February 2019)

74. Canadian Press. B.C. Files Lawsuit Against Pharmaceutical Companies Over Opioids Addictions. *The Huffington Post Canada* 29 August 2018. www.huffingtonpost.ca/2018/08/29/bc-suing-pharma-companies_a_23511989 (cited 1 March 2019)/

75. Cohen D. Dabigatran: how the drug company withheld important analyses. *BMJ Online* 23 July 2014. www.ncbi.nlm.nih.gov/pubmed/25055829 (cited 1 March 2019)

76. Cohen D. Concerns over data in key dabigatran trial. *BMJ* 23 July 2014; 349(12): g4747–g4747. www.bmj.com/cgi/doi/10.1136/bmj.g4747 (cited 1 March 2019)

77. Connolly SJ, Ezekowitz MD, Yusuf S, Eikelboom J, Oldgren J, Parekh A, et al. Dabigatran versus Warfarin in Patients with Atrial Fibrillation. *N Engl J Med* 2009; 361(12): 1139–1151. www.nejm.org/doi/abs/10.1056/NEJMoa0905561 (cited 2 March 2019)

78. Wang S V, Franklin JM, Glynn RJ, Schneeweiss S, Eddings W, Gagne JJ. Prediction of rates of thromboembolic and major bleeding outcomes with dabigatran or warfarin among patients with atrial fibrillation: new initiator cohort study. *BMJ* 2016; 353: i2607. www.ncbi.nlm.nih.gov/pubmed/27221664 (cited 2 March 2019)

79. GlaxoSmithKline. *2012 Annual Report: Do more, feel better, live longer.* London; 2013. www.gsk.com/content/dam/gsk/globals/documents/pdf/GSK-Annual-Report-2012.pdf

80. McGreal C. How big pharma's money – and its politicians – feed the US opioid crisis. *The Guardian* 19 October 2017. www.theguardian.com/us-news/2017/oct/19/big-pharma-money-lobbying-us-opioid-crisis (cited 1 March 2019)

81. Gorski D. The Texas Medical Board lets Stanislaw Burzynski off lightly: A cautionary tale of the failure of regulating medicine.

Science-Based Medicine 2017. https://sciencebasedmedicine.org/
texas-medical-board-lets-off-stanislaw-burzynski-lightly/ (cited
22 February 2019)

82. Canadian Cancer Society. Canadian Cancer Society perspective on
antineoplastons. *Canadian Cancer Society Perspectives* 2006. www.
cancer.ca/en/about-us/news/national/2013/canadian-cancer-
society-perspective-on-antineoplastons/?region=qc (cited 22
February 2019)

83. Chang J. Texas Medical Board sanctions controversial cancer
doctor Burzynski. *The Austin American-Statesman* 3 March 2017.
www.statesman.com/NEWS/20170303/Texas-Medical-Board-
sanctions-controversial-cancer-doctor-Burzynski (cited 22
February 2019)

84. Rouner J. Some of Houston's Most Annoying Residents. Houston
Press 19 July 2015. www.houstonpress.com/news/the-10-most-
embarrassing-houstonians-7681068 (cited 22 February 2019)

85. Walker C, Luke M. Brian Clement, Hippocrates Health Institute
head, ordered to stop practising medicine. *CBC News* 24
February 2015. www.cbc.ca/news/indigenous/brian-clement-
hippocrates-health-institute-head-ordered-to-stop-practising-
medicine-1.2968780 (cited 26 February 2019)

86. CBC. Doctor' treating First Nations girls says can heal themselves.
CBC News 2 December 2014. www.cbc.ca/news/aboriginal/
doctor-treating-first-nations-girls-says-cancer-patients-can-heal-
themselves-1.2832760 (cited 26 February 2019)

87. CBC. Florida spa that treated First Nations girls with cancer faces
lawsuits from ex-staff. *CBC News* 11 December 2014. www.cbc.
ca/news/indigenous/florida-spa-that-treated-first-nations-
girls-with-cancer-faces-lawsuits-from-ex-staff-1.2867597 (cited 26
February 2019)

88. Walker C. Brian Clement, Hippocrates Health Institute head,
ordered to stop practising medicine. *CBC News* 24 February
2015. www.cbc.ca/news/indigenous/brian-clement-
hippocrates-health-institute-head-ordered-to-stop-practising-
medicine-1.2968780 (cited 26 February 2019)

89. Lowson G. Aboriginal girl now receiving both chemo and
traditional medicine. *The Globe and Mail* 24 April 2015. www.
theglobeandmail.com/news/national/case-over-cancer-

treatment-for-native-girl-is-resolved/article24101800/ (cited 26 February 2019)

90. Frketich J. Medical ethicists decry death of aboriginal girl who refused chemo. *The Hamilton Spectator* 23 January 2015. www.thespec.com/news-story/5272164-medical-ethicists-decry-death-of-aboriginal-girl-who-refused-chemo/ (cited 26 February 2019)

91. Norris C. How a survivor of 'conversion therapy' became the driving force behind Canada's first ever ban. *PBS News* 2018; 07. www.pbs.org/newshour/world/how-a-survivor-of-conversion-therapy-became-the-driving-force-behind-canadas-first-ever-ban (cited 4 March 2019)

92. Brittan L. Vancouver to ban businesses offering conversion therapy. *CBC News* 6 June 2018. www.cbc.ca/news/canada/british-columbia/vancouver-conversion-therapy-ban-1.4695117 (cited 4 March 2019)

93. Carey A. Legacy Continues for Pioneer in Reparative Therapy. *Church Militant* 22 March 2018 www.churchmilitant.com/news/article/cm-exclusive-interview-with-dr.-joseph-nicolosi-jr (cited 4 March 2019)

94. Sipp D, Caulfield T, Kaye J, Barfoot J, Blackburn C, Chan S, et al. Marketing of unproven stem cell–based interventions: A call to action. *Sci Transl Med* 2017; 9(397): eaag0426. www.ncbi.nlm.nih.gov/pubmed/28679655 (cited 27 February 2019)

95. Wan W, McGinley L. Miraculous' stem cell therapy has sickened people in five states. *The Washington Post* 27 February 2019. www.washingtonpost.com/national/health-science/miraculous-stem-cell-therapy-has-sickened-people-in-five-states/2019/02/26/c04b23a4-3539-11e9-854a-7a14d7fec96a_story.html?utm_term=.1028d8b65f62 (cited 27 February 2019)

96. Lindsay B. BC naturopath's pricey fecal transplants for autism are experimental and risky, scientists say. *CBC* 10 January 2020. www.cbc.ca/news/canada/british-columbia/bc-naturopath-fecal-transplants-autism-1.5420048 (cited 14 September 2020)

97. Kantor ED, Rehm CD, Du M, White E, Giovannucci EL. Trends in Dietary Supplement Use Among US Adults From 1999-2012. *JAMA* 2016; 316(14): 1464. www.ncbi.nlm.nih.gov/pubmed/27727382 (cited 23 November 2018)

98. Temple NJ. The marketing of dietary supplements: Profit before

health. *Nutritional Health: Strategies for Disease Prevention* 3rd Ed. Springer, 2012; 435–449 pp.

99. Juhn P, Phillips A, Buto K. Balancing Modern Medical Benefits And Risks. *Health Aff* 2007; 26(3): 647–652. www.healthaffairs.org/doi/10.1377/hlthaff.26.3.647 (cited 4 March 2019)

100. Ma X, Xu S. TNF inhibitor therapy for rheumatoid arthritis. *Biomed reports* 2013; 1(2): 177–184. www.ncbi.nlm.nih.gov/pubmed/24648915 (cited 4 March 2019)

101. Sackett DL, Rosenberg WMC, Muir Gray JA, Haynes RB, Richardson WS. Evidence-based medicine: what it is and what it isn't. *BMJ* 1996; 312: 71–72.

102. Garrett B. *Empirical nursing : the art of evidence-based care*. Emerald Publishing Limited; 2018: 283 pp. https://books.emeraldinsight.com/page/detail/Empirical-Nursing/?k=9781787438149 (cited 4 March 2019)

103. Merkley E. Many Americans deeply distrust experts. So will they ignore the warnings about coronavirus? *The Washington Post* 19 March 2020. https://www.washingtonpost.com/politics/2020/03/19/even-with-coronavirus-some-americans-deeply-distrust-experts-will-they-take-precautions/ (cited 12 February 2021).

104. Button M, Leys C. Healthcare fraud in the new NHS market – a threat to patient care. CHPI, London, UK; 2013. http://chpi.org.uk/wp-content/uploads/2012/06/CHPI-Healthcare-Fraud-a-threat-to-patient-care1.pdf

105. England NHS Directorate of Finance. *Tackling Fraud , Bribery and Corruption Corruption*. London, UK: NHS; 2021.

106. Action Fraud. Health scams. 2019. www.actionfraud.police.uk/a-z-of-fraud/health-scams (cited 24 August 2020)

107. Garrett BM. New sophistry: self-deception in the nursing academy. *Nurs Philos* 2016; 17(3): 182–193. www.ncbi.nlm.nih.gov/pubmed/27203787 (cited 19 October 2017)

108. Frankfurt HG. *On bullshit*. Princeton University Press; 2005: 67 pp. https://press.princeton.edu/titles/7929.html (7 March 2019)

109. Wilson J. The rightwing Christian preachers in deep denial over COVID-19's danger. *The Guardian* 4 April 2020. www.theguardian.com/us-news/2020/apr/04/america-rightwing-christian-preachers-virus-hoax (cited 14 September 2020)

110. Zeidler M. B.C. pharmacist fined $25K for selling stolen medication, supplies. *CBC News* 30 August 2020. www.cbc.ca/news/canada/british-columbia/b-c-pharmacist-fined-25k-for-selling-stolen-medication-supplies-1.5705694 (cited 14 September 2020)

111. Hall S. £1m equipment stolen to order, NHS fears. *The Guardian* 14 February 2006. www.theguardian.com/society/2006/feb/14/health.crime (14 September 2020)

112. Anon. Coronavirus: PPE masks worth £160k stolen from Salford warehouse. *BBC News* 7 May 2019. www.bbc.com/news/uk-england-manchester-52582865 (cited 14 September 2020)

113. Grogan S. *Body Image: Understanding Body Dissatisfaction in Men, Women and Children.* Abingdon, Oxford: Routledge & Kegan Paul; 2016. https://books.google.ca/books?hl=en&lr=&id=a0AlDwAAQBAJ&oi=fnd&pg=PP1&dq=body+image+young+men&ots=J1Ny5RzefY&sig=hkaeiD9hSBt8CuuOnDzKEtqM-Q4#v=onepage&q=body

114. Juli MR. Perception of body image in early adolescence. An investigation in secondary schools. *Psychiatr Danub* 2017; 29(Suppl 3): 409–415. www.ncbi.nlm.nih.gov/pubmed/28953800

115. Van Wagoner RM, Eichner A, Bhasin S, Deuster PA, Eichner D. Chemical Composition and Labeling of Substances Marketed as Selective Androgen Receptor Modulators and Sold via the Internet. *JAMA* 2017; 318(20): 2004. http://jama.jamanetwork.com/article.aspx?doi=10.1001/jama.2017.17069

116. Grabe S, Ward LM, Hyde JS. The role of the media in body image concerns among women: A meta-analysis of experimental and correlational studies. *Psychol Bull* 2008; 134(3): 460–476. http://doi.apa.org/getdoi.cfm?doi=10.1037/0033-2909.134.3.460 (cited 1 December 2017)

117. Grogan S, Richards H. Body Image. *Men Masc* 2002; 4(3): 219–32. http://journals.sagepub.com/doi/10.1177/1097184X02004003001 (cited 1 December 2017)

118. United States Attorney's Office. Press Release No. 07-016: Operator of Employers Mutual going to prison for 25 years for operating bogus health insurance provider. United States Attorney's Office Central District of California; 2007. p. 1. www.justice.gov/archive/usao/cac/Pressroom/pr2007/016.html (cited 30 April 2019)

119. Pear P. Federal Officials Shut Down Sales of 'Ruinous' Health

Insurance Plans. *The New York Times* 5 November 2018. www.nytimes.com/2018/11/05/us/politics/ftc-trumpcare-telemarketers-shut-down.html (cited 30 April 2019)

120. Lindsay B. BC dentist who charged for unnecessary procedures suspended from practice. *CBC News* 1 March 2018 www.cbc.ca/news/canada/british-columbia/b-c-dentist-who-charged-for-unnecessary-procedures-suspended-from-practice-1.4558001 (cited 30 April 2019)

121. Freudenheim M. Some Doctors Letting Patients Skip Co-Payments. *The New York Times* 27 December 2003. www.nytimes.com/2003/12/27/business/some-doctors-letting-patients-skip-co-payments.html (cited 30 April 2019.

122. BBC 1 South. BBC - Press Office - Release. Press Release. 06 Oct. 2003. www.bbc.co.uk/pressoffice/pressreleases/stories/2003/10_october/06/winchester_doctor.shtml (cited 2 September 2020)

123. Anon. Tribunal rules Twyford doctor Julian Kenyon who exploited patients can keep job. *Hampshire Chronicle* 19 December 2014. www.hampshirechronicle.co.uk/news/11676249.tribunal-rules-twyford-doctor-julian-kenyon-who-exploited-patients-can-keep-job/ (cited 2 September 2020)

124. Ernst E. Why do patients rarely complain about receiving bogus treatments? *Edzard Ernst's Blog*31 January 2015. https://edzardernst.com/2015/01/why-do-patients-rarely-complain-about-receiving-bogus-treatments/ (cited 2 September 2020)

125. Substance Abuse and Mental Health Services Administration (SAMHSA). National Survey on Drug Use and Health (NSDUH). CBHSQ: Washington, DC; 2017. www.samhsa.gov/data/nsduh/reports-detailed-tables-2017-NSDUH (cited 2 May 2019)

126. Piper C. 10 popular health care provider fraud schemes. *Fraud Magazine* January 2013. www.fraud-magazine.com/article.aspx?id=4294976280 (cited 2 May 2019)

127. McClymont K. Fake doctor conned his way into a job at top medical school. *The Sydney Morning Herald* 27 September 2010 www.smh.com.au/national/fake-doctor-conned-his-way-into-a-job-at-top-medical-school-20100926-15sfs.html (cited 7 March 2019)

128. McClymont K. Bogus psychiatrist caught using forged documents. *The Sydney Morning Herald* 18 October 2018. www.smh.com.

au/national/nsw/bogus-psychiatrist-caught-using-forged-documents-20181016-p50a14.html (cited 7 March 2019)

129. Associated Press. Abortion doctor Kermit Gosnell found guilty of murder. *The Guardian* 13 April 2013. www.theguardian.com/world/2013/may/13/kermit-gosnell-found-guilty-murder (cited 7 March 2019)

130. Anon. Fake doctor Abdul Pirzada jailed over CV lies. *BBC News* 27 September 2012. www.bbc.com/news/uk-england-birmingham-19732950

131. Luk V. Tung Sheng Wu, Illegal Dentist, Sent To Jail. *The Huffington Post Canada* 22 November 2013. www.huffingtonpost.ca/2013/11/22/tung-sheng-wu-illegal-dentist-jail_n_4323956.html

132. Dufresne M. 'Dr. Lipjob' nets suspended sentence for illegally injecting botox. *CBC News* 22 January 2019. www.cbc.ca/news/canada/british-columbia/drlipjob-suspended-sentence-rajdeep-kaur-khakh-1.4987397

133. Edmiston J. Toronto teen - Dr. Kitty - allegedly posed as plastic surgeon, doled out botched procedure in basement. *National Post* 16 October 2017. https://nationalpost.com/news/toronto/toronto-teen-dr-kitty-allegedly-posed-as-plastic-surgeon-doled-out-botched-cosmetic-procedure-in-basement (cited 26 November 2019)

134. Victor D. Man Who Posed as a Doctor at 18 Is Going to Prison at 20. *The New York Times* 5 January 2018. www.nytimes.com/2018/01/05/us/doctor-fraud-charges.html

135. Anon. Quebec woman faked being a nurse for 20 years. *CBC News* 31 May 2019. www.cbc.ca/news/canada/montreal/woman-faked-being-nurse-jonquiere-20-years-1.5157101 (cited 10 September 2020)

136. Anon. Kiwi jailed after working as fake doctor in UK. *Otago Daily Times Online News* 20 November 2018. www.odt.co.nz/news/national/kiwi-jailed-after-working-fake-doctor-uk (10 September 2020)

137. MacAskill A, Stecklow S, Miglani S. Why India's medical schools are plagued with fraud. *Reuters* 16 June 2016. www.cnbc.com/2015/06/16/why-indias-medical-schools-are-plagued-with-fraud.html (cited 26 November 2019)

138. Rankin E, Dufresne M. 1,200 patients 'high and dry' after 2

Chilliwack doctors lose medical licences. *CBC News* 18 April 2018. www.cbc.ca/news/canada/british-columbia/1-200-patients-high-and-dry-after-2-chilliwack-doctors-lose-medical-licences-1.4619764 (cited 7 March 2019)

139. Grierson J. Two arrested for illegally selling COVID-19 home testing kits. *The Guardian* 15 April 2020. www.theguardian.com/uk-news/2020/apr/15/two-arrested-for-illegally-selling-covid-19-home-testing-kits (cited 14 September 2020)

140. Law T. California Doctor Selling 'Cure' for COVID-19 Charged With Fraud. *Time Magazine* 19 April 2020. https://time.com/5823921/california-doctor-cure-covid-19-mail-fraud/ (cited 23 April 2020)

141. O'Kane C. Fake drive-thru coronavirus testing sites investigated in Kentucky. *CBS News* 03 April 2020. www.cbsnews.com/news/coronavirus-testing-sites-drive-thru-fake-kentucky/ (cited 23 April 2020)

142. Braga M. Government coronavirus crackdown angers alternative health providers. *USA Today* 3 September 2020. www.usatoday.com/story/news/investigations/2020/09/03/government-coronavirus-crackdown-angers-alternative-health-providers/5660997002/ (cited 4 September 2020)

143. CBC News. Fighting COVID-19: Supplies, testing and scams: CBC's Marketplace cheat sheet. *CBC Marketplace* 05 April 2020. www.cbc.ca/news/business/fighting-covid-19-supplies-testing-and-scams-cbc-s-marketplace-cheat-sheet-1.5522004 (cited 23 April 2020)

144. CAFC. COVID-19 Fraud. *CAFC Warnings* 18 Dec. 2020. https://antifraudcentre-centreantifraude.ca/features-vedette/2020/covid-19-eng.htm (cited 23 April 2020)

145. Oliver JE, Wood T. Medical Conspiracy Theories and Health Behaviors in the United States. *JAMA Intern Med* 2014; 174(5): 817. http://archinte.jamanetwork.com/article.aspx?doi=10.1001/jamainternmed.2014.190 (cited 3 June 2019)

146. Kestler-D'Amours J. COVID-19 conspiracy theories creating a 'public health crisis' in Canada, experts say. *CBC News* www.cbc.ca/news/politics/covid-19-conspiracy-theories-1.5672766 (cited 4 September 2020)

147. Barnes PM, Bloom B, Nahin RL. Complementary and alternative

medicine use among adults and children: United States, 2007. *Natl Health Stat Report* 2008; (12): 1–23. www.ncbi.nlm.nih.gov/pubmed/19361005 (cited 19 July 2017)

148. University of Bristol. More adults using complementary and alternative medicine in England but access is unequal. *MedicaL XPress* 13 Nov 2018 https://medicalxpress.com/news/2018-11-adults-complementary-alternative-medicine-england.html (cited 28 August 2020)

149. Nahin RL, Barnes PM, Stussman BJ. Expenditures on Complementary Health Approaches: United States, 2012. *Natl Health Stat Report* 2016; (95): 1–11.

150. Public Health Agency of Canada. Complementary and Alternative Health. Canadian Health Network - Public Health Agency Canada. 2019 www.phac-aspc.gc.ca/chn-rcs/cah-acps-eng.php (cited 24 June 2019)

151. Esmail N. Complementary and Alternative Medicine: Use and Public Attitudes 1997, 2006, 2016. *Fraser Inst* 2017; (April): 1–87.

152. Grand View Research. Complementary and Alternative Medicine Market Size, Share & Trends Analysis Report By Intervention (Botanical, Acupuncture, Mind, Body, Yoga), By Distribution (Direct Contact, E-training), And Segment Forecasts, 2019 - 2026. Grand View Research, Inc.: San Francisco, CA; 2019. www.grandviewresearch.com/industry-analysis/aternative-medicine-therapies-market (cited 7 May 2019)

153. Bishop FL, Yardley L, Lewith GT. A systematic review of beliefs involved in the use of complementary and alternative medicine. *J Health Psychol* 2007; 12(6): 851–867. http://journals.sagepub.com/doi/10.1177/1359105307082447 (cited 19 July 2017)

154. Bromfield SG, McGwin G. Use of Complementary and Alternative Medicine for Eye-related Diseases and Conditions. *Curr Eye Res* 2013; 38(12): 1283–1287. www.ncbi.nlm.nih.gov/pubmed/23972126

155. Foltz V, St Pierre Y, Rozenberg S, Rossignol M, Bourgeois P, Joseph L, et al. Use of complementary and alternative therapies by patients with self-reported chronic back pain: a nationwide survey in Canada. *Jt Bone Spine* 2005; 72(6): 571–577. www.ncbi.nlm.nih.gov/pubmed/16256395

156. Rao JK, Mihaliak K, Kroenke K, Bradley J, Tierney WM, Weinberger

M. Use of complementary therapies for arthritis among patients of rheumatologists. *Ann Intern Med* 1999; 131(6): 409–416. www.ncbi. nlm.nih.gov/pubmed/10498556 (cited 19 July 2017)

157. Bernstein BJ, Grasso T. Prevalence of complementary and alternative medicine use in cancer patients. *Oncology* 2001; 15(19): 1267–1272. www.cancernetwork.com/review-article/prevalence-complementary-and-alternative-medicine-use-cancer-patients (cited 4 October 2018)

158. Yeh GY, Eisenberg DM, Davis RB, Phillips RS. Use of complementary and alternative medicine among persons with diabetes mellitus: results of a national survey. *Am J Public Health* 2002; 92(10): 1648–1652. www.ncbi.nlm.nih.gov/pubmed/12356615 (cited 19 July 2017)

159. Nayak S, Matheis RJ, Schoenberger NE, Shiflett SC. Use of unconventional therapies by individuals with multiple sclerosis. *Clin Rehabil* 2003; 17(2): 181–191. http://journals.sagepub.com/doi/10.1191/0269215503cr604oa (cited 19 July 2017)

160. Ganguli SC, Cawdron R, Irvine EJ. Alternative medicine use by Canadian ambulatory gastroenterology patients: secular trend or epidemic? *Am J Gastroenterol* 2004; 99(2): 319–326. www.ncbi. nlm.nih.gov/pubmed/15046224 (cited 19 July 2017)

161. Sirois FM. Provider-based complementary and alternative medicine use among three chronic illness groups: Associations with psychosocial factors and concurrent use of conventional health-care services. *Complement Ther Med* 2008; 16(2): 73–80.

162. Louhiala P. There is no alternative medicine. *Med Humanit* 2010; 36(2): 115–117. www.ncbi.nlm.nih.gov/pubmed/21393295 (cited 3 May 2019)

163. Minchin T. Tim Minchin's Storm the Animated Movie. YouTube 2011 www.youtube.com/watch?v=HhGuXCuDb1U (cited 3 May 2019)

164. Diamond J. *Snake oil and other preoccupations.* Vintage; 2001: 285 pp.

165. Ernst E, Cassileth BR. The prevalence of complementary/alternative medicine in cancer: a systematic review. *Cancer* 15 August 1998.; 83(4): 777–782. www.ncbi.nlm.nih.gov/pubmed/9708945 (cited 19 July 2017)

166. Offit PA. Studying Complementary and Alternative Therapies. *JAMA* 2012; 307(17): 1803–1804. www.ncbi.nlm.nih.gov/pubmed/22550193 (cited 19 July 2017)

167. Yun H, Sun L, Mao JJ. Growth of Integrative Medicine at Leading Cancer Centers Between 2009 and 2016: A Systematic Analysis of NCI-Designated Comprehensive Cancer Center Websites. *JNCI Monogr* 2017; 2017(52). http://www.ncbi.nlm.nih.gov/pubmed/29140485 (cited 6 May 2019)

168. Vyse SA. *Believing in magic : the psychology of superstition*. Oxford, UK: Oxford University Press; 2014: 316 pp.

169. Garrett BM, Cutting RL. Magical beliefs and discriminating science from pseudoscience in undergraduate professional students. *Heliyon* 2017; 3(11): e00433. http://linkinghub.elsevier.com/retrieve/pii/S2405844017321795 (cited 6 November 2017)

170. Rosengren KS, French JA. *Magical Thinking. The Oxford Handbook of the Development of the Imagination*. Oxford, UK: Oxford University Press; 2013: 42–60 pp.

171. Freinkel A, Streltzer J, Blank AJ. Letters: An even closer look at therapeutic touch. *JAMA* 1998; 280(22): 1903.

172. Adhopia V. Why is $350,000 in Canadian aid being used to send homeopaths to Honduras? *CBC News* 23 February 2019. www.cbc.ca/news/health/federal-aid-homeopaths-honduras-1.5030384 (cited 6 May 2019)

173. Ring M, Newmark S. Practice Drift: Are There Risks When Integrative Medicine Physicians Exceed Their Scope? *J Altern Complement Med* 2018; 24(8): 748–751. www.liebertpub.com/doi/10.1089/acm.2018.29051.mlr (cited 6 May 2019)

174. Khorsan R, Coulter ID, Crawford C, Hsiao AF. Systematic review of integrative health care research: Randomized control trials, clinical controlled trials, and meta-analysis. *Evidence-based Complement Altern Med* 2011; 2011. doi:10.1155/2011/636134

175. Gorski D. David Gorski: Integrative Medicine - The Best of Both Worlds? (2017). https://www.youtube.com/watch?v=WYCRd0vqFzg (cited 16 February 2021)

176. Soh K-S, Kang KA, Ryu YH. 50 Years of Bong-Han Theory and 10 Years of Primo Vascular System. *Evidence-Based Complement Altern Med* 31 July 2013. www.hindawi.com/journals/ecam/2013/587827/ (cited 23 May 2019)

177. Park SY, Jung SJ, Bae K-H, Soh K-S. Protocol for Detecting the Primo Vascular System in the Lymph Ducts of Mice. *J Acupunct Meridian Stud* 2015; 8(6): 321–328. www.ncbi.nlm.nih.gov/

pubmed/26742917 (cited 23 May 2019)

178. Hall H. The Primo Vascular System: The N-rays of Acupuncture? *Science-based Medicine* 2016 https://sciencebasedmedicine.org/the-primo-vascular-system-the-n-rays-of-acupuncture/ (cited 23 May 2019)

179. ReShel A. Science Finally Proves Meridians Exist. *Uplift* 20 April 2016. https://upliftconnect.com/science-proves-meridians-exist/

180. Lo Y. Predictive Power of Meridian Theory. *Acupuncture Today* 2007. www.acupuncturetoday.com/mpacms/at/article.php?id=31517 (cited 16 February 2021)

181. Chen CW, Tai CJ, Choy CS, et al. Wave-induced flow in meridians demonstrated using photoluminescent bioceramic material on acupuncture points. *Evidence-based Complement Altern Med* 2013; 2013: 11. doi:10.1155/2013/739293

182. Evans I, Thornton H, Chalmers I, Glasziou P. *Testing Treatments: Better research for better health care.* London. Pinter & Martin. 2011: 199 pp.

183. Khorsan R, Coulter ID, Crawford C, Hsiao A-F. Systematic review of integrative health care research: randomized control trials, clinical controlled trials, and meta-analysis. *Evid Based Complement Alternat Med* 2011; 2011. www.ncbi.nlm.nih.gov/pubmed/20953383 (cited 6 May 2019)

184. Yao S, Wei D, Chen Y, Wang Q, Wang X, Zeng Z, et al. Quality assessment of clinical practice guidelines for integrative medicine in China: A systematic review. *Chin J Integr Med* 2017; 23(5): 381–385. www.ncbi.nlm.nih.gov/pubmed/27909999 (cited 6 May 2019)

185. NHS. Royal London Hospital for Integrated Medicine. www.uclh.nhs.uk/our-services/our-hospitals/royal-london-hospital-integrated-medicine (cited 15 March 2021)

186. Ross S, Blau M, Sheridan K. Medicine with a side of mysticism: Top hospitals promote unproven therapies *STAT* 7 March 2017. www.statnews.com/2017/03/07/alternative-medicine-hospitals-promote/ (cited 15 March 2021)

187. Dashtdar M, Dashtdar MR, Dashtdar B, Kardi K, Shirazi MK. The Concept of Wind in Traditional Chinese Medicine. *J Pharmacopuncture* 2016; 19(4): 293–302. www.ncbi.nlm.nih.gov/pubmed/28097039 (cited 10 May 2019)

188. Dong J. The Relationship between Traditional Chinese Medicine and Modern Medicine. *Evid Based Complement Alternat Med* 2013; 2013: 153148. www.ncbi.nlm.nih.gov/pubmed/23983772 (cited 25 June 2019)

189. Li Z, Dai H, Thurston AF, Nathan AJ, Andrew J. *The private life of Chairman Mao : the memoirs of Mao's personal physician.* London, UK: Random House; 1994: 682 pp.

190. Lu DP, Lu GP. An Historical Review and Perspective on the Impact of Acupuncture on US Medicine and Society. *Med Acupunct* 2013; 25(5): 311–316. www.ncbi.nlm.nih.gov/pubmed/24761180 (cited 25 June 2019)

191. Harper D. The Conception of Illness in Early Chinese Medicine, as Documented in Newly Discovered 3rd and 2nd Century B.C. Manuscripts (Part I). *Sudhoffs Archiv* Stuttgart, Germany: Franz Steiner Verlag; 1990: 210–235 pp. www.jstor.org/stable/20777300 (cited 10 May 2019)

192. Johnson I. Nobel Renews Debate on Chinese Medicine. *The New York Times* 10 October 2015. www.nytimes.com/2015/10/11/world/asia/nobel-renews-debate-on-chinese-medicine.html (cited 10 May 2019)

193. Liu J-P, Han M, Li X-X, Mu Y-J, Lewith G, Wang Y-Y, et al. Prospective registration, bias risk and outcome-reporting bias in randomised clinical trials of traditional Chinese medicine: an empirical methodological study. *BMJ Open* 2013; 3(7): e002968. www.ncbi.nlm.nih.gov/pubmed/23864210 (cited 7 May 2019)

194. Wang Y, Wang L, Chai Q, Liu J. Positive Results in Randomized Controlled Trials on Acupuncture Published in Chinese Journals: A Systematic Literature Review. *J Altern Complement Med* 2014; 20(5): A129–A129. www.liebertpub.com/doi/10.1089/acm.2014.5346.abstract (cited 7 May 2019)

195. Woodhead M. 80% of China's clinical trial data are fraudulent, investigation finds. *BMJ* 2016; 355: i5396. www.ncbi.nlm.nih.gov/pubmed/27707716 (cited 10 May 2019)

196. Haake M, Müller H-H, Schade-Brittinger C, Basler HD, Schäfer H, Maier C, et al. German Acupuncture Trials (GERAC) for chronic low back pain: randomized, multicenter, blinded, parallel-group trial with 3 groups. *Arch Intern Med* 2007; 167(17): 1892–1898. www.ncbi.nlm.nih.gov/pubmed/17893311 (cited 9 May 2019)

197. Brinkhaus B, Witt CM, Jena S, Linde K, Streng A, Hummelsberger J, et al. Physician and treatment characteristics in a randomised multicentre trial of acupuncture in patients with osteoarthritis of the knee. *Complement Ther Med* 2007; 15(3): 180–189. www.ncbi. nlm.nih.gov/pubmed/17709063 (cited 9 May 2019)

198. Barker BR. *Snake Oil science: the truth about complementary and alternative medicine*. Oxford, UK; Oxford University Press: 2007; 324 pp.

199. Melchart D, Streng A, Hoppe A, Brinkhaus B, Becker-Witt C, Hammes M, et al. The Acupuncture Randomised Trial (Art) for Tension-Type Headache - Details of the Treatment. *Acupunct Med* 2005; 23(4): 157–165. www.ncbi.nlm.nih.gov/pubmed/16430123 (cited 9 May 2019)

200. Linde K, Streng A, Jürgens S, Hoppe A, Brinkhaus B, Witt C, et al. Acupuncture for Patients With Migraine. *JAMA* 2005; 293(17): 2118. www.ncbi.nlm.nih.gov/pubmed/15870415 (cited 9 May 2019)

201. Vas J, Aranda J, Modesto M, Benítez-Parejo N, Herrera A, Martínez-Barquín D, et al. True acupuncture for back pain no better than sham or placebo. *Pain Science* 28 June 2015. www. painscience.com/biblio/true-acupuncture-for-back-pain-no-better-than-sham-or-placebo.html (cited 10 May 2019)

202. Colquhoun D, Novella SP. Acupuncture Is Theatrical Placebo. *Anesth Analg* 2013; 116(6): 1360–1363. https://insights.ovid.com/crossref?an=00000539-201306000-00025 (cited 10 May 2019)

203. Burney RO, Giudice LC. Pathogenesis and pathophysiology of endometriosis. *Fertil Steril* 2012; 98(3): 511–519. www.ncbi.nlm. nih.gov/pubmed/22819144 (10 May 2019)

204. Zhou J, Chi H, Cheng TO, Chen T, Wu Y, Zhou W, et al. Acupuncture anesthesia for open heart surgery in contemporary China. *Int J Cardiol* 2011; 150(1): 12–16. www.ncbi.nlm.nih.gov/pubmed/21570137 (cited 10 May 2019)

205. Chernyak G V, Sessler DI. Perioperative acupuncture and related techniques. *Anesthesiology* 2005; 102(5): 1031–1049; quiz 1077–1078. www.ncbi.nlm.nih.gov/pubmed/15851892 (cited 10 May 2019)

206. Canadian Society of Homeopathy. What is Homeopathy? About Homeopathy. 2019 www.csoh.ca/Homeopathy_What_Is_Hx.htm (cited 25 June 2019)

207. Davenas E, Beauvais F, Amara J, Oberbaum M, Robinzon B, Miadonnai A, et al. Human basophil degranulation triggered by very dilute antiserum against IgE. *Nature* 1988; 333(6176): 816–818. www.nature.com/articles/333816a0 (cited 15 May 2019)

208. Hirst SJ, Hayes NA, Burridge J, Pearce FL, Foreman JC. Human basophil degranulation is not triggered by very dilute antiserum against human IgE. *Nature* 1993; 366(6455): 525–527. www.nature.com/articles/366525a0 (cited 15 May 2019)

209. Cowan ML, Bruner BD, Huse N, Dwyer JR, Chugh B, Nibbering ETJ, et al. Ultrafast memory loss and energy redistribution in the hydrogen bond network of liquid H2O. *Nature* 2005; 434(7030): 199–202. www.nature.com/articles/nature03383 (cited 15 May 2019)

210. Manzalini A, Galeazzi B. Explaining Homeopathy with Quantum Electrodynamics. *Homeopathy* 22 March 2019. www.ncbi.nlm.nih.gov/pubmed/30901775 (cited 15 May 2019)

211. Milgrom LR. Towards a New Model of the Homeopathic Process Based on Quantum Field Theory. *Complement Med Res* 2006; 13(3): 174–183. www.ncbi.nlm.nih.gov/pubmed/16868363 (cited 16 May 2019)

212. Stenger VJ. *The unconscious quantum : metaphysics in modern physics and cosmology*. New York. NY, US. Prometheus Books; 1995; 322 pp. www.goodreads.com/book/show/339253. The_Unconscious_Quantum (cited 15 May 2019)

213. Ernst E. A systematic review of systematic reviews of homeopathy. *Br J Clin Pharmacol* 2002; 54(6): 577–582. www.ncbi.nlm.nih.gov/pubmed/12492603 (cited 15 May 2019)

214. Hawke K, van Driel ML, Buffington BJ, McGuire TM, King D. Homeopathic medicinal products for preventing and treating acute respiratory tract infections in children. *Cochrane Database Syst Rev* 2018; (9). http://doi.wiley.com/10.1002/14651858. CD005974.pub5 (cited 15 May 2019)

215. Jonas WB, Anderson RL, Crawford CC, Lyons JS. A systematic review of the quality of homeopathic clinical trials. *BMC Complement Altern Med* 2001; 1: 12. www.ncbi.nlm.nih.gov/pmc/articles/PMC64638/ (cited 15 May 2019)

216. Mathie RT, Frye J, Fisher P. Homeopathic Oscillococcinum ® for preventing and treating influenza and influenza-like

illness. *Cochrane Database Syst Rev* 2015; (1). http://doi.wiley.com/10.1002/14651858.CD001957.pub6

217. Mathie RT, Ramparsad N, Legg LA, Clausen J, Moss S, Davidson JRT, et al. Randomised, double-blind, placebo-controlled trials of non-individualised homeopathic treatment: systematic review and meta-analysis. *Syst Rev* 2017; 6(1): 63. www.ncbi.nlm.nih.gov/pubmed/28340607 (cited 15 May 2019)

218. Donnelly L. High Court backs NHS decision to stop funding homeopathy. *The Telegraph* 5 May 2018. www.telegraph.co.uk/science/2018/06/05/high-court-backs-nhs-decision-stop-funding-homeopathy/ (cited 15 May 2019)

219. Canadian Association of Naturopathic Doctors. About Naturopathic Medicine. What is Naturopathic Medicine? 2018. www.cand.ca/about-naturopathic-medicine/ (cited 25 June 2019)

220. Cayleff SE. *Nature's path: a history of naturopathic healing in America.* Baltimore. John-Hopkins University Press: 2016; 397 pp.

221. Murdoch B, Carr S, Caulfield T. Selling falsehoods? A cross-sectional study of Canadian naturopathy, homeopathy, chiropractic and acupuncture clinic website claims relating to allergy and asthma. *BMJ Open* 2016; 6(12): e014028. www.ncbi.nlm.nih.gov/pubmed/27986744 (cited 8 December 2017)

222. Ellis E. IV vitamin therapy hits the road in Vancouver bringing a drip to your door. *Vancouver Sun* 17 August 2016. https://vancouversun.com/news/local-news/iv-vitamin-therapy-hits-the-road-in-vancouver-bringing-a-drip-to-your-door (cited 16 May 2019)

223. Caulfield T. The IV therapy myth. *National Post* 11 July 2016. https://nationalpost.com/opinion/timothy-caulfield-the-iv-therapy-myth (cited 16 May 2019)

224. Kirkey S. Hooking up to an IV drip is the latest health fad, but critics say there is little proof it works. *National Post* 21 July 2015. https://nationalpost.com/health/0801-na-vitamin-drip (cited 16 May 2019)

225. The British Nutrition Foundation. Intravenous vitamin therapy. *Nutrition in the News* 23 December 2014. www.nutrition.org.uk/nutritioninthenews/headlines/ivvitamins.html (cited 16 May 2019)

226. Cerritelli F, Pizzolorusso G, Ciardelli F, et al. Effect of osteopathic manipulative treatment on length of stay in a population of

preterm infants: A randomized controlled trial. *BMC Pediatr* 2013; 13(1): 65. doi:10.1186/1471-2431-13-65

227. Bekowsky B. Nature's Therapies - The Germ Theory: The Traditional Naturopathic Perspective - Part I. *Natural Health Science* 2019. https://naturalhealthscience.com/article_Natures-Therapies_090114.php (cited 15 May 2019)

228. Downey L, Tyree PT, Huebner CE, Lafferty WE. Pediatric Vaccination and Vaccine-Preventable Disease Acquisition: Associations with Care by Complementary and Alternative Medicine Providers. *Matern Child Health J* 2010; 14(6): 922–930. www.ncbi.nlm.nih.gov/pubmed/19760163 (15 May 2019)

229. CNPBC. CNPBC Media Release. College of Naturopathic Physicians of British Columbia. 2019. www.cnpbc.bc.ca/media-release/ (cited 16 May 2019)

230. WHO. Ten threats to global health in 2019. World Health Organization Website 2019. www.who.int/emergencies/ten-threats-to-global-health-in-2019 (cited 9 July 2019)

231. Young L. Here's what naturopaths and chiropractors shouldn't be advising you about. *Global News* 2 May 2018. https://globalnews.ca/news/4248401/naturopath-chiropractor-advice-vaccination/ (cited 15 May 2019)

232. Lindsay B. Controversial naturopath gives up licence, says work 'not going to change.' *CBC News* 8 November 2018. www.cbc.ca/news/canada/british-columbia/naturopath-rabid-dog-saliva-zimmerman-1.4897090 (cited 16 May 2019)

233. Schwarcz J. Homeopathy and the Flu. Office for Science and Society - McGill University. 2017.: 1 pp. www.mcgill.ca/oss/article/science-science-everywhere/homeopathy-and-flu (cited 6 November 2019)

234. Jarry J. Naturopath Sues Whistleblower for Denouncing Quack Treatments. Office for Science and Society - McGill University 25 January 2018. www.mcgill.ca/oss/article/quackery/naturopath-sues-whistleblower-denouncing-quack-treatments (cited 16 May 2019)

235. Jaiswal YS, Williams LL. A glimpse of Ayurveda - The forgotten history and principles of Indian traditional medicine. *J Tradit Complement Med* 2017; 7(1): 50–53. www.ncbi.nlm.nih.gov/pubmed/28053888 (cited 26 June 2019)

236. Anon. Prince Charles cured by ayurveda, homoeopathy: Minister. *The Tribune India* 7 April 2020. www.tribuneindia.com/news/ nation/prince-charles-cured-by-ayurveda-homeopathy-minister-66905 (cited 4 September 2020)

237. Sridharan K, Mohan R, Ramaratnam S, Panneerselvam D. Ayurvedic treatments for diabetes mellitus. *Cochrane Database Syst Rev* 2011; (12). http://doi.wiley.com/10.1002/14651858. CD008288.pub2 (cited 26 June 2019)

238. FTC. FTC Brings First-ever Action Targeting 'iV Cocktail' Therapy *Federal Trade Commision News* September 2018. www.ftc.gov/ news-events/press-releases/2018/09/ftc-brings-first-ever-action-targeting-iv-cocktail-therapy (cited 7 May 2019)

239. Lazarus D. Chiropractic treatment, a $15-billion industry, has its roots in a ghost story. *Los Angeles Times* 30 June 2017 www. latimes.com/business/lazarus/la-fi-lazarus-chiropractic-quackery-20170630-story.html (cited 13 May 2019)

240. Gorski D, Novella S, Atwood KC, Crislip MA, Hal H. Science-Based Medicine - Chiropractic. *Science-based Medicine* 2019. https://sciencebasedmedicine.org/?s=chiropractic&category_ name=&submit=Search

241. Atwood KC. Naturopathy: a critical appraisal. *MedGenMed* 2003; 5(4): 39. www.ncbi.nlm.nih.gov/pubmed/14745386 (cited 7 June 2019)

242. Goncalves G, Le Scanff C, Leboeuf-Yde C. Effect of chiropractic treatment on primary or early secondary prevention: A systematic review with a pedagogic approach. Vol. 26, *Chiropractic and Manual Therapies* BioMed Central Ltd.; 2018.

243. Rubinstein SM, van Middelkoop M, Assendelft WJ, de Boer MR, van Tulder MW. Spinal manipulative therapy for chronic low-back pain. *Cochrane Database Syst Rev* 2011; (2). http://doi.wiley. com/10.1002/14651858.CD008112.pub2 (cited 13 May 2019)

244. Thomas JS, Clark BC, Russ DW, France CR, Ploutz-Snyder R, Corcos DM. Effect of Spinal Manipulative and Mobilization Therapies in Young Adults With Mild to Moderate Chronic Low Back Pain: A Randomized Clinical Trial. *JAMA Netw open*2020; 3(8): e2012589. https://jamanetwork.com/ (cited 28 August 2020)

245. Singh S, Ernst E. *Trick or treatment : the undeniable facts about alternative medicine.* New York, US: WW Norton; 2008: 342 pp.

246. Robbins M. Furious backlash from Simon Singh libel case puts chiropractors on ropes. *The Guardian* 1 March 2010. www.theguardian.com/science/2010/mar/01/simon-singh-libel-case-chiropractors (cited 13 May 2019)

247. Boseley S. Simon Singh libel case dropped. *The Guardian* 15 April 2010. www.theguardian.com/science/2010/apr/15/simon-singh-libel-case-dropped (cited 13 May 2019)

248. Vara S. Defamation laws take effect. London, UK: GovUK; 2013. www.gov.uk/government/news/defamation-laws-take-effect (cited 13 May 2019)

249. Portolese T. Portolese Family Chiropractic - Chiropractor in Lansdale, PA US. Chirogal. Published 2020. www.chirogal.com/ (cited 16 February 2021).

250. Cuthbert SC, Barras M. Developmental Delay Syndromes: Psychometric Testing Before and After Chiropractic Treatment of 157 Children. *J Manip Physiol Ther*; 32(8): 660–669. www.jmptonline.org/article/S0161-4754(09)00198-5/abstract (cited 21 May 2019)

251. Spigelblatt L. Chiropractic care for children: Controversies and Issues. *Paediatrics & Child Health.* 2002; 7(2) 85–89. (cited 14 May 2019). https://doi.org/10.1093/pch/7.2.85

252. Gotlib A, Rupert R. Chiropractic manipulation in pediatric health conditions – an updated systematic review. *Chiropr Osteopat* 2008; 16(1): 11. www.ncbi.nlm.nih.gov/pubmed/18789139 (cited 14 May 2019)

253. Homola S. Pediatric Chiropractic Care: Scientifically Indefensible? *Science-Based Medicine* 03 May 2010. https://sciencebasedmedicine.org/pediatric-chiropractic-care-scientifically-indefensible/ (cited 14 May 2019)

254. Gorman M. Halifax chiropractor investigated for anti-vaccination views. *CBC News* 25 May 2018. www.cbc.ca/news/canada/nova-scotia/health-care-vaccines-cancer-chiropractor-dena-churchill-1.4676037 (cited 14 May 2019)

255. Lindsay B. Vancouver chiropractor resigns from college board over anti-vaccine video. *CBC News* 4 May 2018. www.cbc.ca/news/canada/british-columbia/vancouver-chiropractor-resigns-from-college-board-over-anti-vaccine-video-1.4649019 (cited 14 May 2019)

256. Gallup. *Gallup Poll - Honesty/Ethics in Professions*. New York, NY: Gallup; 2016. https://news.gallup.com/poll/1654/honesty-ethics-professions.aspx (cited 15 May 2019)

257. SANOFI. The Sanofi Canada Healthcare Survey. Ottawa, ON; 2018. www.sanofi.ca/l/ca/en/layout.jsp?cnt=65B67ABD-BEF6-487B-8FC1-5D06FF8568ED

258. Benjamin A, Birnholtz J, Baecker R, Gromala D, Furlan A. Impression Management Work: How Seniors With Chronic Pain Address Disruptions in Their Interactions. *Cscw* 12; 2012; 799–808.

259. Loew LM, Brosseau L, Tugwell P, Wells GA, Welch V, Shea B, et al. Deep transverse friction massage for treating lateral elbow or lateral knee tendonitis. *Cochrane Database Syst Rev* 2014; (11): CD003528. www.ncbi.nlm.nih.gov/pubmed/25380079 (cited 26 June 2019)

260. Pichonnaz C, Bassin J-P, Lécureux E, Christe G, Currat D, Aminian K, et al. Effect of Manual Lymphatic Drainage After Total Knee Arthroplasty: A Randomized Controlled Trial. *Arch Phys Med Rehabil* 2016; 97(5): 674–682. www.ncbi.nlm.nih.gov/pubmed/26829760 (cited 26 June 2019)

261. Garrett B, Mallia E, Anthony J. Public perceptions of internet-based health scams, and factors that promote engagement with them. *Health Soc Care Community* 2019; 27(5): hsc.12772. www.ncbi.nlm.nih.gov/pubmed/31194273 (cited 26 August 2019)

262. Garagarza CA, Valente AT, Oliveira TS, Caetano CG. Effect of personalized nutritional counseling in maintenance hemodialysis patients. *Hemodial Int* 2015; 19(3): 412–418. www.ncbi.nlm.nih.gov/pubmed/25560538 (cited 26 June 2019)

263. De Waele E, Mattens S, Honoré PM, Spapen H, De Grève J, Pen JJ. Nutrition therapy in cachectic cancer patients. The Tight Caloric Control (TiCaCo) pilot trial. *Appetite* 2015; 91: 298–301. www.ncbi.nlm.nih.gov/pubmed/25912786 (cited 26 June 2019)

264. Harman D. Aging: A Theory Based on Free Radical and Radiation Chemistry. *J Gerontol* 1956; 11(3): 298–300. https://academic.oup.com/geronj/article-lookup/doi/10.1093/geronj/11.3.298 (cited 22 May 2019)

265. Leopold JA. Antioxidants and coronary artery disease: from pathophysiology to preventive therapy. *Coron Artery Dis* 2015;

26(2): 176–183. www.ncbi.nlm.nih.gov/pubmed/25369999 (cited 22 May 2019)

266. Harvard TH. Chan School of Public Health. Antioxidants: Beyond the Hype. *The Nutrition Source* 2015. www.hsph.harvard.edu/nutritionsource/antioxidants/ (cited 22 May 2019)

267. Which. Nutritional therapists: gambling with your health? *Which? News* 16 January 2012. www.which.co.uk/news/2012/01/nutritional-therapists-gambling-with-your-health-276653/ (cited 11 September 2020)

268. Goldacre B. Ben Goldacre: why I'm battling it out with Gillian McKeith again. *The Guardian* 18 July 2010. www.theguardian.com/science/2010/jul/18/ben-goldacre-gillian-mckeith-twitter (cited 11 September 2020)

269. Krokowski JT, Lang P, Bell A, Broad N, Clayton J, Milne I, et al. A review of the incidence of cyanobacteria (blue-green algae) in surface waters in Scotland including potential effects of climate change, with a list of the common species and new records from the Scottish Environment Protection Agency. *Scottish Environment Protection Agency* 2012; 25.

270. Jarry J. 'CANCER IS A GOOD THING!!!'; says Montreal's Own "Food Babe. McGill University Office for Science and Society. March 2018 www.mcgill.ca/oss/article/quackery/cancer-good-thing-says-montreals-own-food-babe (cited 22 May 2019)

271. Lee MS, Choi J, Posadzki P, Ernst E. Aromatherapy for health care: An overview of systematic reviews. *Maturitas* 2012;71(3): 257–260. www.ncbi.nlm.nih.gov/pubmed/22285469 (cited 26 June 2019)

272. Broughan C. The psychological aspects of aromatherapy. *Int J Aromather* 2005; 15(1): 3–6. http://search.ebscohost.com/login.aspx?direct=true&db=ccm&AN=2009144636&site=ehost-live

273. Hines S, Steels E, Chang A, Gibbons K. Aromatherapy for treatment of postoperative nausea and vomiting. *Cochrane Database Syst Rev* 2012; (4): CD007598. www.ncbi.nlm.nih.gov/pubmed/22513952 (cited 26 June 2019)

274. Clarke TC, Black LI, Stussman BJ, Barnes PM, Nahin RL. Trends in the use of complementary health approaches among adults: United States, 2002-2012. *Natl Health Stat Report* 2015; (79): 1–16. www.ncbi.nlm.nih.gov/pubmed/25671660 (cited 27 June 2019)

275. Büssing A, Michalsen A, Khalsa SBS, Telles S, Sherman KJ. Effects of yoga on mental and physical health: a short summary of reviews. *Evid Based Complement Alternat Med* 2012; 2012: 165410. www.ncbi.nlm.nih.gov/pubmed/23008738 (cited 27 June 2019)

276. Kim THM, Pascual-Leone J, Johnson J, Tamim H. The mental-attention Tai Chi effect with older adults. *BMC Psychol* 2016; 4(1): 29. www.ncbi.nlm.nih.gov/pubmed/27245444 (cited 27 June 2019)

277. Prathikanti S, Rivera R, Cochran A, Tungol JG, Fayazmanesh N, Weinmann E. Treating major depression with yoga: A prospective, randomized, controlled pilot trial. *PLoS One* 2017; 12(3): e0173869. www.ncbi.nlm.nih.gov/pubmed/28301561 (cited 27 June 2019)

278. Qaseem A, Wilt TJ, McLean RM, Forciea MA. Noninvasive treatments for acute, subacute, and chronic low back pain: A clinical practice guideline from the American College of Physicians. *Ann Intern Med* 2017; 166(7): 514–530.

279. Cramer H, Lauche R, Klose P, Lange S, Langhorst J, Dobos GJ. Yoga for improving health-related quality of life, mental health and cancer-related symptoms in women diagnosed with breast cancer. *Cochrane Database Syst Rev* 2017 ; 1(1): CD010802. www.ncbi.nlm.nih.gov/pubmed/28045199 (cited 27 June 2019)

280. Marks R. Qigong Exercise and Arthritis. *Med (Basel, Switzerland)* 27 September 2017; 4(4). www.ncbi.nlm.nih.gov/pubmed/28953263 (cited 27 June 2019)

281. Yang G-Y, Wang L-Q, Ren J, Zhang Y, Li M-L, Zhu Y-T, et al. Evidence base of clinical studies on Tai Chi: a bibliometric analysis. *PLoS One* 2015; 10(3): e0120655. www.ncbi.nlm.nih.gov/pubmed/25775125 (cited 27 June 2019)

282. McNeely ME, Duncan RP, Earhart GM. A comparison of dance interventions in people with Parkinson disease and older adults. *Maturitas* 2015; 81(1): 10–16. www.ncbi.nlm.nih.gov/pubmed/25771040 (cited 27 June 2019)

283. Tortora S. Children Are Born to Dance! Pediatric Medical Dance/Movement Therapy: The View from Integrative Pediatric Oncology. *Child (Basel, Switzerland)* 2019; 6(1). www.ncbi.nlm.nih.gov/pubmed/30669668 (cited 27 June 2019)

284. Campo M, Shiyko MP, Kean MB, Roberts L, Pappas E. Musculoskeletal pain associated with recreational yoga

participation: A prospective cohort study with 1-year follow-up. *J Bodyw Mov Ther* 2018; 22(2): 418–423.

285. Original Goat Yoga. Health Benefits of Original Goat Yoga. Original Goat YogaTM & Goat Happy Hour® Website. 2019. https://goatyoga.net/2018/04/10/health-benefits-of-goat-yoga-2/ (cited 31 August 2020)

286. Kocovski NL, Fleming JE, Blackie RA, MacKenzie MB, Rose AL. Self-Help for Social Anxiety: Randomized Controlled Trial Comparing a Mindfulness and Acceptance-Based Approach With a Control Group. *Behav Ther* 2019; 50(4): 696–709. www.ncbi.nlm.nih.gov/pubmed/31208680 (cited 27 June 2019)

287. Ma Y, Fang S. Adolescents' Mindfulness and Psychological Distress: The Mediating Role of Emotion Regulation. *Front Psychol* 2019; 10: 1358. www.ncbi.nlm.nih.gov/pubmed/31231292 (cited 27 June 2019)

288. Nyklíček I, Dijksman SC, Lenders PJ, Fonteijn W a, Koolen JJ. A brief mindfulness based intervention for increase in emotional well-being and quality of life in percutaneous coronary intervention (PCI) patients: the MindfulHeart randomized controlled trial. *J Behav Med* 2014; 37(1): 135–144. www.ncbi.nlm.nih.gov/pubmed/23180285 (cited 30 January 2014)

289. Spears CA, Abroms LC, Glass CR, Hedeker D, Eriksen MP, Cottrell-Daniels C, et al. Mindfulness-Based Smoking Cessation Enhanced With Mobile Technology (iQuit Mindfully): Pilot Randomized Controlled Trial. *JMIR mHealth uHealth* 2019; 7(6): e13059. www.ncbi.nlm.nih.gov/pubmed/31237242 (cited 27 June 2019)

290. Badaoui A, Kassm SA, Naja W. Fear and Anxiety Disorders Related to Childbirth: Epidemiological and Therapeutic Issues. *Curr Psychiatry Rep* 2019; 21(4): 27. www.ncbi.nlm.nih.gov/pubmed/30868272 (cited 27 June 2019)

291. Birnie KA, Noel M, Chambers CT, Uman LS, Parker JA. Psychological interventions for needle-related procedural pain and distress in children and adolescents. *Cochrane Database of Systematic Reviews* 2018; 2018.

292. Hirsch JA. Integrating Hypnosis with Other Therapies for Treating Specific Phobias: A Case Series. *Am J Clin Hypn* 2018; 60(4): 367–377. www.ncbi.nlm.nih.gov/pubmed/29485374 (cited 27 June 2019)

References

293. Barnes J, McRobbie H, Dong CY, Walker N, Hartmann-Boyce J. Hypnotherapy for smoking cessation. *Cochrane Database Syst Rev* 2019; 6: CD001008. www.ncbi.nlm.nih.gov/pubmed/31198991 (cited 27 June 2019)

294. Clarke-Billings L. Hypnotist jailed for ten years after sexually assaulting woman under his spell. *The Telegraph* 28 September 2015. www.telegraph.co.uk/news/uknews/crime/11897562/Hypnotist-jailed-for-ten-years-after-sexually-assaulting-woman-under-his-spell.html (cited 31 August 2020)

295. Dossey BM, Keegan L, Barrere CC, Blaszko Helming MA. *Holistic nursing : A handbook for practice*. 7th ed. Burlington, MA: Jones & Bartlett Learning; 2018: 936 pp.

296. Koerner JG. *Healing presence : the essence of nursing*. New York, NY, US: Springer Pub Co; 2007. https://trove.nla.gov.au/work/26321835?selectedversion=NBD41283055 (cited 21 May 2019)

297. Hanley MA, Coppa D, Shields D. A Practice-Based Theory of Healing Through Therapeutic Touch: Advancing Holistic Nursing Practice. *J Holist Nurs* 2017; 35(4): 369–381. http://journals.sagepub.com/doi/10.1177/0898010117721827 (cited 21 May 2019)

298. Rosa L. A Close Look at Therapeutic Touch. *JAMA* 1998; 279(13): 1005. http://jama.jamanetwork.com/article.aspx?articleid=187390 (11 September 2013)

299. Jhaveri A, Walsh SJ, Wang Y, McCarthy M, Gronowicz G. Therapeutic touch affects DNA synthesis and mineralization of human osteoblasts in culture. *J Orthop Res* 2008; 26(11): 1541–1546.

300. O'Mathúna DP. Therapeutic touch for healing acute wounds. *Cochrane Database Syst Rev* 1 September 2016. http://doi.wiley.com/10.1002/14651858.CD002766.pub6 (cited 22 May 2019)

301. Robinson J, Biley FC, Dolk H. Therapeutic touch for anxiety disorders. *Cochrane Database Syst Rev* 2007; (3). http://doi.wiley.com/10.1002/14651858.CD006240.pub2 (cited 22 May 2019)

302. So PS, Jiang JY, Qin Y. Touch therapies for pain relief in adults. *Cochrane Database Syst Rev* 2013; 2013(11). http://doi.wiley.com/10.1002/14651858.CD006535.pub3 (cited 22 May 2019)

303. Van Wijk R, Van Wijk E. The search for a biosensor as a witness of a human laying on of hands ritual. *Altern Ther Heal Med* 2003; 9(2): 48–55.

304. Opp JW. *The Lord for the body : religion, medicine and Protestant faith healing in Canada, 1880-1930.* Montreal, QC: McGill-Queen's University Press; 2005: 274 pp.

305. Cha KY, Wirth DP, Lobo RA. Does prayer influence the success of in vitro fertilization-embryo transfer? Report of a masked, randomized trial. *J Reprod Med* 2001; 46(9): 781–787. www.ncbi.nlm.nih.gov/pubmed/11584476 (cited 27 May 2019)

306. Benson H, Dusek JA, Sherwood JB, Lam P, Bethea CF, Carpenter W, et al. Study of the Therapeutic Effects of Intercessory Prayer (STEP) in cardiac bypass patients: A multicenter randomized trial of uncertainty and certainty of receiving intercessory prayer. *Am Heart J* 2006; 151(4): 934–942. www.ncbi.nlm.nih.gov/pubmed/16569567 (cited 27 May 2019)

307. Leibovici L. Effects of remote, retroactive intercessory prayer on outcomes in patients with bloodstream infection: randomised controlled trial. *BMJ* 2001; 323(7327): 1450–1451. www.ncbi.nlm.nih.gov/pubmed/11751349 (cited 27 May 2019)

308. Struve AR, Lu D-F, Hart LK, Keller T. The Use of Intercessory Prayer to Reduce Disruptive Behaviors of Patients With Dementia. *J Holist Nurs* 2016; 34(2): 135–45. www.ncbi.nlm.nih.gov/pubmed/26025094 (cited 27 May 2019)

309. Hoşrik EM, Cüceloğlu AE, Erpolat S. Therapeutic Effects of Islamic Intercessory Prayer on Warts. *J Relig Health* 2017; 56(6): 2053–2060. www.ncbi.nlm.nih.gov/pubmed/24535044 (cited 27 May 2019)

310. Tindle HA, Wolsko P, Davis RB, Eisenberg DM, Phillips RS, McCarthy EP. Factors associated with the use of mind body therapies among United States adults with musculoskeletal pain. *Complement Ther Med* 2005; 13(3): 155–164. http://linkinghub.elsevier.com/retrieve/pii/S0965229905000440 (cited 19 July 2017)

311. Masters KS, Spielmans GI. Prayer and Health: Review, Meta-Analysis, and Research Agenda. *J Behav Med* 2007; 30(4): 329–338. www.ncbi.nlm.nih.gov/pubmed/17487575 (cited 27 May 2019)

312. Hodge DR. A Systematic Review of the Empirical Literature on Intercessory Prayer. *Res Soc Work Pract* 2007; 17(2): 174–187. http://journals.sagepub.com/doi/10.1177/1049731506296170 (cited 27 May 2019)

313. Rath LL. Scientific Ways to Study Intercessory Prayer as an

Intervention in Clinical Research. *J Perinat Neonatal Nurs* 2009; 23(1): 71–77. www.ncbi.nlm.nih.gov/pubmed/19209063

314. de Aguiar PRDC, Tatton-Ramos TP, Alminhana LO. Research on Intercessory Prayer: Theoretical and Methodological Considerations. *J Relig Health* 2017; 56(6): 1930–1936. www.ncbi.nlm.nih.gov/pubmed/26743876 (cited 27 May 2019)

315. Stroumboulopoulos G. Adam The Dream Healer. YouTube - The Hour with George Stroumboulopoulos. 7 December 2007. www.youtube.com/watch?v=ry7qbNIKiLk (cited 27 May 2019)

316. Mendleson R. A trail of victims from Woodbridge to the U.K. *The Star* 20 February 2015. www.thestar.com/news/crime/2015/02/20/a-trail-of-victims-from-woodbridge-to-the-uk.html (cited 31 August 2020)

317. Dowswell T, Bedwell C, Lavender T, Neilson JP. Transcutaneous electrical nerve stimulation (TENS) for pain management in labour. *Cochrane Database Syst Rev* 2009; (2): CD007214. www.ncbi.nlm.nih.gov/pubmed/19370680 (cited 22 May 2019)

318. Gibson W, Wand BM, O'Connell NE. Transcutaneous electrical nerve stimulation (TENS) for neuropathic pain in adults. *Cochrane Database Syst Rev* 14 September 2017. http://doi.wiley.com/10.1002/14651858.CD011976.pub2 (cited 22 May 2019)

319. Fishbein M. *The new medical follies: an encyclopedia of cultism and quackery in these United States, with essays on the cult of beauty, the craze for reduction, rejuvenation, eclecticism, bread and dietary fads.* New York: Boni and Liveright; 1927. www.worldcat.org/title/new-medical-follies-an-encyclopedia-of-cultism-and-quackery-in-these-united-states-with-essays-on-the-cult-of-beauty-the-craze-for-reduction-rejuvenation-eclecticism-bread-and-dietary-fads-physical-therapy-and-a-forecast-as-to-the-physician-of-the-future/oclc/1450871 (cited 22 May 2019)

320. Radionics and Dowsing Institute of Canada. *Advances in Radionics equipment.* 20 January 2018. http://radionicsinstitute.com/radionic_equipment.html (cited 22 May 2019)

321. Wang S-M, Maranets I, Lin EC, DeZinno P. Is Commercially Available Point Finder Accurate and Reliable in Detecting Active Auricular Acupuncture Points? *J Altern Complement Med* 2012;18(9): 860. www.ncbi.nlm.nih.gov/pubmed/22834870 (cited 23 May 2019)

322. Ahn AC, Martinsen OG. Electrical characterization of acupuncture points: technical issues and challenges. *J Altern Complement Med*2007; 13(8): 817–824. www.ncbi.nlm.nih.gov/pubmed/17983337 (cited 23 May 2019)

323. Barrett S. ZYTO Scanning: Another Test to Avoid. *Device Watch* 28 August 2018. www.devicewatch.org/reports/zyto/overview.shtml (cited 23 May 2019)

324. ZYTO Corporation. 10Q Filing with the Securities and Exchange Commission. 20 September 2011. www.secinfo.com/d11f65.q2Wa.s.htm#1stPage

325. ASBCE. Consent Agreement and Findings of Fact, Conclusions of Law and Order for Cease and Desist; Probation and Civil Penalty Consent Agreement 2015. www.casewatch.net/board/chiro/bean/order_2015.pdf (cited 24 May 2019)

326. Mitchel LM. FDA Warning Letter to ZYTO Technologies Inc. *FDA Letter*. 21 May 2015. www.casewatch.net/fdawarning/prod/2015/zyto.shtml (24 May 2019)

327. FDA. Class 2 Device Recall ZYTO Select Software and ZYTO Elite Software. *FDA* 01 Jul. 2016. www.accessdata.fda.gov/scripts/cdrh/cfdocs/cfres/res.cfm?id=147046 (cited 24 May 2019)

328. Shaughnessy A. Is the 'Q-ray ionized bracelet' effective for muscle or joint pain? *Evidence-Based Pract* 2003; 6(3): 6–7. http://search.ebscohost.com/login.aspx?direct=true&db=c8h&AN=2003123300&login.asp&site=ehost-live

329. Federal Trade Commission. FTC Returns More Than $11.8 Million to Consumers Defrauded by Q-Ray Bracelet Scam. FTC Press Release 6 May 2011. www.ftc.gov/news-events/press-releases/2011/05/ftc-returns-more-118-million-consumers-defrauded-q-ray-bracelet (cited 22 May 2019)

330. Karlamangla S. A California doctor is selling hissing sounds to patients. The medical board isn't buying it. *Los Angeles Times* 25 May 2018. www.latimes.com/local/california/la-me-ln-doctor-license-threat-20180524-story.html (cited 29 May 2019)

331. Krugel L. Sentencing decision for Calgary couple convicted in toddler's infection death. *CTV News* 5 June 2019. www.ctvnews.ca/canada/sentencing-decision-for-calgary-couple-convicted-in-toddler-s-infection-death-1.4452332 (cited 5 June 2019)

332. Hartley-Parkinson R. Mum who went vegan and shunned NHS

treatment dies from cancer. *Metro News* 5 June 2019. https://metro.co.uk/2019/06/03/mum-went-vegan-shunned-nhs-treatment-dies-cancer-9777871/ (cited 5 June 2019)

333. Johnson SB, Park HS, Gross CP, Yu JB. Complementary Medicine, Refusal of Conventional Cancer Therapy, and Survival Among Patients With Curable Cancers. *JAMA Oncol* 2018; 4(10): 1375. http://oncology.jamanetwork.com/article.aspx?doi=10.1001/jamaoncol.2018.2487 (cited 5 June 2019)

334. Offit PA. *Do You Believe in Magic?: The Sense and Nonsense of Alternative Medicine*. New York: Harper Collins; 2013.

335. Caulfield TA. *Is Gwyneth Paltrow wrong about everything? : when celebrity culture and science clash*. Boston, MA: Beacon Press; 2015: 381 pp.

336. Jha A. Homeopaths 'endangering lives' by offering malaria remedies. *The Guardian* 14 July 2006. www.theguardian.com/science/2006/jul/14/medicineandhealth.lifeandhealth (cited 16 May 2019)

337. Jones M, Ghosh P. Cases dropped against malaria homeopaths. *BBC News* 11 January 2011. www.bbc.com/news/health-12153074 (16 May 2019)

338. Smith S. Homeopathic 'vaccine pills' should be withdrawn, says regulator. *BBC News* 14 January 2013. www.bbc.com/news/uk-england-devon-20991335 (cited 2 September 2020)

339. Hayward E, Adams G. Fury as royal chemist Ainsworths backs anti-vaxxers. *The Daily Mail* 2 September 2019. www.dailymail.co.uk/news/article-7623623/Fury-royal-chemist-Ainsworths-backs-anti-vaxxers.html (cited 2 September 2020)

340. Bajic C. Homeopathic doctors help in Liberia. *Zeitschrift Homoeopathie* 24 November 2014. www.homoeopathie-online.info/homoeopathische-aerzte-helfen-in-liberia/ (cited 16 May 2019)

341. Boseley S. Homeopaths offer services 'to help fight' Ebola epidemic in west Africa. *The Guardian* 30 October 2014. www.theguardian.com/world/2014/oct/30/homeopaths-offer-services-fight-ebola (cited 16 May 2019)

342. Chivers G. Canadian government will stop paying for homeopaths to go to Honduras. *CBC News* 6 March 2019. www.cbc.ca/news/health/government-funding-homeopaths-honduras-1.5046056 (cited 16 May 2019)

343. Ireland N. Stronger action urged against homeopathic products touted as alternatives to vaccines. *CBC News* 18 March 2018. www.cbc.ca/news/health/health-canada-homeopathy-vaccine-hesitancy-1.5058393 (cited 15 May 2019)

344. Loeb M, Russell ML, Neupane B, Thanabalan V, Singh P, Newton J, et al. A randomized, blinded, placebo-controlled trial comparing antibody responses to homeopathic and conventional vaccines in university students. *Vaccine* 2018; 36(48): 7423–7429. www.ncbi.nlm.nih.gov/pubmed/30352746 (cited 16 May 2019)

345. Lindsay B. 'Dangerous' claims that homeopathic remedies prevent infectious disease under review by feds. *CBC News* 1 March 2019. www.cbc.ca/news/canada/british-columbia/homeoprophylaxis-vaccination-health-canada-bc-homeopaths-1.5036538 (cited 16 May 2019)

346. Young L. B.C. naturopath who prescribed rabid dog saliva remedy to a child surrenders her licence. *Global News* 8 November 2018. https://globalnews.ca/news/4644439/bc-naturopath-license-dog-saliva/ (cited 30 April 2019)

347. Ali A, Vitulano L, Lee R, Weiss TR, Colson ER. Experiences of patients identifying with chronic Lyme disease in the healthcare system: a qualitative study. *BMC Fam Pract* 2014; 15: 79. www.ncbi.nlm.nih.gov/pubmed/24885888 (cited 29 May 2019)

348. Lantos PM. Chronic Lyme disease. *Infect Dis Clin North Am* 2015; 29(2): 325–340. www.ncbi.nlm.nih.gov/pubmed/25999227 (cited 29 May 2019)

349. Gallagher S. Homeopaths 'forbidden' from offering autism 'treatment' by government watchdog. *The Independent* 14 January 2020. www.independent.co.uk/life-style/health-and-families/homeopathy-autism-treatment-banned-a9333796.html (cited 2 September 2020)

350. Holden M. Chinese herbal pills destroyed UK woman's health. *Reuters UK News* 17 February 2010. https://uk.reuters.com/article/uk-britain-doctor/chinese-herbal-pills-destroyed-uk-womans-health-idUKTRE61G3N420100217 (cited 10 May 2019)

351. Hermes B-M. Confirmed: Licensed Naturopathic Doctor Gave Lethal 'Turmeric' Injection. *Forbes* 10 April 2017. www.forbes.com/sites/brittmariehermes/2017/04/10/confirmed-licensed-naturopathic-doctor-gave-lethal-turmeric-

injection/#48b57a976326 (cited 2 September 2020)

352. Smith WS, Johnston SC, Skalabrin EJ, Weaver M, Azari P, Albers GW, et al. Spinal manipulative therapy is an independent risk factor for vertebral artery dissection. *Neurology* 2003; 60(9): 1424–1428. www.ncbi.nlm.nih.gov/pubmed/12743225 (cited 20 July 2017)

353. Ernst E. Deaths after acupuncture: A systematic review. *Int J Risk Saf Med* 2010; 22(3): 131–136. http://content.iospress.com/articles/international-journal-of-risk-and-safety-in-medicine/jrs503 (cited 20 July 2017)

354. Lee MS, Ernst E. Acupuncture for surgical conditions: an overview of systematic reviews. *Int J Clin Pract* 2014; 68(6): 783–789. www.ncbi.nlm.nih.gov/pubmed/24447388 (cited 26 July 2017)

355. Paulus YM, Belill N. Preretinal hemorrhages following chiropractor neck manipulation. *Am J Ophthalmol Case Reports* 2018; 11: 181–183. https://doi.org/10.1016/j.ajoc.2018.04.017

356. Whedon JM, Song Y, Mackenzie TA, Phillips RB, Lukovits TG, Lurie JD. Risk of stroke after chiropractic spinal manipulation in medicare B beneficiaries aged 66 to 99 years with neck pain. *J Manipulative Physiol Ther* 2015; 38(2): 93–101. www.ncbi.nlm.nih.gov/pubmed/25596875 (cited 5 June 2019)

357. Hufnagel A, Hammers A, Schönle PW, Böhm KD, Leonhardt G. Stroke following chiropractic manipulation of the cervical spine. *J Neurol* 1999; 246(8): 683–688. www.ncbi.nlm.nih.gov/pubmed/10460445 (cited 5 June 2019)

358. Laycock M. John Lawler suffered broken neck during chiropractor treatment, inquest told. *York Press* 11 November 2019. www.yorkpress.co.uk/news/18028898.john-lawler-suffered-broken-neck-chiropractor-treatment-inquest-told/ (cited 14 September 2020)

359. Ernst E. 'We hope that the publicity surrounding this event will highlight the dangers of chiropractic...' A statement of the family of the man who died after treatment of a 'vertebral subluxation complex'. *Edzard Ernst Blog* 19 November 2019. https://edzardernst.com/2019/11/we-hope-that-the-publicity-surrounding-this-event-will-highlight-the-dangers-of-chiropractic-a-statement-of-the-family-of-the-man-who-died-after-treatment-of-a-vertebral-subluxation-complex/ (cited 14 September 2020)

360. Drewett Z. Chiropractor 'broke patient's neck' during treatment for sore leg. *Metro News* 14 November 2019. https://metro.co.uk/2019/11/14/chiropractor-broke-patients-neck-treatment-sore-leg-11123778/ (cited 15 November 2019)

361. Norris JW, Beletsky V. Update from the Canadian Stroke Consortium. *CMAJ* 2001; 165(7).

362. Beletsky V. Chiropractic manipulation may be underestimated as cause of stroke. In: *American Stroke Association's 27th International Stroke Conference - 7-8th February*. San Antonio, TX, TX; 2002.

363. Zimmerman AW, Kumar AJ, Gadoth N, Hodges FJ. Traumatic vertebrobasilar occlusive disease in childhood. *Neurology* 1978; 28(2): 185–188. www.ncbi.nlm.nih.gov/pubmed/563999 (cited 5 June 2019)

364. Shafrir Y, Kaufman BA. Quadriplegia after chiropractic manipulation in an infant with congenital torticollis caused by a spinal cord astrocytoma. *J Pediatr* 1992; 120(2 Pt 1): 266–269. www.ncbi.nlm.nih.gov/pubmed/1735825 (cited 5 June 2019)

365. Medew J, Corderoy A. Call for age limit after chiropractor breaks baby's neck. *The Age* 29 September 2013. www.theage.com.au/healthcare/call-for-age-limit-after-chiropractor-breaks-babys-neck-20130928-2ul6e.html (cited 14 May 2019)

366. Humphreys BK. Possible adverse events in children treated by manual therapy: a review. *Chiropr Osteopat* 2010; 18: 12. www.ncbi.nlm.nih.gov/pubmed/20525194 (cited 5 June 2019)

367. Zhang J, Shang H, Gao X, Ernst E. Acupuncture-related adverse events: a systematic review of the Chinese literature. *Bull World Health Organ* 2010; 88(12): 915–921. www.who.int/bulletin/volumes/88/12/10.076737.pdf (cited 5 June 2019)

368. Ernst E. Acupuncture - a treatment to die for? *J R Soc Med* 2010; 103(10): 384–385. www.ncbi.nlm.nih.gov/pubmed/20929887

369. Yamashita H, Tsukayama H, White AR, Tanno Y, Sugishita C, Ernst E. Systematic review of adverse events following acupuncture: the Japanese literature. *Complement Ther Med* 2001; 9(2): 98–104. https://linkinghub.elsevier.com/retrieve/pii/S0965229901904467 (cited 5 June 2019)

370. Norheim AJ. Adverse effects of acupuncture: a study of the literature for the years 1981-1994. *J Altern Complement Med* 1996; 2(2): 291–297. www.liebertpub.com/doi/10.1089/acm.1996.2.291

(cited 5 June 2019)

371. Peuker ET. Traumatic Complications of Acupuncture: Therapists Need to Know Human Anatomy. *Arch Fam Med* 1999; 8(6): 553–558. http://archfami.ama-assn.org/cgi/doi/10.1001/archfami.8.6.553 (cited 5 June 2019)

372. Australian Associated Press. Naturopath whose diet nearly starved baby vows to never work with children again. *The Guardian* 5 April 2018. www.theguardian.com/australia-news/2018/apr/05/naturopath-whose-diet-nearly-starved-baby-vows-to-never-work-with-children-again (29 May 2019)

373. Shermer M. Skeptic What's the Harm ? *Sci Am* 2003; 289(6).

374. Roser M, Ortiz-Ospina E. Tertiary Education - Higher education Today and in the Future. *OurWorldInData* 2 January 2013; 409 pp. https://ourworldindata.org/tertiary-education (cited 6 June 2019)

375. Statistics Canada. Canadian postsecondary enrolments and graduates. Ottawa, ON; 2017. www150.statcan.gc.ca/n1/daily-quotidien/181128/dq181128c-eng.htm

376. d'Entremont Y. Chiropractors are bullshit. *The Outline* June 2017 https://theoutline.com/post/1617/chiropractors-are-bullshit?zd=3&zi=d2b3agfd (cited 6 June 2019)

377. Palmer College of Chiropractic. Published Completion rates 2021. www.palmer.edu/about-us/accreditation/completion-rates/ (cited 17 February 2021)

378. Hermes B-M. Naturopathic Student's Guide. *Naturopathic Diaries* 2015. www.naturopathicdiaries.com/students-guide-naturopathic-school/ (cited 7 June 2019)

379. Devlin H. The naturopath whistleblower: 'It is surprisingly easy to sell snake oil.' *The Guardian* 27 May 2018 www.theguardian.com/lifeandstyle/2018/mar/27/naturopath-whistleblower-snake-oil-multi-billion-dollar (cited 7 June 2019)

380. Hermes B. Justice prevails! Cancer quack Colleen Huber loses her defamation suit against me. *Naturopathic Diaries*. 3 June 2019. www.naturopathicdiaries.com/justice-prevails-cancer-quack-colleen-huber-loses-her-defamation-suit-against-me/ (cited 10 June 2019)

381. Anon. Montreal-based vlogger faces ire over alternative cancer remedies. *CTV News Montreal* 27 April 2018. https://montreal.ctvnews.ca/montreal-based-vlogger-faces-ire-over-alternative-

cancer-remedies-1.3905110 (cited 22 May 2019)

382. Auerbach B. The Big C: The Truth about Cancer and How to Reverse it Naturally! . *Montreal Healthy Girl Blog* 23 August 2013. https://montrealhealthygirl.com/cancer/ (cited 22 May 2019)

383. Benedetti P, Macphail W. Straightening out chiropractic's claim as a treatment for autism. *Spectrum* 12 June 2019.www. spectrumnews.org/features/deep-dive/straightening-chiropractics-claim-treatment-autism/ (cited 12 June 2019)

384. Haigh T. Did V.A. Shiva Ayyadurai Invent Email? Special Interest Group for Computing, Information and Society. 4 August 2015. www.sigcis.org/ayyadurai (cited 3 September 2020)

385. Mullis KB. *Dancing naked in the mind field*. Vintage Books; 2000: 222 pp.

386. Bartz D, Flaherty M. Herbalife settles pyramid scheme case with regulator, in blow to Pershing's Ackman. *Reuters* 15 July 2015. www.reuters.com/article/us-herbalife-probe-ftc-idUSKCN0ZV1F7 (cited 27 November 2019)

387. Johnson K. Herbalife Nutrition to pay $20 million to settle false disclosure charges: U.S. SEC. *Reuters* 27 September 2019. www.reuters.com/article/us-usa-sec-herbalife/herbalife-nutrition-to-pay-20-million-to-settle-false-disclosure-charges-u-s-sec-idUSKBN1WC1YS (cited 27 November 2019)

388. Pershing Square Capital. Who wants to be a millionairre? Herbalife Presentation. 2012; 53 pp.

389. Evans D. Nobel Prize Winner Didn't Disclose His Herbalife Contract. *Bloomberg News* 26 December 2004. https://culteducation.com/group/969-herbalife/9601-nobel-prize-winner-didnt-disclose-his-herbalife-contract.html (cited 27 November 2019)

390. Montagnier L, Aïssa J, Ferris S, Montagnier JL, Lavalléee C. Electromagnetic signals are produced by aqueous nanostructures derived from bacterial DNA sequences. *Interdiscip Sci Comput Life Sci* 2009; 1(2): 81–90.

391. Coghlan A. Scorn over claim of teleported DNA. *New Scientist* 12 January 2011. www.newscientist.com/article/mg20927952-900-scorn-over-claim-of-teleported-dna/ (cited 27 November 2019)

392. Myers PZ. It almost makes me disbelieve that HIV causes AIDS! *Science Blogs* 11 January 2011. https://scienceblogs.com/

pharyngula/211/01/24/it-almost-makes-me-disbelieve (cited 11
September 2020)

393. Interdisciplinary Sciences: Computational Life Sciences. Editorial
Board Members. Interdisciplinary Sciences: Computational Life
Sciences. 2 August 2019 www.springer.com/journal/12539/
editors (cited 27 November 2019)

394. Eserink M. Luc Montagnier. French Nobelist escapes "intellectual
terror" to pursue radical ideas in China. *Science* 2010; 330(6012).
doi:10.1126/science.330.6012.1732

395. Bast F. A Nobel Laureate Said the New Coronavirus Was Made
in a Lab. He's Wrong. *Wire Sci* April 2020. https://science.
thewire.in/the-sciences/luc-montagnier-coronavirus-wuhan-lab-
pseudoscience/ (cited 18 February 2021)

396. Cancer Research UK. Vitamin C as a cancer treatment: the
evidence so far. *Cancer Science* 25 April 2018. https://scienceblog.
cancerresearchuk.org/2018/04/25/vitamin-c-as-a-treatment-for-
cancer-the-evidence-so-far/ (cited 18 February 2021)

397. Mayo Clinic. High-dose vitamin C: Can it kill cancer cells? 20
December 2020. www.mayoclinic.org/diseases-conditions/
cancer/expert-answers/alternative-cancer-treatment/faq-
20057968 (cited 18 February 2021)

398. Jacobs C, Hutton B, Ng T, Shorr R, Clemons M. Is There a Role for
Oral or Intravenous Ascorbate (Vitamin C) in Treating Patients
with Cancer? A Systematic Review. *The Oncologist* 2015; 20(2):
210-223. doi:10.1634/theoncologist.2014-0381

399. Cabanillas F. Vitamin C And cancer: What can we conclude - 1,609
patients and 33 years later? *P R Health Sci J* 2010; 29(3): 215–217.

400. Schetter L. A community-based study of vitamin C (ascorbic acid)
in patients with advanced cancer. In: *Proceedings of the American
Society of Clinical Oncology (ASCO)* 1983.

401. Creagan ET, Moertel CG, O'Fallon JR, Schutt AJ, O'Connell MJ,
Rubin J, et al. Failure of High-Dose Vitamin C (Ascorbic Acid)
Therapy to Benefit Patients with Advanced Cancer. *N Engl J Med*
1979; 301(13): 687–690. www.ncbi.nlm.nih.gov/pubmed/384241
(cited 18 June 2019)

402. Moertel CG, Fleming TR, Creagan ET, Rubin J, O'Connell
MJ, Ames MM. High-Dose Vitamin C versus Placebo in the
Treatment of Patients with Advanced Cancer Who Have Had No

Prior Chemotherapy. *N Engl J Med* 1985; 312(3): 137–141. www.
ncbi.nlm.nih.gov/pubmed/3880867 (cited 18 June 2019)

403. Gao P, Zhang H, Dinavahi R, Li F, Xiang Y, Raman V, et al.
HIF-Dependent Antitumorigenic Effect of Antioxidants In
Vivo. *Cancer Cell* 2007; 12(3): 230–238. www.ncbi.nlm.nih.gov/
pubmed/17785204 (cited 18 June 2019)

404. Suh S-Y, Bae WK, Ahn H-Y, Choi S-E, Jung G-C, Yeom CH.
Intravenous vitamin C administration reduces fatigue in office
workers: a double-blind randomized controlled trial. *Nutr J* 2012;
11(1): 7. www.pubmedcentral.nih.gov/articlerender.fcgi?artid=32
73429&tool=pmcentrez&rendertype=abstract

405. Manson JAE, Bassuk SS. Vitamin and mineral supplements what
clinicians need to know. *JAMA* 2018; 319(9): 859–860.

406. Klimant E, Wright H, Rubin D, Seely D, Markman M. *Current
Oncology* 2018; 25: 139–148. https://current-oncology.com/index.
php/oncology/article/view/3790/2712 (cited 18 June 2019)

407. McHugh GJ, Graber ML, Freebairn RC. Fatal vitamin C-associated
acute renal failure. *Anaesth Intensive Care* 2008; 36(4): 585-588.
doi:10.1177/0310057x0803600413

408. Barrett S. The Dark Side of Linus Pauling's Legacy.
Quackwatch 14 September 2014. www.quackwatch.
org/01QuackeryRelatedTopics/pauling.html (cited 18 June 2019)

409. Oprah Winfrey. Nasal Probe Surgery - Video Oprah.com Website.
2010 www.oprah.com/own-oprahshow/nasal-probe-surgery-
video

410. Korownyk C, Kolber MR, McCormack J, Lam V, Overbo K, Cotton
C, et al. Televised medical talk shows--what they recommend and
the evidence to support their recommendations: a prospective
observational study. *BMJ* 2014; 349: g7346. www.ncbi.nlm.nih.
gov/pubmed/25520234 (cited 11 July 2019)

411. Leggett AJ. The quantum measurement problem. *Science* 2005;
307(5711): 871–872. www.ncbi.nlm.nih.gov/pubmed/15705838
(cited 11 July 2019)

412. Schneiderman LJ. The (Alternative) Medicalization of Life. *J Law,
Med Ethics* 2003; 31(2): 191–197. http://journals.sagepub.com/
doi/10.1111/j.1748-720X.2003.tb00080.x (cited 11 July 2011)

413. Mnookin S. *The panic virus : the true story behind the vaccine-autism
controversy*. Toronto, Canada: Simon & Schuster; 2012: 439 pp.

414. McCarthy J. Questions About Autism with Jenny McCarthy. Oprah. 2007. www.oprah.com/relationships/questions-about-autism (cited 9 July 2019)

415. Wellcome Trust. Wellcome Global Monitor 2018. London, UK: Wellcome Trust; 2019. https://wellcome.ac.uk/reports/wellcome-global-monitor/2018 (cited 6 August 2019)

416. BC Centre for Disease Control. *Communicable Disease Control Manual of Relative Risks of Diseases and Immunization.* May 2009 www.bccdc.ca/resource-gallery/Documents/Guidelines%20and%20Forms/Guidelines%20and%20Manuals/Epid/CD%20Manual/Chapter%202%20-%20Imms/RelativeRisks.pdf (cited 15 March 2021)

417. Centers for Disease Control and Prevention. Questions About Measles. CDC Measles. 2021. www.cdc.gov/measles/about/faqs.html (cited 22 February 2021)

418. BBC. Covid: Anti-vaccination protests held in Australia ahead of rollout. *BBC News.* www.bbc.com/news/world-australia-56137597 (cited 22 February 2021)

419. Rao TSS, Andrade C. The MMR vaccine and autism: Sensation, refutation, retraction, and fraud. *Indian Journal of Psychiatry* 2011; 53: 95–96.

420. Hussain A, Ali S, Ahmed M, Hussain S. The Anti-vaccination Movement: A Regression in Modern Medicine. *Cureus* 2018; 10(7): e2919. www.ncbi.nlm.nih.gov/pubmed/30186724 (cited 6 August 2019)

421. Enserink M, Cohen J. Fact-checking Judy Mikovits, the controversial virologist attacking Anthony Fauci in a viral conspiracy video. *Science* 8 May 2020. doi:10.1126/science.abc7103

422. Kasten J. What Judy Mikovits Gets Wrong. MedPage Today. *MedPage Today* 12 May 2020. www.medpagetoday.com/infectiousdisease/generalinfectiousdisease/86461 (cited 18 February 2021)

423. D'Zurilla C. Gwyneth Paltrow cracks a coronavirus joke while wearing a face mask. *Los Angeles Times* 26 February 2020. www.latimes.com/entertainment-arts/story/2020-02-26/gwyneth-paltrow-kate-hudson-face-mask-coronavirus (cited 3 September 2020)

424. Peters JW. From Jerry Falwell Jr. to Dr. Drew: 5 Coronavirus Doubters. *The New York Times* 18 March 2020. www.nytimes.com/2020/03/18/us/politics/coronavirus-doubters-falwell-drew.html (cited 3 September 2020)

425. Kruger J, Kruger J, Dunning D. Unskilled and Unaware of It: How Difficulties in Recognizing One's Own Incompetence Lead to Inflated Self-Assessments. *J Pers Soc Psychol* 1999;77: 1121--1134. https://citeseerx.ist.psu.edu/viewdoc/summary?doi=10.1.1.64.2655 (cited 6 August 2019)

426. Tehrani J. Did our brains evolve to foolishly follow celebrities? *BBC News - Viewpoint* June 2013. www.bbc.com/news/magazine-23046602 (cited 6 August 2019)

427. Raffaele P. In John They Trust. The Smithsonian - History. 2006. www.smithsonianmag.com/history/in-john-they-trust-109294882/ (cited 6 August 2019)

428. Gallagher B, Berger K. Why Misinformation Is About Who You Trust, Not What You Think. *Nautilus* February 2019. http://nautil.us/issue/69/patterns/why-misinformation-is-about-who-you-trust-not-what-you-think (cited 6 August 2019)

429. Gallagher S. Mary Berry 'appalled' to be affiliated with CBD oil scam.. *The Independent* 19 February 2020. www.independent.co.uk/life-style/mary-berry-cbd-hoax-adverts-facebook-a9344326.html (cited 14 September 2020)

430. Sakoui A. Clint Eastwood calls out fake cannabis product endorsements. *Los Angeles Times* 22 July 2020. www.latimes.com/entertainment-arts/business/story/2020-07-22/clint-eastwood-sues-cannabis-products-cbd (cited 14 September 2020)

431. Jalimnson G. Beware Of Fake Celebrity Cannabidiol Endorsements. *Hemp Gazette* 27 January 2020. https://hempgazette.com/news/cannabis-cannabidiol-celebrities-hg1097/ (cited 14 September 2020)

432. Better Business Bureau. Subscription Traps and Deceptive Free Trials Scam Millions with Misleading Ads and Fake Celebrity. *BBB Report* New York NY; 2018. www.bbb.org/article/investigations/18929-subscription-traps-and-deceptive-free-trials-scam-millions-with-misleading-ads-and-fake-celebrity-endorsements (cited 14 September 2020)

433. Gilbert DT, Krull DS, Malone PS. Unbelieving the unbelievable:

some problems in the rejection of false information. *J Pers Soc Psychol* 1990; 59: 601–613.

434. Greenspan S. *Annals of gullibility: why we get duped and how to avoid it*. Westport, CT: Praeger Publishers; 2009: 199 pp.

435. Sperber D, Clément F, Heintz C, Mascaro O, Mercier H, Origgi G, et al. Epistemic Vigilance. *Mind Lang* 2010; 25(4): 359–393. http://onlinelibrary.wiley.com/store/10.1111/j.1468-0017.2010.01394.x/asset/j.1468-0017.2010.01394.x.pdf?v=1&t=hp5idvy6&s=83b fd48795bb02b7bc19b28ad0963a5eafe90e02%5Cnpapers2://publication/uuid/27F8D50F-53D5-4CC4-B7D2-DB22D954C180

436. Hogenbroom M. The devious art of lying by telling the truth. *BBC Future* 15 November 2017. www.bbc.com/future/story/20171114-the-disturbing-art-of-lying-by-telling-the-truth

437. Rogers T, Zeckhauser R, Gino F, Schweitzer M, Norton M. Artful Paltering : The Risks and Rewards of Using Truthful Statements to Mislead Others Faculty Research Working Paper Series Harvard Business School. *J Pers Soc Psychol* 2017; 112(3): 456–473. http://dx.doi.org/10.1037/pspi0000081.supp%0AJim

438. Kessler Glann, Rizzo S, Kelly M. President Trump has made 10,796 false or misleading claims over 869 days. *The Washington Post* 10 June 2019. https://www.washingtonpost.com/politics/2019/06/10/president-trump-has-made-false-or-misleading-claims-over-days/ (cited 13 August 2019)

439. Shermer M. *Why People Believe Weird Things: Pseudoscience, Superstition, and Other Confusions of Our Time, Vol 2*. New York: Henry Holt; 2002.

440. Sullivan ME. Creationism in the Classroom: Trump's 'Alternative Facts'. *The National Law Review* 11 March 2019. www.natlawreview.com/article/alternative-facts-classroom-creationist-educational-policy-and-trump-administration (cited 22 February 2021)

441. Hobson A. Teaching Relevant Science for Scientific Literacy. *J Coll Sci Teach* 2001; 30(4): 23–243.

442. Ayala MO. Avocado: the 'green gold' causing environment havoc. *World Economic Forum* 24 February 2020. www.weforum.org/agenda/2020/02/avocado-environment-cost-food-mexico/ (cited 22 February 2021)

443. Wilcox C. Mythbusting 101: Organic Farming vs Conventional

Agriculture. *Scientific American* 18 August 2011. https://blogs. scientificamerican.com/science-sushi/httpblogsscientificameric ancomscience-sushi20110718mythbusting-101-organic-farming-conventional-agriculture/ (cited 22 February 2021)

444. Watson S. Organic food no more nutritious than conventionally grown food. *Harvard Health Blog* 2012. www.health.harvard.edu/blog/organic-food-no-more-nutritious-than-conventionally-grown-food-201209055264 (cited 22 February 2021)

445. Industry S of C. Organic Food Has No More Nutritional Value than Food Grown with Pesticides, Study Shows. *Science Daily* 2008. www.sciencedaily.com/releases/2008/08/080807082954. htm (cited 22 February 2021)

446. Rodriguez F, Rhodes RE, Miller KF, Shah P. Examining the influence of anecdotal stories and the interplay of individual differences on reasoning. *Think Reason* 2016; 22(3): 274–296. www.tandfonline.com/doi/full/10.1080/13546783.2016.1139506 (cited 5 September 2019)

447. Aarnio K, Lindeman M. Magical food and health beliefs: A portrait of believers and functions of the beliefs. *Appetite* 2004; 43(1): 65–74. www.ncbi.nlm.nih.gov/pubmed/15262019 (cited 8 May 2014)

448. Lindeman M, Aarnio K. The Origin of Superstition, Magical Thinking, and Paranormal Beliefs - an Integrative Model. *Skeptic* 2007; 13(1): 58–65.

449. Tobacyk JJ, Wilkinson L V. Magical thinking and paranormal beliefs. *Journal of Social Behaviour and Personality* 1990; 5(4): Spec-264.

450. Kinard BR, Webster C. The Effects of Advertising, Social Influences, and Self-Efficacy on Adolescent Tobacco Use and Alcohol Consumption. *Journal of Consumer Affairs* 2010; 44: 24–43. www.jstor.org/stable/23859774 (cited 22 August 2019)

451. Gross RE. *Key studies in psychology*. London: Hodder Arnold; 2008.

452. Fifel K. Readiness Potential and Neuronal Determinism: New Insights on Libet Experiment. *J Neurosci* 2018; 38(4): 784–786. www.ncbi.nlm.nih.gov/pubmed/29367289 (cited 26 August 2019)

453. Brown D. Derren Brown Advertising Agency Task. YouTube 2012, www.youtube.com/watch?v=YQXe1CokWqQ (cited 26 August 2019)

454. Alhabash S, McAlister AR, Kim W, Lou C, Cunningham C, Quilliam ET, et al. Saw It on Facebook, Drank It at the Bar! Effects of Exposure to Facebook Alcohol Ads on Alcohol-Related Behaviors. *J Interact Advert* 2016; 16(1): 44–58. www.tandfonline.com/doi/full /10.1080/15252019.2016.1160330 (cited 23 August 2019)

455. Hudson S, Huang L, Roth MS, Madden TJ. The influence of social media interactions on consumer–brand relationships: A three-country study of brand perceptions and marketing behaviors. *Int J Res Mark* 2016; 33(1): 27–41. www.sciencedirect.com/science/ article/abs/pii/S0167811615000841 (cited 26 August 2019)

456. Bond RM, Fariss CJ, Jones JJ, Kramer ADI, Marlow C, Settle JE, et al. A 61-million-person experiment in social influence and political mobilization. *Nature* 2012; 489(7415): 295–298. www. nature.com/articles/nature11421 (cited 26 August 2019)

457. Hutchinson A. New Listing Shows Just How Much Celebrities are Being Paid Per Sponsored Instagram Post. *Social Media Today* 24 July 2019. www.socialmediatoday.com/news/new-listing-shows-just-how-much-celebrities-are-being-paid-per-sponsored-in/559360/ (cited 26 August 2019)

458. Bakshy E, Hofman JM, Mason WA, Watts DJ. Everyone's an Influencer: Quantifying Influence on Twitter. In: *Proceedings of the fourth ACM international conference on Web search and data mining*. Hong Kong, China; 2011: 65–74. http://snap.stanford.edu/class/ cs224w-readings/bakshy11influencers.pdf (cited 26 August 2019)

459. National Crime Agency. Cyber Crime. *NCA Website* 2020. www. nationalcrimeagency.gov.uk/what-we-do/crime-threats/cyber-crime (cited 8 September 2020)

460. Federal Bureau of Investigation. 2018 internet Crime Report. Washington, DC; 2019. https://pdf.ic3.gov/2018_IC3Report.pdf (cited 9 September 2019)

461. McAfee. The Economic Impact of Cybercrime—No Slowing Down Executive Summary. www.mcafee.com/enterprise/en-us/ assets/executive-summaries/es-economic-impact-cybercrime. pdf (cited 9 September 2019)

462. Fischer P, Modic D, Lea SEG, Evans KM. Why do Individuals Respond to Fraudulent Scam Communication and Lose Money? *J Appl Soc Psychol* 2013; 43(102060–2072). https://research. deception.org.uk/sites/research.deception.org.uk/files/

research/Modic%2C D. and Lea%2C S. %282013%29 Scam
Compliance.pdf (cited 19 October 2017)

463. Rusch JJJ. The ' Social Engineering ' of internet Fraud. *IOSC
99* 2003; 1–12. www.isoc.org/isoc/conferences/inet/99/
proceedings/3g/3g_2.htm (cited 13 August 2015)

464. Modic D, Anderson R, Palomäki J. We will make you like our
research: The development of a susceptibility-to-persuasion scale.
PLoS One 2018; 13(3): 1–21.

465. Modic, D, Anderson, RJ. We Will Make You Like Our Research:
The Development of a Susceptibility-to-Persuasion Scale. 28
April, 2014. *SSRN*. https://ssrn.com/abstract=2446971 or http://
dx.doi.org/10.2139/ssrn.2446971 (cited 24 August 2019)

466. Kenrick DT, Goldstein NJ, Braver SL. *Six degrees of social influence :
science, application, and the psychology of Robert Cialdini*. Oxford,
UK: Oxford University Press; 2012: 185 pp.

467. Centre for Collaboration Motivation and Innovation. CCMI
Resources. *Health Literacy Resources* 21 November 2019. https://
centrecmi.ca/resources/ (cited 8 September 2020)

468. Moseley JB, O'Malley K, Petersen NJ, Menke TJ, Brody BA,
Kuykendall DH, et al. A Controlled Trial of Arthroscopic Surgery
for Osteoarthritis of the Knee. *N Engl J Med* 2002; 347(2): 81–88.
www.ncbi.nlm.nih.gov/pubmed/12110735 (cited 12 September
2019)

469. Laupattarakasem W, Laopaiboon M, Laupattarakasem P,
Sumananont C. Arthroscopic debridement for knee osteoarthritis.
Cochrane Database Syst Rev 2008; (1): CD005118. www.ncbi.nlm.
nih.gov/pubmed/18254069 (cited 12 September 2019)

470. American Academy of Orthopaedic Surgeons, Academy A,
Aaos. Treatment Of Osteoarthritis Of The Knee Evidence-
Based Guideline 2nd Edition. Am Acad Orthop Surg
Board Dir 2013; 973. www.aaos.org/research/guidelines/
TreatmentofOsteoarthritisoftheKneeGuideline.pdf

471. Kise NJ, Risberg MA, Stensrud S, Ranstam J, Engebretsen L, Roos
EM. Exercise therapy versus arthroscopic partial meniscectomy
for degenerative meniscal tear in middle aged patients:
randomised controlled trial with two year follow-up. *BMJ* 2016;
354: i3740. www.ncbi.nlm.nih.gov/pubmed/27440192 (cited 12
September 2019)

472. Evidence Development and Standards Branch, Health Quality Ontario ED and S, Ontario HQ. Arthroscopic Debridement of the Knee: An Evidence Update. Ont Health Technol Assess Ser. 2014; 14(13): 1–43. www.ncbi.nlm.nih.gov/pubmed/26330895 (cited 12 September 2019)

473. Katz JN, Brophy RH, Chaisson CE, de Chaves L, Cole BJ, Dahm DL, et al. Surgery versus Physical Therapy for a Meniscal Tear and Osteoarthritis. *N Engl J Med* 2013; 368(18): 1675–1684. www.ncbi.nlm.nih.gov/pubmed/23506518 (cited 12 September 2019)

474. van de Graaf VA, Noorduyn JCA, Willigenburg NW, Butter IK, de Gast A, Mol BW, et al. Effect of Early Surgery vs Physical Therapy on Knee Function Among Patients With Nonobstructive Meniscal Tears. *JAMA* 2018; 320(13): 1328. http://jama.jamanetwork.com/article.aspx?doi=10.1001/jama.2018.13308 (cited 12 September 2019)

475. Monk AP, Davies LJ, Hopewell S, Harris K, Beard DJ, Price AJ. Surgical versus conservative interventions for treating anterior cruciate ligament injuries. *Cochrane Database Syst Rev* 3 April 2016. http://doi.wiley.com/10.1002/14651858.CD011166.pub2 (cited 12 September 2019)

476. Mirza SK, Deyo RA. Systematic Review of Randomized Trials Comparing Lumbar Fusion Surgery to Nonoperative Care for Treatment of Chronic Back Pain. *Spine* 2007; 32(7): 816–823. https://insights.ovid.com/crossref?an=00007632-200704010-00018 (cited 13 September 2019)

477. Kolata G. Why 'Useless' Surgery Is Still Popular. *The New York Times* 3 August 2016. www.nytimes.com/2016/08/04/upshot/the-right-to-know-that-an-operation-is-next-to-useless.html

478. Kallmes DF, Comstock BA, Heagerty PJ, Turner JA, Wilson DJ, Diamond TH, et al. A Randomized Trial of Vertebroplasty for Osteoporotic Spinal Fractures. *N Engl J Med* 2009; 361(6): 569–579. www.nejm.org/doi/abs/10.1056/NEJMoa0900563 (cited 13 September 2019)

479. Barnett AG, van der Pols JC, Dobson AJ. Regression to the mean: what it is and how to deal with it. *Int J Epidemiol* 2005; 34(1): 215–220.

480. Skrabanek P (Petr), McCormick J, James S. *Follies Fallacies in Medicine*. London, UK: Prometheus Books; 1990: 13–14 pp.

481. Doheny K. Where Is My Excedrin? *WebMD News* 17 September 2012. www.webmd.com/migraines-headaches/news/20120917/where-is-my-excedrin#2 (cited 17 September 2019)

482. Safran JD. The Curious Case of the Growing Placebo Effect. *Psychology Today Canada* 20 March 2018. www.psychologytoday.com/ca/blog/straight-talk/201803/the-curious-case-the-growing-placebo-effect (cited 17 September 2019)

483. Meador CK. Hex death: voodoo magic or persuasion? *South Med J* 1992; 85(3): 244–247. www.ncbi.nlm.nih.gov/pubmed/1546347 (cited 19 September 2019)

484. Guess HA. *The science of the placebo: toward an interdisciplinary research agenda.* London, UK: BMJ Books; 2002: 332 pp.

485. Voelker R. Nocebos contribute to host of ills. *JAMA* 1996; 275(5): 345–345. www.ncbi.nlm.nih.gov/pubmed/8568997 (cited 19 September 2019)

486. Lederman D. A Low Bar for Passage. *Inside Higer Ed* 23 March 2019. www.insidehighered.com/news/2018/03/23/new-data-bar-passage-show-wide-variation-law-schools-rates

487. Das N, Panjabi M. Plagiarism: Why is it such a big issue for medical writers? *Perspect Clin Res* 2011; 2(2): 67. doi:10.4103/2229-3485.80370

458. Harvey HB, Weinstein DF. Predatory Publishing. *Acad Med* 2017; 92(2): 150-151. doi:10.1097/ACM.0000000000001521

Index

Index

Index

Index

influenza (flu) vaccination, 160–161,
    262
injuries
    chiropractic, 210–213
    risk *see* risk
    weapon salve for healing of,
        72–73
    see also do no harm principle
Institut de Formation Naturopathique
    (IFN), 225
insurance (health), 48–50
integrative medicine, 129–138
    bogus clinic, 112
    downside, 133–134
    research, 134–136
intention (to deceive), 37, 38
    diagnoses or procedures and, 52
intercessory prayer, 189–191
International Association of
    Naturopathy Hygionomists
    (AINH), 225
International University of Health
    Sciences, 106
Internet *see* online
intravenous delivery
    chelation therapy, 158
    supplements, 158–159
        megadose vitamins, 210
        turmeric, 28, 210
ionisation bracelets, 203
Iowa, Palmer College of Chiropractic,
    220
IV Health Centre/Wellness Boutique
    (Vancouver), 158, 159

Jacobsen, Carlyle F, 77
Jim the Horse episode, 81–82
John of God, 248–249, 251
Johnson & Johnson, 93, 94
journal publication in self-interest,
    231, 345
Junger, Dr Alejandro, 258

Kallmes, Dr David, 332
Kawchuk, Greg, 239
Kelly, Kim, 210
Kenyon, Dr Julian, 52–53
Khakh, Rajdeep Kaur, 51, 56
Kim Bong-han, 135
Klop, Jason, 114
knee, arthroscopic surgery, 330–332
Kokolulu Farm and Cancer Retreat,
    113–114

Kokott, William, 49
Kreiman's experiments on
    subconscious influences in
    decision-making, 309–310
Kruger–Dunning, 270–271, 270–271

LaBelle, Patti, 304–305
Lalini, Dr Kaim, 50–51
Langara College, 227
law (incl. legislation/regulations/
    litigation/lawsuits), 217–228
    alternative healthcare sector, 113,
        217–228
    anti-vaccination advocacy and,
        160–162
    celebrities, 250–251
    chiropractic critics sued by
        chiropractors, 169–170
    cybercrime, 315
    drugs, 89, 90, 92–99
        approval, 90
    medical devices/products, 87
    private clinics, 103–104, 105,
        107–108, 109
    see also crime
Lawler, John, 211
laying on of hands, 188–189, 188–189
leaders, influence of, 271–272, 272, 273
lenalidomide, 97
leucotomy (lobotomy), 77–79
Libert's experiments on subconscious
    influences in decision-
    making, 309–310
life force (vital) energy, 133, 135,
    141–142
    acupuncture (*Qi*), 144, 145, 147,
        150, 199, 200
    homeopathy, 139, 151
lifestyles
    alternative medicine and, 123
    healthy, 48, 325
    targeting people based on,
        283–284
limb deformities, thalidomide, 85
Lister, Joseph, 70
litigation *see* law
Liu Changhua, Dr, 142
lobotomy (leucotomy), 77–79
Louhiala, Pekka, 125
Love-Robinson, Malachi, 51, 56
lung disease, chronic, 233
Lust, Benedict, 156, 160
Lyme disease, chronic, 209, 241

Also from Hammersmith Health Books...

Blind Trust

How parents with a sick child can escape the labyrinth of lies, hypocrisy and false promises

Klaus Rose MD PhD

A former pharmaceutical company insider looks at so-called 'paediatric' pharmaceutical studies to show how they have become an international multi-billion business with many careers in academia, regulatory authorities and the pharmaceutical industry based on this work, yet much of this activity is founded on a series of flawed concepts that have led to immeasurable wastage of resources and serious, ongoing medical abuse.